BEST LOOP HIKES

New Hampshire's White Mountains to the Maine Coast

BEST LOOP HIKES
New Hampshire's White Mountains to the Maine Coast

Jeffrey Romano

THE MOUNTAINEERS BOOKS

THE MOUNTAINEERS BOOKS
is the nonprofit publishing arm of The Mountaineers Club, an organization founded in 1906 and dedicated to the exploration, preservation, and enjoyment of outdoor and wilderness areas.

1001 SW Klickitat Way, Suite 201, Seattle, WA 98134

First edition, 2006

Manufactured in the United States of America

Acquiring Editor: Cassandra Conyers
Project Editor: Laura Drury
Copy Editor: Jane Crosen
Cover and Book Design: The Mountaineers Books
Layout: Mayumi Thompson
Cartographer: Moore Creative Design
Photographer: All photographs by author unless otherwise noted

Cover photograph: *Pisgah Reservoir Pisgah State Park (Hike 1)*
Frontispiece: *The Presidentials from the Imp Face (Hike 27)*

Maps shown in this book were produced using National Geographic's *TOPO!* software. For more information, go to *www.nationalgeographic.com/topo.*

Library of Congress Cataloging-in-Publication Data
Romano, Jeff.
Best loop hikes New Hampshire's White Mountains to the Maine coast / Jeff Romano.-- 1st ed.
p. cm.
Includes bibliographical references and index.
ISBN 0-89886-985-4 (pbk.)
1. Hiking--New Hampshire--Guidebooks. 2. Hiking--Maine--Guidebooks. 3. New Hampshire--Guidebooks. 4. Maine--Guidebooks. I. Title.
GV199.42.N4R66 2005
796.5109742--dc22

2005027138

Printed on recycled paper

CONTENTS

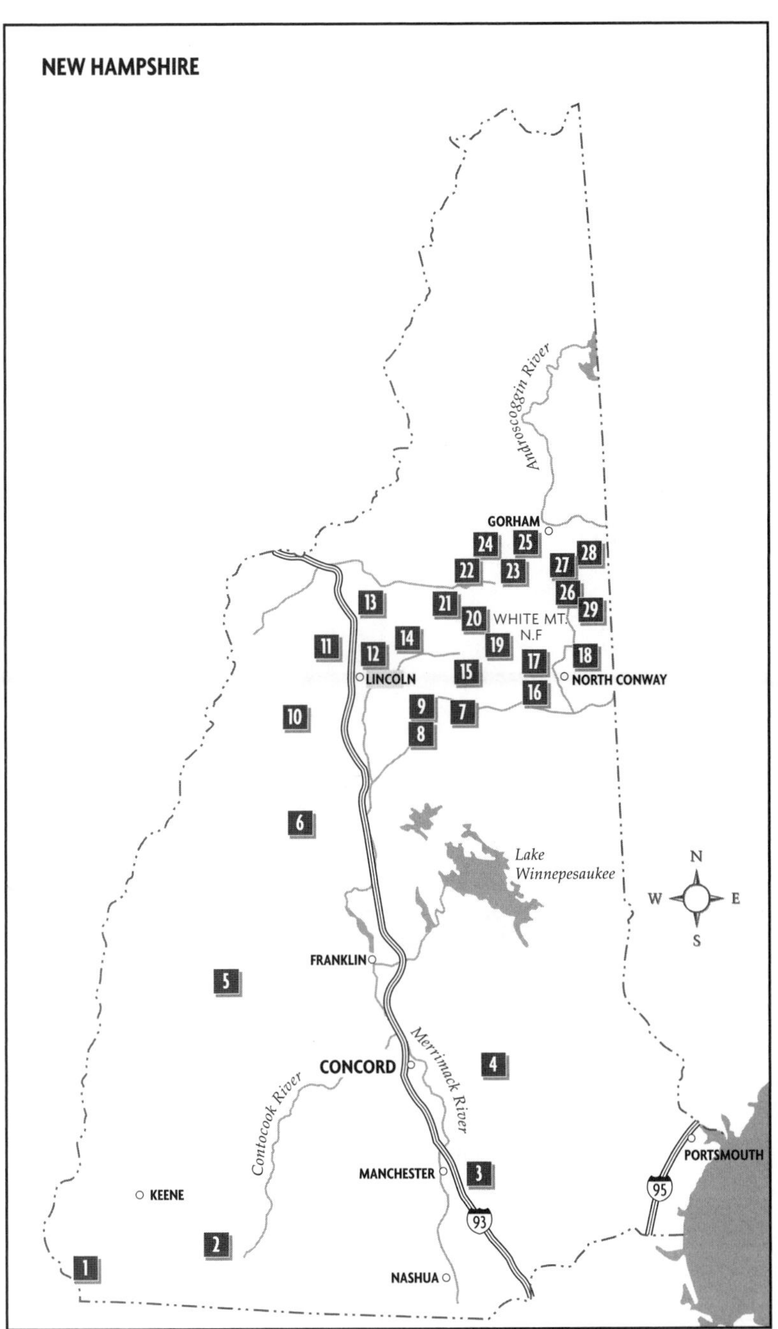
NEW HAMPSHIRE
Androscoggin River
GORHAM
24
25
28
27
22
23
26
13
21
29
20
WHITE MT.
N.F
14
11
19
12
18
17
15
LINCOLN
NORTH CONWAY
16
9
7
10
8
6
Lake
Winnepesaukee
N
W
E
S
FRANKLIN
5
Merrimack River
4
CONCORD
Contocook River
PORTSMOUTH
MANCHESTER
3
95
KEENE
93
2
1
NASHUA

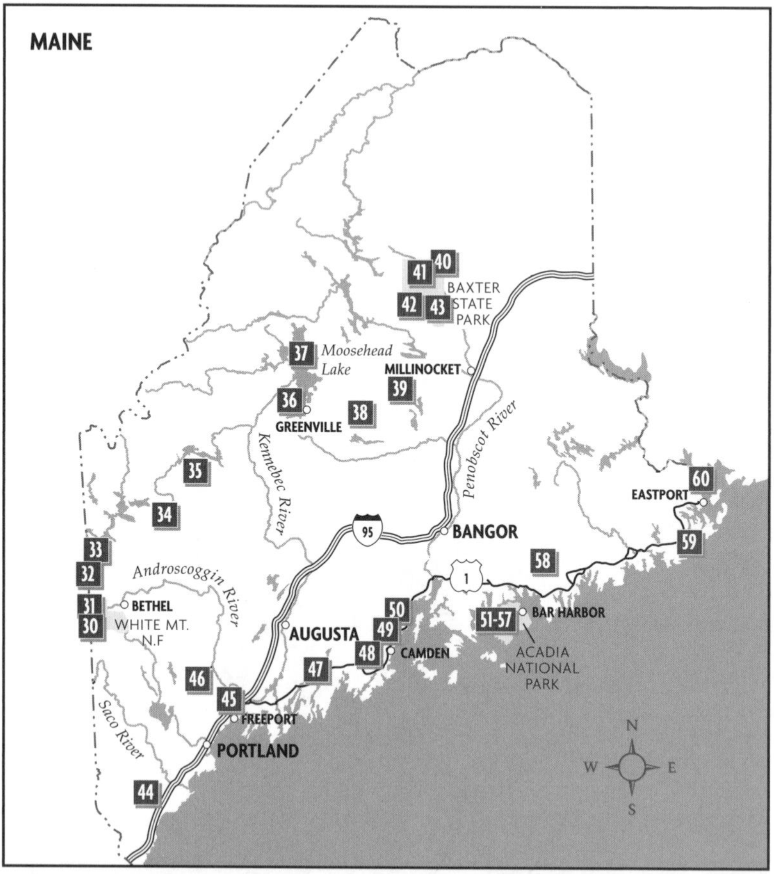

MAINE
40
41
42
43
BAXTER
STATE
PARK
37
Moosehead
Lake
MILLINOCKET
39
36
38
GREENVILLE
Kennebec River
Penobscot River
35
34
95
BANGOR
EASTPORT
60
59
58
33
32
Androscoggin River
1
31
BETHEL
30
WHITE MT.
N.F
50
49
AUGUSTA
51-57
BAR HARBOR
48
CAMDEN
ACADIA
NATIONAL
PARK
47
46
45
FREEPORT
PORTLAND
Saco River
44
N
W
E
S

MAP LEGEND

Interstate highway
Paved road
Unpaved road
Featured trail
Connecting trail
Cross-country trail
Railroad
River/creek
Lake
Building/structure
95
Interstate
1
U.S. highway
139
State or County road
9712
Forest road
Trailhead
Parking
Campground or Site
Peak
Scenic point

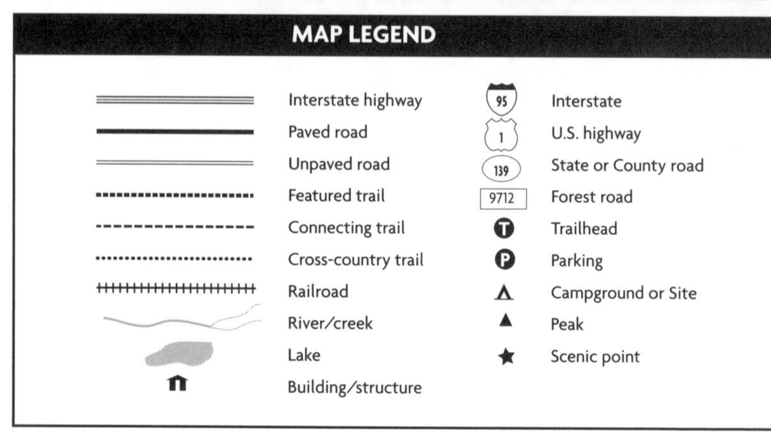

Hike Number and Name	Distance (miles)	Elevation Gain (feet)	Hike Duration	Season to Hike	Features
1 Pisgah State Park	8	1350	Day	All year	Wetlands and views
2 Pack Monadnock	8	2000	Day	All year	Scenic ridge and cliff
3 Lake Massabesic	4	60	Half-day	All year	Bird-watching and history
4 North Pawtuckaway Mountain	4.9	900	Half-day	May–November	Geology and forests
5 Mount Kearsarge	2.8	1100	Half-day	May–October	Views
6 Mount Cardigan	7.6	2350	Day	May–November	Scenic ridges and views
7 Mount Whiteface	11.5	3800	Full-day	May–October	Solitude and ledges
8 Jennings Peak	6.5	2100	Day	All year	Views and brook
9 Tripyramids	11.1	3000	Full-day	May–October	Rock slides and peaks
10 Mount Moosilauke	11	2750	Full-day	May–October	Alpine and history
11 Franconia Notch	6.2	1300	Half-day	All year	Cascades and pond
12 Flume and Liberty	9.9	3500	Full-day	All year	Views and slide
13 Franconia Ridge	8.8	4000	Full-day	All year	Alpine and waterfalls
14 Pemigewasset Wilderness	25.5	4750	Multi-day	May–October	Scenic ridge and wilderness
15 Hedgehog Mountain	4.8	1350	Half-day	All year	Views and ledges
16 Mount Chocorua and the Three Sisters	9.8	2950	Full-day	All year	Scenic ridges and views
17 North Moat Mountain	10	2750	Full-day	All year	Scenic ridges and waterfalls
18 Green Hills Preserve	5.6	1600	Half-day	All year	Rare plants and views
19 Mount Carrigain	13.5	3900	Full-day	May–October	Solitude and views
20 Arethusa Falls and Frankenstein Cliff	5	1600	Half-day	May–November	Waterfalls and cliff
21 Zealand Notch	17	3300	Full-day/ overnight	May–October	Wildlife viewing and notch

Hike Summary Table (continued)

Hike Number and Name	Distance (miles)	Elevation Gain (feet)	Hike Duration	Season to Hike	Features
22 Crawford Notch	10	3100	Full-day	All year	Views and peaks
23 Mount Washington	10.5	4600	Full-day	May–October	Alpine and ravine
24 Mount Jefferson	10.5	4250	Full-day	June–October	Alpine and ravine
25 Mount Madison	9.6	4300	Full-day	May–October	Alpine and waterfalls
26 Carter Dome	11.9	3160	Full-day	May–October	Notch and rivers
27 Imp Face	6.5	2125	Half-day	All year	Scenic ledge
28 Wild River	16.4	3550	Full-day/ overnight	May–October	Solitude and scenic ridges
29 Baldfaces	9.7	3450	Full-day	April–November	Scenic ridges and views
30 Speckled Mountain	8.6	2550	Day	All year	Views and waterfalls
31 Caribou Mountain	6.9	1950	Day	May–October	Views and waterfalls
32 Goose Eye Mountain	9.5	2800	Full-day	May–October	Cirque and views
33 Grafton Notch	4.9	1950	Half-day	May–October	Scenic ledges and waterfalls
34 Tumbledown Mountain	6.5	2400	Day	June–October	Geology and views
35 Bigelows	13.2	3690	Full-day/ overnight	May–October	Scenic ridge and wetlands
36 Little Moose Mountain	4.8	600	Half-day	May–November	Ponds and views
37 Mount Kineo	6	760	Day	May–October	Cliff and lake
38 Gulf Hagas	9	670	Day	May–October	Waterfalls and gorge
39 Turtle Ridge	8.5	1200	Day	May–November	Ponds and views
40 Trout Brook Mountain	3.4	1050	Half-day	May–October	Views
41 South Branch Mountain	6.8	2175	Day	May–October	Wildlife viewing and views

Hike Number and Name	Distance (miles)	Elevation Gain (feet)	Hike Duration	Season to Hike	Features
42 Brothers and Coe	10.9	3870	Full-day	May–October	Solitude and slide
43 Mount Katahdin	9.8	4050	Full-day	May–October	Alpine and geology
44 Wells Estuary	5	60	Half-day	All year	Bird-watching and beach
45 Wolfe's Neck Woods	2.8	160	Half-day	All year	Ocean and forests
46 Bradbury Mountain	3.2	280	Half-day	All year	History and ledges
47 Dodge Point	4.2	450	Half-day	All year	Tidal river and forests
48 Mount Megunticook and Maiden Cliff	6.8	1670	Day	All year	Scenic ledges and views
49 Zekes Lookout	7.2	1100	Day	All year	Wildlife viewing
50 Ducktrap River	4.4	120	Half-day	All year	Salmon river and forests
51 Champlain Mountain	5.5	1400	Day	June–September	Scenic ridge and ocean
52 Dorr and Cadillac Mountains	6.5	1700	Day	April–November	Views and cascades
53 Jordan Pond	5.4	1670	Day	April–November	Geology and views
54 Sargent Mountain	5.2	1900	Day	April–November	Scenic ridges and views
55 Beech Mountain and Cliff	3.6	780	Half-day	April–November	Cliffs and views
56 Western Mountain	4.9	1500	Half-day	April–November	Notches and forests
57 Ship Harbor	1.4	35	Half-day	All year	Ocean and wildlife viewing
58 Black Mountain	5.1	900	Half-day	April–November	Views and lake
59 Cutler Coast	10	1000	Full-day	All year	Cliffs and wildlife viewing
60 Shackford Head	3	300	Half-day	All year	Ocean and history

Key:
Half-day = less than 4 hours; Day = 4–7 hours; Full-day = more than 7 hours; Overnight = 2 days; Multi-day = more than 2 days.

Hikes by Interest

Feature	Hike Number	Hike Name
Panoramic views	6	Mount Cardigan
	24	Mount Jefferson
	52	Dorr and Cadillac Mountains
Solitude	28	Wild River
	39	Turtle Ridge
	42	Brothers and Coe
Kid-friendly trail	5	Mount Kearsarge
	15	Hedgehog Mountain
	46	Bradbury Mountain
Waterfalls and rivers	11	Franconia Notch
	20	Arethusa Falls and Frankenstein Cliff
	38	Gulf Hagas
Wildlife viewing	19	Mount Carrigain
	41	South Branch Mountain
	51	Champlain Mountain
Bird-watching	3	Lake Massabesic
	21	Zealand Notch
	44	Wells Estuary
Natural splendor	14	Pemigewasset Wilderness
	43	Mount Katahdin
	59	Cutler Coast
History	1	Pisgah State Park
	10	Mount Moosilauke
	60	Shackford Head
Cliffs	37	Mount Kineo
	48	Mount Megunticook and Maiden Cliff
	53	Jordan Pond
Scenic ridges	2	Pack Monadnock
	13	Franconia Ridge
	35	Bigelows

The Travelers from Trout Brook Mountain

PREFACE

In 2004 I embarked upon this labor of love to compile the sixty best loop hikes in Maine and New Hampshire. The sixteen-month effort was the latest chapter in a more than three-decade-long journey enjoying the hiking trails of northern New England. I have scaled most of the region's highest summits, many of them in winter, and journeyed on miles and miles of northern New England's hiking trails. The more than 450 miles of hiking, countless hours of writing, and toil of creating trail maps greatly exceed any other hiking-related endeavor I have tackled to date. However, like most adventures in the outdoors, especially those which test one's endurance and capabilities, writing this book is something I will savor for many years. I hope you are able to enjoy the special places I have chronicled in this guidebook. New Hampshire and Maine are blessed with an abundance of natural places to explore.

ACKNOWLEDGMENTS

I would be remiss in failing to acknowledge the many people who played a part in the evolution of this project, especially those who joined me on the trail, posed for photographs, and reviewed draft material. I owe a great deal of appreciation to Eric Aldrich, Julie Clemons, Paul Dest, Jean Hoekwater, Andy Kekacs, Vern Labbe, Iain MacLeod, Roger Merchant, Seth Mercier, Wanda Moran, Tom Morrison, Doug Romano, Blake Romano, Judy Romano, Richard Romano, Peter Smith, Heather B. Scott, Bob Spoerl, and Conrad Welzel. Special thanks to Craig Romano for his inspiration, guidance, and encouragement. Extra special thanks to my wife Maria and my son Anthony for their love, support, and patience, and for joining me on so many adventures. I will especially remember scrambling up Kearsarge,

Young moose, South Branch Pond

falling asleep coming down Caribou, hiking along the Bold Coast, crashing across Moosehead Lake to the Kineo trailhead, stumbling upon the mother moose, calf, and bear cub, and standing atop Mount Katahdin.

INTRODUCTION

The sixty loop hikes described in this guidebook cover areas throughout Maine and New Hampshire. The first half dozen hikes explore the rolling hills and small mountains of southern New Hampshire. Located within islands of green space and surrounded by rapidly growing municipalities, these hikes showcase the many features of the region, including: a patchwork landscape of fields, farms, and orchards; growing forests dominated by white pine and red oak; countless ponds, rivers, and small wetlands; and small, classic New England communities. While the region may be short on dramatic scenery, it abounds in wildlife diversity, history, and beauty.

Moving northward the guidebook begins a journey through the deep notches, expansive scenery, and towering summits of the White Mountains. With a large cluster of high peaks, forty-eight of them above 4000 feet in elevation, and with well over 1000 miles of trails, the White Mountains region has been the premier hiking destination in the Northeast for more than a

Maine's Acadia coastline

century. In its lower elevations the forest is dominated by stands of maturing northern hardwoods—maple, birch, ash, and beech—while the highest elevations are filled with dense spruce-fir forests and wide-open areas of stunted trees, rock, and alpine vegetation. The White Mountains offer hikers of all abilities trails to mountains, ponds, waterfalls, and numerous unique natural features.

Next the guidebook meanders through northern Maine, paralleling and joining the Appalachian Trail's journey toward the top of the state. This region, the most sparsely populated area of New England, is noteworthy for its large lakes and rivers; moose, loons, and abundant wildlife; millions of acres of actively managed forests; long logging roads to obscure natural areas; and its people's rugged independence. Largely privately owned throughout the twentieth century by paper companies and other landowners focused on timber harvesting, much of the region has been protected in large blocks of public and private conservation land in the past decade. The most recent conservation acquisitions have built on a tradition started by the late Governor Percival Baxter, whose foresight led to the jewel of northern Maine: the more than 200,000 acres that compose Baxter State Park.

The guidebook ends where America's day begins, on the long, rocky coastline of Maine. Thousands of miles long, the Maine coast, with its countless peninsulas, bays, and islands, offers visitors cool breezes in the dog days of summer, glimpses of spouting whales and bobbing seals offshore, and steep cliffs bombarded with crashing surf, mist, and fog. While the central hiking attraction of the Maine coast is Acadia National Park with its many miles of trails and panoramic vistas, locations east and west of the park offer tremendous (and usually less crowded) opportunities for outdoor adventure, as well. The Maine coast is also noteworthy for its lobster and fishing industries. Fortunately, there are ample places to enjoy the day's catch.

Permits, Fees, and Regulations

The hikes described in this guidebook take place on lands owned and managed by a number of different organizations, individuals, and governmental entities. While in Maine and New Hampshire the vast majority of land is held privately, roughly 94 and 84 percent respectively, most of the hikes in this book occur primarily on publicly owned and managed lands. The book also includes hikes accessible over private roads, hikes with sections of private land, and hikes on conservation land owned by private nonprofit organizations. Each landowner and land manager associated with hikes in this book has unique missions and regulations. For your enjoyment, and to ensure that others that follow can enjoy these same special places, it is important to know and obey all regulations and to be especially considerate of private landowners. The list of landowners that follows serves as an introduction to applicable rules, camping regulations, and fees. Please turn to the appendix for contact information and websites for additional materials, updates, and more complete lists of regulations.

White Mountain National Forest pay station

White Mountain National Forest

Established in 1911, the White Mountain National Forest comprises more than 780,000 acres of land in New Hampshire and Maine. The Forest Service charges $3 a day to park at trailheads within the forest. Many trailheads have self-service fee stations. Other options include a seven-consecutive-days parking pass ($5), and an annual pass ($20 for one vehicle, $25 for a two-vehicle "household"). Parking passes are available at all Forest Service offices and from many local vendors. All backcountry camping within the national forest must occur at designated sites or at least 200 feet from trails or water sources. Additional camping restrictions apply within scenic areas, wilderness areas, near certain bodies of water, above tree line, and around developed camping areas. The Forest Service also operates more than twenty developed campgrounds of various sizes. Sites at each are available on a first-come, first-served basis. Reservations can also be made in advance for some campgrounds.

Acadia National Park

Acadia National Park in Downeast Maine encompasses more than 47,000 acres and over 120 miles of hiking trails. Backcountry camping is not permitted in the park. Camping is restricted to Blackwoods and Seawall campgrounds. Campsites range from $14 to $20 per night, and reservations can be made in advance. The National Park Service charges a per-vehicle entrance fee of $20 for seven days or an individual permit fee (for pedestrians or people on motorcycles or bicycles) of $5 for seven days. Visitors can also purchase an annual pass for $40. To help reduce traffic and air pollution, and the stress of finding a parking space, take advantage of the Island Explorer, a propane-powered shuttle bus service that provides free transportation throughout the park, stopping at major trailheads and other popular destinations. Contact the National Park Service for shuttle stops and schedules.

Appalachian National Scenic Trail

The Appalachian National Scenic Trail is a 2174-mile footpath along the ridges and across the major valleys of the Appalachian Mountains from Mount Katahdin in Maine to Springer Mountain in northern Georgia. It was designated as the first national scenic trail by the National Trails System Act of 1968. No fees or permits are required for walking on the Appalachian Trail. Camping options vary according to the trail management district, and are addressed in specific hike descriptions.

New Hampshire Division of Parks and Recreation

The New Hampshire Division of Parks and Recreation, a division of the Department of Resource and Economic Development, manages New Hampshire's state parks and houses the Bureau of Trails, which administers multiple-use trails on state, federal, and private lands. Day-use fees for most New Hampshire State Parks are $3 for adults, $1 for children ages six to eleven, free for children ages five and under, and free for New Hampshire residents ages sixty-five and over.

Maine Bureau of Parks and Lands

The Maine Bureau of Parks and Lands, a bureau of the Department of Conservation, manages more than thirty state parks and the almost half million acres of the state's public reserved lands. Per-person day-use fees at Maine's state parks vary depending on the facilities provided ($2 or $3), and admission is free for persons over sixty-five and under five. The state also sells two types of annual park passes: a $60 pass to cover everyone in a vehicle, and a $30 pass for individuals. Maine's public reserved lands are not staffed as state parks. Generally, fees are not charged to visit these lands; funds generated from careful timber harvesting cover land management costs. Campsites on public reserved lands are generally in remote locations, free to use, and available on a first-come, first-served basis.

Baxter State Park

Baxter State Park includes 204,733 acres of land and more than 200 miles of hiking trails. Day use is free for Maine residents. For non-Maine residents, a $12-per-vehicle entrance fee is required. A season pass can also be purchased for $37. Day use is limited to the parking lot capacity at each trailhead in the park. Camping is limited to developed locations by reservation only.

Opposite: Classic White Mountain rock formation, Mount Chocorua

Camping accommodations range from tent sites to lean-tos to cabins, from large campgrounds to remote backcountry sites; reservations are processed through the Baxter State Park Authority. Baxter State Park, although a state park, is governed by the Baxter State Park Authority according to trust documents developed by the park's donator, the late Governor Percival Baxter. Pets and motorcycles are not allowed in the park.

Baxter State Park trailheads can be accessed in three ways. One approach is to secure camping reservations at trailheads with overnight facilities

Bog at Tumbledown Mountain

(lean-tos, tent sites, or cabins). Also, there is limited day-use parking at each trailhead on a first-come, first-served basis. Finally, Maine residents may call in advance to reserve one of a handful of day use parking spaces available at each trailhead; these spaces are reserved on a first-come, first-served basis as well.

Wells National Estuarine Reserve

The Wells Reserve is a 1600-acre research, education, and recreation facility, a public-private partnership within the National Estuarine Research Reserve System. The reserve has 7 miles of hiking and cross-country skiing trails that provide access to woodlands, fields, wetlands, beach, and dunes. The reserve is open every day, 7:00 AM to dusk. Admission fees are in effect on weekends from May to October and daily in July and August. Fees are $1 for ages six to sixteen and $2 for those over sixteen.

KI-Jo-Mary Multiple-Use Forest

Two hikes in this book are accessed across private lands and private roads managed by the KI–Jo-Mary Multiple-Use Forest management organization, a consortium of landowners who collectively own more than 175,000 acres of working forestland. KI–Jo-Mary, Inc. contracts with North Maine Woods, Inc. (NMW) to manage recreation in the KI–Jo-Mary Forest. All roads and bridges in the KI–Jo-Mary Forest are maintained primarily for forest management activities. Trucks ALWAYS have the right-of-way. The KI–Jo-Mary Forest charges a per-person per day fee to access their roads, $5 for Maine residents and $8 for non-residents, and they sell seasonal passes as well. Access is free for people under fifteen years of age and older than seventy.

Private Nonprofit Landowners

A number of hikes in this book occur on land owned and managed by private nonprofit organizations including Dartmouth College, New Hampshire Audubon, the Appalachian Mountain Club, and the New Hampshire Chapter of The Nature Conservancy. With different missions ranging from outdoor recreation to the protection of biodiversity, these five landowners provide public access to their land. In addition, Dartmouth College and the Appalachian Mountain Club offer overnight accommodations including lodges at the base of Mount Cardigan and Mount Moosilauke. The Appalachian Mountain Club also manages numerous huts and tent site areas. With the exception of tent sites, reservations to these facilities should be made in advance.

Trail and Camping Etiquette

With more folks enjoying hiking and backpacking each year, the need for outdoor ethics has never been greater. Few things on a hike are more frustrating, for example, than encountering improper or inconsiderate camping. It is amazing how often tents are perched on the banks of streams or right

Author and son, Mount Kearsarge (photo by Maria Fuentes)

off of trails. Similarly, watching a mountainside erode due to hikers taking shortcuts off the trail, or having a peaceful day in the woods interrupted by a loud group of oblivious people to the enjoyment of others, can leave a sour taste after an otherwise glorious day in the outdoors. In some cases, these transgressions violate the rules that govern a particular area, but more importantly these activities diminish the experiences of other hikers.

To ensure we all can enjoy the same opportunity to renew our spirits in the wilds of Maine and New Hampshire, it is essential for each of us to commit to basic outdoor ethical principles. The Leave No Trace Center for Outdoor Ethics, a national nonprofit organization dedicated to promoting and inspiring responsible outdoor recreation through education, research, and partnerships, has developed seven simple principles that all hikers should follow. They are:

Plan Ahead and Prepare

This includes knowing applicable regulations and special concerns for each area visited; being prepared for extreme weather, hazards, and emergencies; scheduling trips to avoid times of high use; and understanding how to use a map, guidebook, and compass.

Travel and Camp on Durable Surfaces

Durable surfaces means using established trails and campsites, rock, gravel, dry grasses, or snow. Remember that good campsites are found, not made, and should never be located closer than 200 feet from wetlands. Also, walking single-file in the middle of the trail, even when it is wet or muddy, minimizes erosion.

Dispose of Waste Properly

We should all follow the basic rule of waste disposal: Pack it in and pack it out. In the absence of a pit privy or other toilet facilities, bag and pack out human waste or bury it in a cathole. When depositing solid human waste, dig a small hole 6 to 8 inches deep at least 200 feet from water, camp, and trails. Cover and disguise the hole when finished. The same goes for dog waste if you are hiking with your pet. Avoid washing yourself or your dishes within 200 feet of streams or lakes, and use small amounts of biodegradable soap.

Leave What You Find

You are not the first to visit any of these places and likely will not be the last. Preserve the experience for others who follow: examine, but do not touch, cultural or historic structures and artifacts; leave rocks, plants, and other natural objects as you find them; avoid introducing or transporting non-native species; and do not build structures, furniture, or trenches.

Minimize Campfire Impacts

Lightweight stoves and candle lanterns leave less impact than campfires. Where fires are permitted, use established fire rings, fire pans, or mound fires and keep fires small. Only use sticks from the ground that can be broken by hand. When done, burn all wood to ash, and then scatter cool ashes. Put campfires out completely.

Respect Wildlife

Wildlife is best observed from a distance and should never be fed. Feeding wild animals damages their health, alters natural behaviors, and exposes them to predators and other dangers. Protect wildlife and your food by storing rations and trash securely. Control pets at all times or leave them at home.

Be Considerate of Other Visitors

Respect other visitors and protect the quality of their experience. Be courteous, and yield to other users on the trail. Let nature's sounds prevail—avoid loud voices and noises.

Weather and Seasons

Hiking in Maine and New Hampshire is enjoyable for a number of reasons, not the least of which is the constant change of seasons. The endless cycle of spring, summer, fall, and winter is probably not more pronounced in any other place in the United States. While each season is uniquely special, it is important to remember that all four seasons have unique challenges as well.

Spring

It is always exhilarating to see the first trillium poke out of the sunny hillside where recently melted snow has left small channels within the compressed layer of last year's leaves—or the thick carpet of Canada mayflowers that soon accelerates the greening process. Climbing under an open canopy of trees whose small buds do little to shade the increasingly strong sunlight invigorates and refreshes after a long harsh winter, while the chorus of songbirds welcomes back long-lost friends returning after six months in the tropics. Spring is a great time to head for the trails to enjoy comfortable daytime temperatures. It is also a good time to visit popular destinations, like Acadia National Park, that can be overrun in the summer. Late spring is also fabulous for venturing above tree line in the White Mountains when alpine flowers are blooming and before school is out.

Spring hiking can also be deceptively winter-like. Warm weather at lower elevations and in southern parts of New England does not mean spring has arrived in northern Maine or in the higher elevations of the White Mountains. In fact, it is not unusual for snow and ice to be abundant throughout April in both of these locations and present into May and early June. Proper equipment like snowshoes, crampons, and warm clothing may be necessary additions to your backpack. When considering a spring hike,

Painted trilliums

keep in mind that slopes melt faster, especially south-facing slopes, and that flat areas, particularly when shaded by evergreens, stay snowy longer.

Though winter-like in some respects, spring can also be summer-like. The sun's ultraviolet rays, for example, can burn as quickly in April as in August. Adding to the sunburn threat is light reflecting off snow and the lack of leaves to provide shade. Be sure to add sunscreen to your pack by March. Insects are also a concern on spring hikes. The arrival of the swarming, biting, and eye-, mouth-, and ear-filling blackflies usually begins in early May in the southern areas described in this book. By Memorial Day most places have ushered in their arrival. Although short-lived, the blackfly season can be frustrating. Spring also marks the start of tick season; these blood-sucking parasites seem to be spreading farther north each year. Some of these ticks carry diseases, including Lyme disease, a debilitating illness that requires immediate treatment.

Finally, spring can also be very spring-like, and nothing says spring more than water, the result of spring rains and snowmelt runoff. A constant issue on many spring hikes is the number and size of water crossings. It is hard to hike in Maine and New Hampshire without encountering running water, particularly in the spring when streams and water tables are full. To ensure that the worst-case scenario is only wet boots, it is essential to use caution at all stream crossings and be prepared to turn around if necessary. The water also creates muddy trails that may lead to wet feet and increased erosion. To avoid mud, pick hikes in the southern and coastal areas earlier in the spring and slowly work your way north.

Summer

Long days and warm temperatures: a tempting combination that draws the most avid among us to long journeys deep into the forest and high above tree line. Regardless of the length of one's hike, summer is also a great time to enjoy the abundant wildlife that inhabits the region, from the diminutive hummingbird darting between flowers to the massive bull moose foraging in the murky bottom of a secluded pond. The hottest months of the year also bring forth a spectacular array of wildflowers, including the region's frequently encountered collection of bunchberries, starflowers, and blue-bead lilies. Consider these factors when choosing a hike in the summer: much of northern Maine and some parts of the White Mountains are only accessible in the summer and fall; the sea breezes along the Maine coast offer a refreshing reprieve from the summer's hottest days; and popular destinations can be overrun on nice weekend days.

Few things put a damper on a summer hike more than swarming insects. Swarms of mosquitoes lurking in shady, moist areas and deerflies circling on the hottest, most humid days of July can be annoying and painful. To ease the situation, be prepared with effective bug repellent; avoid low, wet areas; and smile—without the insects, we would not be blessed with so many different and colorful songbirds.

Pileated woodpecker cavities, Mount Pisgah

Summer heat and humidity are other factors to consider. This combination, most common in July, quickly saps one's energy. Try to start hikes early in the day, and make sure to drink plenty of fluids. Heat and humidity also may trigger thunderstorms. Many of the hikes described in this book have a lot of exposure. These are excellent hikes when the weather cooperates, but potentially very dangerous when lightning is in the air. Storms most frequently hit later in the day, but often come on suddenly. Be alert and seek cover quickly at the sound of thunder. Lastly, heat and humidity tend to mix with smog from the Midwest, diminishing views that can be far more impressive other times of the year. If you are looking for the optimum summer day, wait for the day after a strong thunderstorm, often the result of a cold front ushering in cooler, cleaner air from Canada.

Autumn

As the days grow shorter, the insects become less prevalent, the air drier, and the temperatures cooler. Autumn is prime time for hiking. Nothing beats hitting the trail on a crisp fall day; you feel like you can hike forever. Adding to the lure of the season is the dizzying array of colors that splash across the landscape as the deciduous tree leaves change from green to orange, red, yellow, purple, and rust. Typically peaking in late September in the northern areas covered in this book, the changing foliage quickly moves south through the region. As fast as it appears, it ends, leaving a forest devoid of cover, save evergreen needles and the hearty leaves of beech and oak trees. Autumn is also marked with numerous migrations, most notably the movement of moose from lowly marshland to higher elevations and the waves of raptors taking advantage of the strong northerly winds.

While autumn hiking can be very enjoyable, remember that the days shorten quickly. Conditions may tempt you to long adventures, but be prepared to finish before the sun sets. Unlike the summer, in autumn once the sun goes down the temperatures quickly follow. In fact, it is not uncommon to experience winter-like conditions during the day, especially in northern Maine and the White Mountains. Be sure to have plenty of warm clothing, including a hat and gloves. The cool temperatures often make water crossings more difficult, too. When crossing rocks that look icy, it is safer to step on sections slightly submerged by water than on wet spots in the open air.

A final consideration for the autumn is that while excellent for hiking, it is also prime hunting season throughout the region. (Hunting occurs other times of the year as well. Check with the New Hampshire Fish & Game Department and the Maine Department of Inland Fisheries and Wildlife for more information.) Many of the trails described in this book

Red squirrel, Mount Kineo

Winter in the Green Hills Preserve

occur in areas open for hunting. Although it is quite uncommon to encounter hunters near hiking trails, it is good policy to wear bright colors such as blaze orange. To avoid hunters altogether, head for Maine on a Sunday, when hunting is prohibited.

Winter

Shadows, silence, and solitude—the three S's that best describe winter hiking. The angle of the sun's rays in the dead of winter can create such vivid images highlighting the many curves and edges of mountains, trees, and rocks. With most animals farther south or hibernating, it is amazing how quiet the forest can be while shrouded in a thick blanket of snow. On some excursions, the only sounds breaking the silence are whistling winds and an occasional chickadee. Winter is also the time of year when fewer people head for the trails. Although snowshoeing and backcountry skiing are becoming increasingly popular, winter is still the best time of year to find solitude.

Before choosing a winter hike, it is important to keep in mind that many trailheads are inaccessible by November or December. Before heading to a particular hike, make sure to check on the accessibility of the access road and/or be prepared to change plans. Also, loop hikes are not always the easiest choices in winter months, particularly after heavy snowfall or in areas with minimal use. As opposed to going up and down the same way, loop hikes will require you to break trail throughout the day. Be prepared for a longer, more tiring day, and bring a few extra friends.

The margin for error in winter hiking is slim. It is a good policy to carry more than what you think you will need of clothes, water, and food. It is especially helpful to have dry clothes in case you get wet from precipitation or from perspiration. In winter, the sun sets around 4:00 PM in January and slowly grows later and later. On cloudy days or on northern, forested slopes it can get darker even earlier.

Finally, always bring and expect to use snowshoes. Surprisingly, many hikers shy away from using snowshoes and focus more on ice axes and crampons. While ice axes and crampons are essential in certain circumstances, they are needed infrequently, even when climbing most 4000-footers. On the contrary, snowshoes are required on the vast majority of winter hikes. Why people rebel against wearing snowshoes is a mystery, especially with the compact lightweight designs and easy-to-fasten bindings now available; sinking deep in the snow or constantly sliding backwards is much more difficult. When choosing snowshoes, opt for narrow, oval-shaped ones with metal crampons underneath. This design will allow maximum control and maneuverability, particularly in mountainous terrain.

Weather Above Tree Line

When choosing a hike that climbs above tree line, such as Mount Katahdin, the Brothers, and Bigelow in Maine, and Moosilauke, Franconia Ridge, the

National Forest alpine weather sign

Pemigewasset Wilderness, and the Presidential Range in New Hampshire, weather should be of increased concern. The weather in all of these areas can be ferocious, and in most cases there is no safe shelter once you are above tree line. Pay attention not only to the existing conditions but also to the afternoon forecast that day and any incoming systems noted on the weather report. Remember that weather conditions above tree line are not reflective of conditions in the lowlands. Expect a minimum of 3 degrees Fahrenheit drop in ambient air temperature for each 1000 feet in elevation gain, combined with the wind chill from increased wind velocity as you climb. Plan for the best possibilities, but be prepared to change plans to accommodate weather conditions. Do not try to outsmart the weather or push hesitant members of your party if conditions are not ideal. The mountain will be there another day and hopefully you will get a chance to try again, made all the sweeter by the fact that you have exercised discipline and respect for the elements.

Gear

Before hitting the trails, it is prudent to be prepared with proper gear. While it is often tempting to head up the trail with less, you never know what may occur: injury, change of weather, illness, a wrong turn. The bottom line for any hike is to bring more than you think you will need; at worst you will build stronger back and shoulder muscles. For any hike, it is wise to include the following Ten Essentials:

1. Extra clothing. Even on the hottest days of summer, at a minimum you should carry a rain jacket and a water-resistant layer of clothing (fleece works well). An extra pair of socks is insurance against wet feet any time of year. During colder times of year or while venturing above tree line, lots of additional layers are a must, including warm hats and gloves. The highest locations described in this book can experience winter-like conditions throughout the year.
2. Extra food and water. Hiking is a strenuous activity that burns calories quickly. Fill your pack with high-energy food and more than you expect to eat. In addition, bring on each hike at least two quarts of water per person, even during colder months. Few things put a damper on an otherwise enjoyable hike as effectively—and unnecessarily—as headaches resulting from dehydration and hunger.
3. Sunglasses and sunscreen. Sun protection is a must throughout the year. In fact, the low angle of the sun and the reflection off snow and ice can make sunglasses very important during colder months. Sunscreen is also necessary, especially from late February to October. Hikers can be most vulnerable from late winter through mid-spring, when the sun is strong and bare trees provide little protection.
4. Knife or multitool and repair kit. A pocketknife or multitool with pliers is a handy device to carry. While seldom needed, the one time it is you will be happy to have brought it along. The same goes for repair items you may need to fix a critical piece of gear.
5. First-aid kit. Cuts, stings, twisted ankles, and other afflictions are distinct possibilities even for the most prepared hiker. Bandages, pain relievers, and ointments can help to significantly alleviate many injuries. Knowledge of first-aid procedures and how to react in certain emergency situations should ensure an injured party receives the necessary help.
6. Firestarter and matches. Having something that will catch fire, even when sticks and brush are wet, can be a huge help in an emergency, such as having to spend an unplanned night in the woods. Always carry dry matches in a waterproof container.
7. Emergency shelter. In an emergency situation, improvised shelter can make a critical difference in comfort or survival. An aluminized emergency space blanket will deflect wind and rain while reflecting body heat, and adds little weight to your pack. It can also be used in hot weather to provide shade.
8. Flashlight or head lamp. If forced to spend the night outdoors or when still on the trail after sunset, artificial light can be a big help in returning to the trailhead safely.

9. Maps. Having a map of the area and knowing how to read it provides options in the case of emergency. For example, often there are multiple trails in an area that provide shorter or easier alternatives. Know where you are and how to get someplace safely in an emergency.
10. Compass. While the trails in this book are generally well marked and easy to follow, harsh weather and snow can sometimes obscure the way. If for some reason you lose your way, the use of a compass can be a valuable tool in safely returning home.

In addition to these ten items, there are other gear considerations to make. Many of the hikes in this book, and throughout the region, take place on rocky terrain. To provide optimum comfort and effectiveness, choose sturdy boots with good ankle protection. It is also desirable to treat the boots with a waterproof coating or waterproofing agent, even if already applied by the manufacturer. There are a number of commercially available products that will cause water to bead up and run off boots, leaving your feet dry. Gaiters that wrap around your lower leg are also handy for keeping water and debris out of your boots. Lastly, when choosing socks avoid cotton, because it provides poor insulation when wet.

From May to September, you may not encounter insects on every hike in northern New England, but it is wise to be prepared for them: blackflies, mosquitoes, deerflies, and ticks in particular. Insect repellents, hats, and other gear can help ward off the annoyance and pain inflicted by these critters. Tucking clothes in and wearing light colors is also helpful when thinking about ticks.

Finally, include gear essential for enjoyment, such as a camera and binoculars. Similarly, bringing books that help in the identification of birds, wildlife, trees, and wildflowers can add many new dimensions to a hiking adventure.

Water

Unless faced with extreme dehydration, you should not drink any water you find on the trail before treating it. In fact, the cleanest mountain streams may be home to microscopic viruses and bacteria that will wreak havoc on your digestive system. Treating water can be as simple as boiling it, chemically purifying it with iodine tablets, or pumping it through one of the many commercially available water filter and purifier systems. Drinking untreated water is a mistake you will remember for a long time, and one that will provide you ample time to sit down to think about the poor decision you have made.

Cell Phones Are Not Safety Equipment

Cell phones cannot receive signals in many regions throughout Maine and New Hampshire. Never depend on cell phones for help in a hiking emergency. Technology should not be a replacement for preparedness and common sense.

Hiker Responsibility Code

(Recommended by Hike Safe, a program sponsored by the White Mountain National Forest and the New Hampshire Fish and Game Department)

You are responsible for yourself, so be prepared:

With knowledge and gear. Become self-reliant by learning about the terrain, conditions, local weather, and your equipment before you start.

To leave your plans. Tell someone where you are going, the trails you are hiking, when you will return, and your emergency plans.

To stay together. When you start as a group, hike as a group and end as a group. Pace your hike to the slowest person.

To turn back. Weather changes quickly in the mountains. Fatigue and unexpected conditions can also affect your hike. Know your limitations and when to postpone your hike. The mountains will be there another day.

For emergencies, even if you are headed out for just an hour. An injury, severe weather, or a wrong turn can become life threatening. Don't assume you will be rescued; know how to rescue yourself.

To share the hiker code with others.

Wildlife

From the low, rocky Maine coast to the highest elevations of the White Mountains, northern New England offers a wide array of land and habitat types. Within the diversity lives a broad spectrum of wildlife species. In the

Frog enjoying mid-day sun, Ethan Pond

more than sixteen months of hiking to research this guidebook, I encountered many wildlife species in their native habitats. Highlights included a moose cow and calf browsing in a marsh, a black bear scurrying across a rocky ridge, dozens of snakes sunning themselves, peregrine falcons and bald eagles gliding through thin mountain air, a beaver swimming beneath a pond covered by two inches of ice, and two red squirrels so focused on the survival of their species that they would not leave the trail. You never know what you will encounter around the next bend in the trail. Stay alert, walk softly, and eventually you will be pleasantly surprised.

Author's List of Wildlife Observed

While not exhaustive, the following list of species witnessed while researching illustrates the breadth of wildlife encounters possible in the region:

Mammals

Beaver
Black bear
Chipmunk
Gray squirrel
Harbor seal
Moose
Otter
Porcupine
Red fox
Red squirrel
White-tailed deer

Reptiles/Amphibians

American toad
Eastern newt
Garter snake
Green frog
Green snake
Milk snake
Spring peeper
Wood frog

Birds

American crow
American goldfinch
American kestrel
American redstart
American robin
American woodcock
Bald eagle
Barn swallow
Barred owl
Bicknell's thrush
Black-and-white warbler
Black-capped chickadee
Black guillemot
Black-throated blue warbler
Black-throated green warbler
Black-backed woodpecker
Blackburnian warbler
Blackpoll warbler
Blue jay
Bobolink
Bohemian waxwing
Boreal chickadee
Broad-winged hawk
Brown creeper
Bufflehead duck
Canada warbler
Cedar waxwing
Chestnut-sided warbler
Chipping sparrow
Common eider duck
Common flicker
Common goldeneye duck
Common loon
Common merganser
Common raven
Common yellowthroat
Dark-eyed junco
Double-crested cormorant
Downy woodpecker
Eastern bluebird
Eastern phoebe
Evening grosbeak
Fox sparrow
Golden-crowned kinglet
Gray jay
Great blue heron
Great black-backed gull
Hairy woodpecker

Hermit thrush
Herring gull
Horned lark
Indigo bunting
Least flycatcher
Long-tailed duck
Magnolia warbler
Mallard duck
Mourning dove
Northern parula warbler
Osprey
Ovenbird
Peregrine falcon
Pileated woodpecker
Purple finch
Red-breasted nuthatch
Red-eyed vireo
Red-winged blackbird
Rose-breasted grosbeak
Ruby-crowned kinglet
Ruby-throated hummingbird
Ruffed grouse
Sanderling
Sharp-shinned hawk
Solitary vireo
Song sparrow
Spotted sandpiper
Spruce grouse
Swainson's thrush
Tree swallow
Turkey vulture
Veery
Water pipit
White-breasted nuthatch
White-throated sparrow
White-winged crossbill
Wild turkey
Winter wren
Wood duck
Wood thrush
Yellow warbler
Yellow-bellied flycatcher
Yellow-bellied sapsucker
Yellow-rumped warbler

Land Conservation

Land conservation in Maine and New Hampshire has a long and proud tradition. Before 1900, most land in the region was worked hard, the forests stripped and burned, the watersheds polluted, and wildlife over-hunted. However, over the past hundred years much has changed. Numerous land conservation successes have led to healthier forests, cleaner water, and more diverse wildlife habitat. The hikes described in this book visit the region's oldest conservation areas and many areas protected in recent years.

Conservation land in Maine and New Hampshire from the beginning has been a partnership between private people and organizations with local, state, and federal governments. The combination of public and private interests has worked to protect special places, as well as to build and maintain hiking trails so the public can safely access these areas. Today, these efforts continue throughout the region. Maine and New Hampshire host a healthy community of private land conservation organizations that raise funds to protect and maintain thousands of acres of land each year. These private efforts are often supported in part by local, state, and federal programs, like the Land and Community Heritage Investment Program, the Land for Maine's Future Program, the Forest Legacy Program, and the Land and Water Conservation Fund.

Established in 1998 by New Hampshire's state legislature, the Land and Community Heritage Investment Program conserves and preserves the state's most important natural, cultural, and historical resources of local, regional, and statewide significance, in partnership with the state's municipalities and the private sector, to ensure the perpetual contribution of these resources to the state's economy, environment, and overall quality of life. The Land for

Maine's Future Program, established in 1987, finances and coordinates acquisition of lands for conservation, water access, outdoor recreation, wildlife and fish habitat, and farmland conservation. Since its creation, the Land for Maine's Future Program has assisted in the protection of more than 215,000 acres of land from willing sellers, through acquisition and conservation easements. The Forest Legacy Program is administered by the U.S. Forest Service. It has supported state efforts to protect thousands of acres of environmentally sensitive forestlands throughout the region. Created by the U.S. Congress in 1964, the Land and Water Conservation Fund provides money to federal, state, and local governments to purchase land for recreational opportunities, clean water, wildlife habitat, scenic vistas, archaeological and historical sites, and wilderness areas. The fund receives money mostly from fees paid by companies drilling offshore for oil and gas.

The appendix includes contact information for land conservation organizations and programs. It is important to keep these organizations and programs in mind after enjoying a wonderful hike in the open spaces of Maine and New Hampshire. Consider supporting the private organizations financially or through volunteering, and do not hesitate to contact

Fragile plants cling to exposed ledge

your legislators to ensure that public conservation programs remain sufficiently funded.

Using This Book

No guidebook can provide all the details of a trail, nor stay current with constantly changing conditions of trails, stream crossings, and access roads. So before starting a hike, it is often helpful to check in with the respective landowner. Contact information for landowners can be found in the appendix.

When referring to the hiking time stated at the beginning of each hike, please bear in mind that this is an estimate for the average hiker. Depending on your pace as a hiker, you may find the estimates are too high or too low. Use the estimated times as a tool, rather than a way to judge success or failure. Hikes are rated easy, moderate, difficult, or strenuous, an estimation based on length of hike, elevation change, and terrain.

The recommended best season to go is another subjective tool meant to be a guide, not an absolute. Anyone who has lived in New England long enough knows that the weather can be quite unpredictable. The amount of snow and ice on a given trail or access road varies from year to year. In most cases, hikes that have trailheads accessible twelve months a year are listed as year-round destinations. Some hikes with year-round-accessible trailheads are recommended only for times of the year when snow and/or ice are not a factor; however, with proper equipment and experience many of these hikes are possible year round as well.

The loop direction given for each hike is a recommendation that has been made primarily based on the terrain. As a general rule, it is preferable to ascend steep trails and descend the gradual ones when there is a choice.

Each hike includes a number of elevation statistics. Starting elevation refers to the trailhead; high point refers to the highest elevation reached on the loop; elevation gain cumulatively calculates all of the ups that occur on a hike. An elevation profile is also included with each hike description.

In choosing the sixty best hikes from New Hampshire's White Mountains to the Maine coast, special consideration was given to trailheads with multiple loop-hike options. Many of the longer hikes in the book describe shorter, easier loop hikes leaving from the same trailhead, and conversely, many of the shorter loop descriptions provide information on ways to extend or make a loop more challenging. There is information in this guidebook for more than one hundred loop hikes of various lengths and difficulties, providing different options depending on skill level, interest, or time of the year.

One of the natural attractions of northern New England is the diversity of its bird life. As an added feature, each chapter in the book includes a short, detailed description of at least one of the birds likely to be encountered on the hike. In total there are seventy-five different bird descriptions found throughout the book. For more assistance in identification, consider purchasing a pair of binoculars and a field guide to Northeastern birds and birding.

See you on the trails.

A Note About Safety

Safety is an important concern in all outdoor activities. No guidebook can alert you to every hazard or anticipate the limitations of every reader. Therefore, the descriptions of roads, trails, routes, and natural features in this book are not representations that a particular place or excursion will be safe for your party. When you follow any of the routes described in this book, you assume responsibility for your own safety. Under normal conditions, such excursions require the usual attention to traffic, road and trail conditions, weather, terrain, the capabilities of your party, and other factors. Keeping informed on current conditions and exercising common sense are the keys to safe, enjoyable outings.

—*The Mountaineers Books*

SOUTHERN NEW HAMPSHIRE

1 Pisgah State Park

Round trip ■ 8 miles
Loop direction ■ Counterclockwise
Rating ■ Moderate–Difficult
Hiking time ■ 5 hours
Starting elevation ■ 1080 feet
High point ■ 1410 feet
Elevation gain ■ 1350 feet
Best season ■ Year round
Map ■ USGS Hinsdale
Contact ■ New Hampshire Division of Parks and Recreation

Driving directions: From the junction of Routes 9 and 101 in Keene, follow Route 9 west for 9 miles, then turn left onto Route 63. Continue straight for 4.5 miles until reaching the Kilburn Road parking area on the left.

Pisgah State Park, 13,500 acres of rolling hills and sprawling wetlands, is quietly nestled in the southwest corner of New Hampshire. A year-round haven for outdoor activities, the park is a perfect destination for spring bird-watchers, summer wildflower enthusiasts, autumn leaf peepers, and winter wildlife trackers. Once the domain of local paper mill owners and rural farmers, today the land is a permanently protected preserve where hikers of all abilities can find beauty and be rejuvenated. With more than 50 miles of trails and six separate trailheads, the park also offers countless loop hiking possibilities.

One of the more scenic and quiet loops begins on Kilburn Road, a wide footpath that meanders over easy grades 0.6 mile to the north shore of Kilburn Pond, where it meets the western branch of the popular 5-mile Kilburn Loop leading straight along the pond's shore. To reach Mount Pisgah, stay left on Kilburn Road. After a sharp right turn the path narrows and crosses a small stream, before gradually climbing up a hemlock-covered hillside.

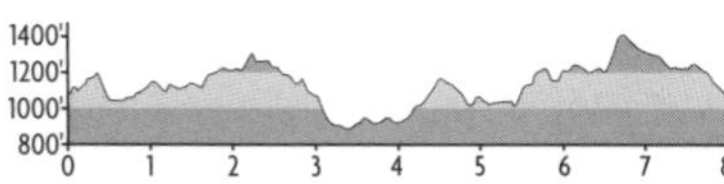

At an intersection with the Kilburn Loop's east branch, veer left, reaching the Pisgah Ridge Trail a half-mile farther.

Begin the steady climb south along the narrowing ridgeline. Soon the trail emerges onto an open ledge where views of Mount Monadnock dominate the eastern skyline. A curiously shaped cairn stands guard over

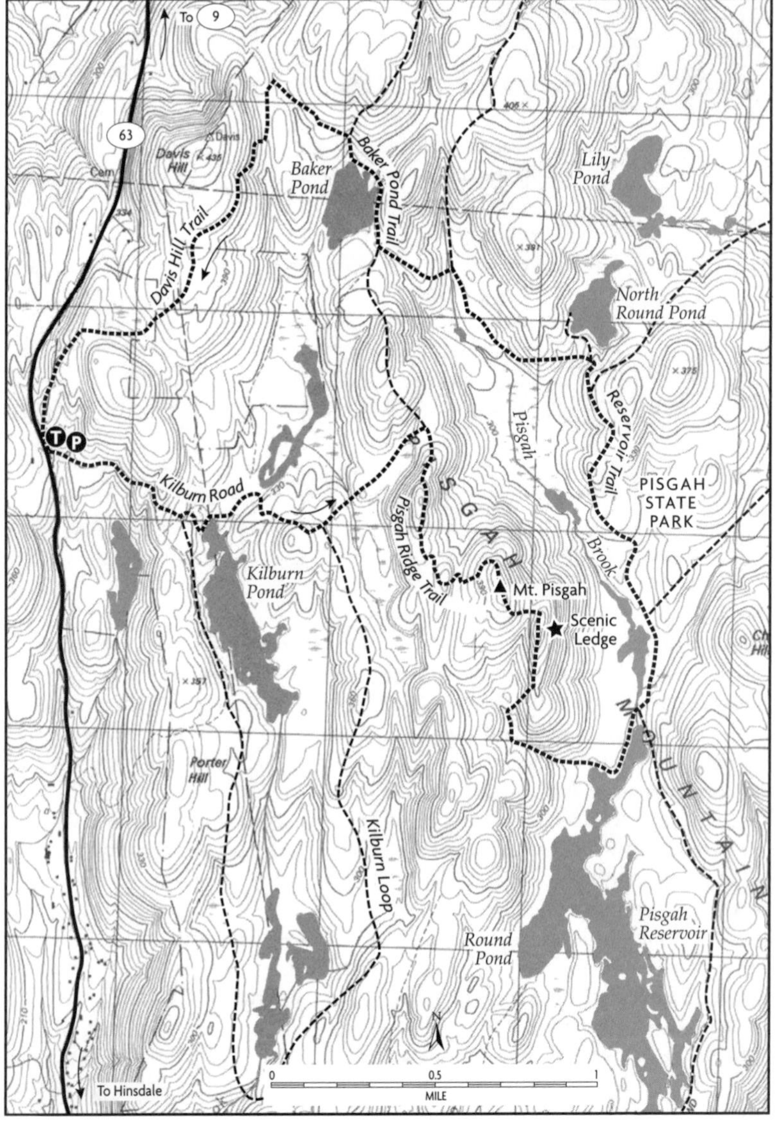

Kilburn Pond

a western viewpoint pointing to the rolling hills of southern Vermont. The trail descends into a small saddle and then quickly ascends to the 1329-foot wooded summit of Mount Pisgah. While little vegetation grows beneath the evergreen canopy, the trail's footing is greatly eased by the padded carpet of discarded needles.

Continue down the ridge to the finest viewpoint of the day where the trail reaches the top of a scenic ledge. This is a great spot to enjoy the park's tranquil scenery, which has changed greatly in the last one hundred years from open fields to today's thick forests. In fact, the area's most famous descendant, Harlan Fiske Stone, was born in 1872 on farmland now owned by the park. A lifelong Republican, Stone was appointed the twelfth chief justice of the U.S. Supreme Court by President Franklin Roosevelt in 1941. Stone's most enduring legacy occurred in the 1937 Carolene Products case, when he laid the foundation for decades of decisions upholding individual rights. What else would one expect from a justice born in the "Live free or die" state?

Beyond the ledge the trail passes a large rock, enters a small notch, and descends the gradual slope to the shore of Pisgah Reservoir. Approach the water quietly and you may stumble upon one of the many resident species of waterfowl, including the hooded merganser, a small duck easily recognized by the male's fan-shaped black-and-white head. The sheltered reservoir provides ideal habitat for these shy "hoodies," which often dive underwater for food.

After hugging the shoreline the path crosses a small bridge and ends at the Reservoir Trail, a multi-use trail also enjoyed by snowmobilers and mountain bikers. Turn left and follow the wide route 1.8 miles up and over a number of low ridges, by many small wetlands, and past a few side trails. The 0.2-mile spur to North Round Pond is a nice diversion to a quiet corner of the park and a great location to see mountain laurel, a showy flowering shrub of southern New England common in the park but uncommon in New Hampshire. Upon reaching the Baker Pond Trail, turn left onto the old roadway and travel 0.8 mile around the serene pond to a three-way intersection. Here a path leads right 0.5 mile up to scenic Hubbard Hill.

The journey back begins left on the Davis Hill Trail, a series of old roads that dissect the wooded landscape. While cresting Davis Hill, scan the trailside for small American chestnut trees. Once abundant in the Appalachian Mountains, the chestnut is now rare, decimated by a blight imported from Asia. As the bark on these small trees becomes grooved, they too will likely endure the fate of their predecessors. Over the final stretch the trail passes two town boundaries and briefly leaves state land before ending at the parking area.

2 Pack Monadnock

Round trip ■ 8 miles
Loop direction ■ Counterclockwise
Rating ■ Moderate–Difficult
Hiking time ■ 5 hours
Starting elevation ■ 1480 feet
High point ■ 2290 feet
Elevation gain ■ 2000 feet
Best season ■ Year round
Maps ■ USGS Peterborough South, Peterborough North, Greenville, and Greenfield
Contact/fee ■ New Hampshire Division of Parks and Recreation

Driving directions: Beginning at the junction of Routes 101 and 101A in Milford, head west on Route 101. Travel 10.8 miles and turn right into Miller State Park. (Approaching from the junction of Routes 202 and 101 in Peterborough, follow Route 101 east for 3.9 miles and turn left into the state park entrance.) The large parking area is at the base of the auto road.

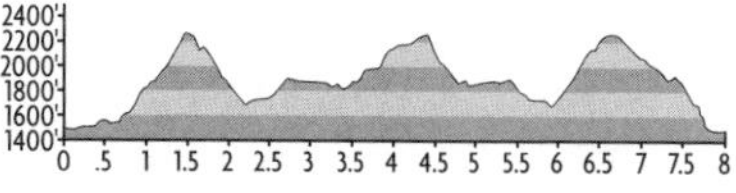

Two loops in one, a relaxing trek across a scenic ridge, and views stretching from New England's highest point to its largest city highlight this adventure in southwestern New Hampshire. The hike takes place within nearly 3000 acres of contiguous conservation land protected from encroaching development through a partnership of public and private initiative at the local, state, and federal levels. Together, these protected lands provide valuable habitat for moose, deer, fisher, and countless songbirds. Thanks to the collaborative efforts that have protected Pack Monadnock, we can all enjoy its natural and recreational values for many years to come.

Begin the journey in Miller State Park, established in 1891 as New Hampshire's first state park. In 1892 it was named in honor of General James Miller, a hero of the War of 1812's Battle of Lundy's Lane. The centerpiece of the park, which now encompasses 550 acres of land, is 2290-foot South Pack Monadnock. While many reach the summit via the 1.3-mile auto road, hiking up remains the most pleasurable option.

Two footpaths leave the eastern side of the parking area. Leading left is the Wapack Trail, a 21-mile route established in 1923 running from Mount Watatic in Massachusetts to North Pack Monadnock; you will be joining this trail later. Turn right onto the 1.4-mile trail named in honor of Wapack Trail co-founder Marion Davis. The Marion Davis Trail gradually winds through a rock-shrouded forest before arriving at the summit parking area. While South Pack Monadnock is mostly wooded, there are views from an old lookout tower and from the short 0.4-mile Summit Loop Trail, blazed in red, which passes a number of vistas while circling the summit. When ready for a quieter destination, hike north along the Wapack Trail. Past an open ledge and a junction with the Raymond Trail, the route reenters the forest and swings right where a short spur leads to a viewpoint. Beyond, a steady descent through the dark evergreen forest leads to a flat ridge carpeted in fern, where a large sign welcomes you to the Joanne Bass Bross Preserve, a 500-acre parcel protected in 2000 by the New Hampshire Chapter of the Nature Conservancy. Continuing along the ridge, you soon enter the Wapack National Wildlife Refuge (no signs or markers). This 1672-acre refuge, which encompasses much of North Pack Monadnock, is managed primarily for the protection of nesting songbirds, upland mammals, and migrating hawks.

On the right, 1.7 miles from South Pack Monadnock, lies the start of the Cliff Trail. Look for its sign painted on a rock, and if you have any trouble, ask one of the slithering snakes sunning on the dry ridge. The 1.2-mile trek past the most scenic spot on the mountain first descends to a small stream, but quickly rises to the base of a talus slope. Swing right and climb steeply through the woods to the cliff's edge where expansive views of Mount Monadnock, Mount Wachusett, and the Boston skyline await. This infrequently visited spot is a great location to scan the sky for turkey vultures.

With long wingspans resembling outstretched fingertips, these eerie-looking birds gracefully soar on the wind.

Ahead, the trail passes through woods and across open ledges before reaching the summit of North Pack Monadnock, which stands slightly lower

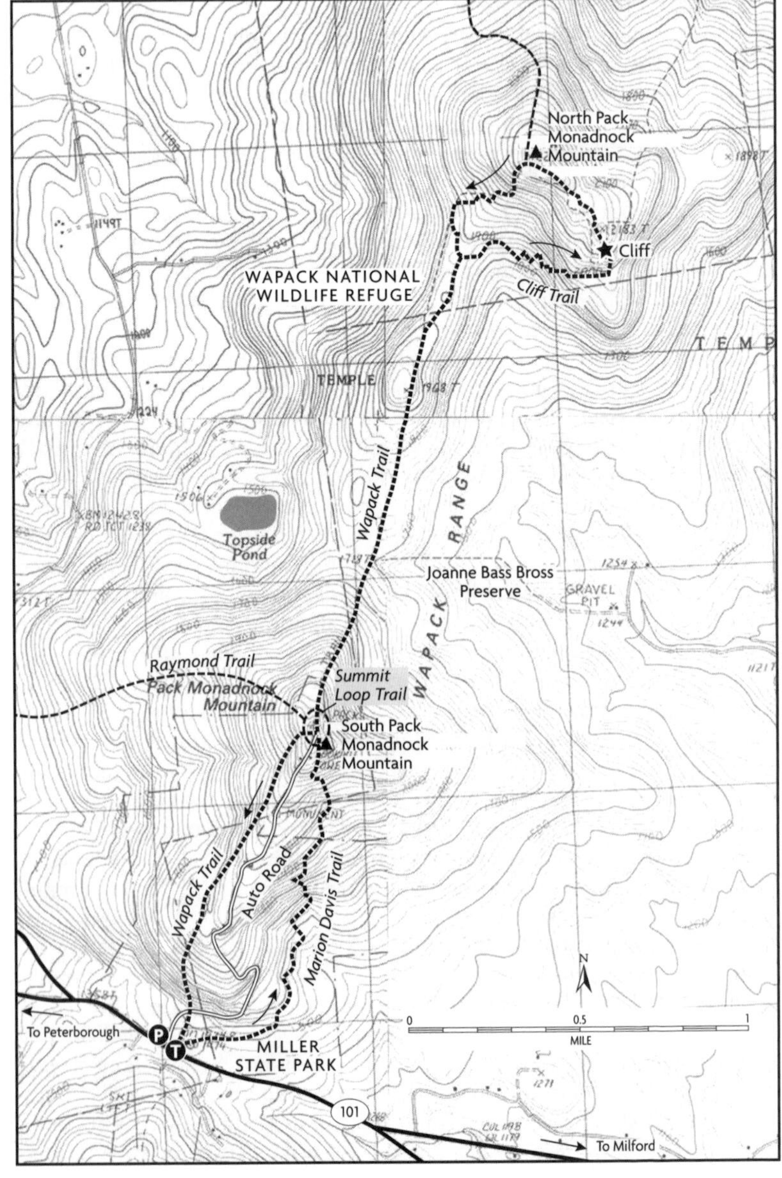

The Cliff Trail, North Pack Monadnock

than its southern neighbor. While trees continue to restrict the views, there are plenty of places to relax and enjoy the fields and rolling hills of western New Hampshire.

The 3.7-mile return trip follows the Wapack Trail exclusively. Beginning at a large cairn, the path gradually winds west, then south through the shady forest before returning to the start of the Cliff Trail. Stay right and remain on the ridge until reaching South Pack Monadnock. From the summit parking area the Wapack Trail begins its descent at a western viewpoint of Mount Monadnock. Dropping steadily over rocky terrain, the trail becomes steeper as you approach the highway. A series of switchbacks leads down oak-covered ledges with occasional views until reaching the auto road. Cross the road and hike a few hundred yards to the trail's end.

If 8 miles sounds too long, limit the loop to South Pack Monadnock. The Wapack and Marion Davis Trails easily combine for a 2.8-mile hike. Including the red-blazed Summit Loop Trail would add another 0.4 mile.

3 Lake Massabesic

Round trip ■ 4 miles
Loop direction ■ Counterclockwise
Rating ■ Easy
Hiking time ■ 2 hours
Starting elevation ■ 295 feet
High point ■ 310 feet
Elevation gain ■ 60 feet
Best season ■ Year round
Maps ■ USGS Derry and Candia
Contact/fee ■ New Hampshire Audubon

Driving directions: From Interstate 93 in Manchester, take Exit 7 onto Route 101 east. Turn right on Exit 1 onto Bypass 28 and head south. Drive 2.1 miles on Bypass 28, then turn left onto Spofford Road. Continue for 0.3 mile before turning left again onto Audubon Way. A parking area is located on the left across from the Massabesic Audubon Center.

Located minutes from Manchester, northern New England's largest city, the Massabesic Audubon Sanctuary boasts 130 acres of fields and forests owned and managed by New Hampshire Audubon. From the parcel's nature center, open year round Tuesday through Sunday (except in the summer when open Monday through Saturday), a 1.5-mile interpretive trail loops around the property through many diverse habitats. The loop provides access to additional trails that lead to the end of scenic Battery Point. The combination of trails is ideal for a half-day adventure of leisurely hiking and wildlife observation. The shoreline and end of Battery Point is owned and managed by the Manchester Water Works, and there is a seamless transition from Audubon to Water Works land. Both organizations have a cooperative management agreement on the whole of Battery Point that includes a no-hunting policy.

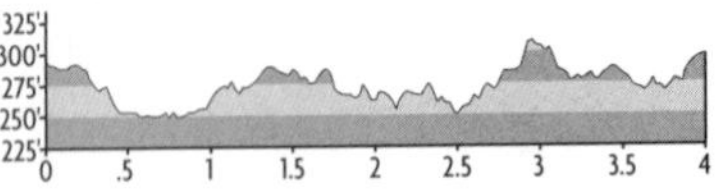

The first stop on the trip is the nature center. Inside there are a number of displays and information on the sanctuary and the work

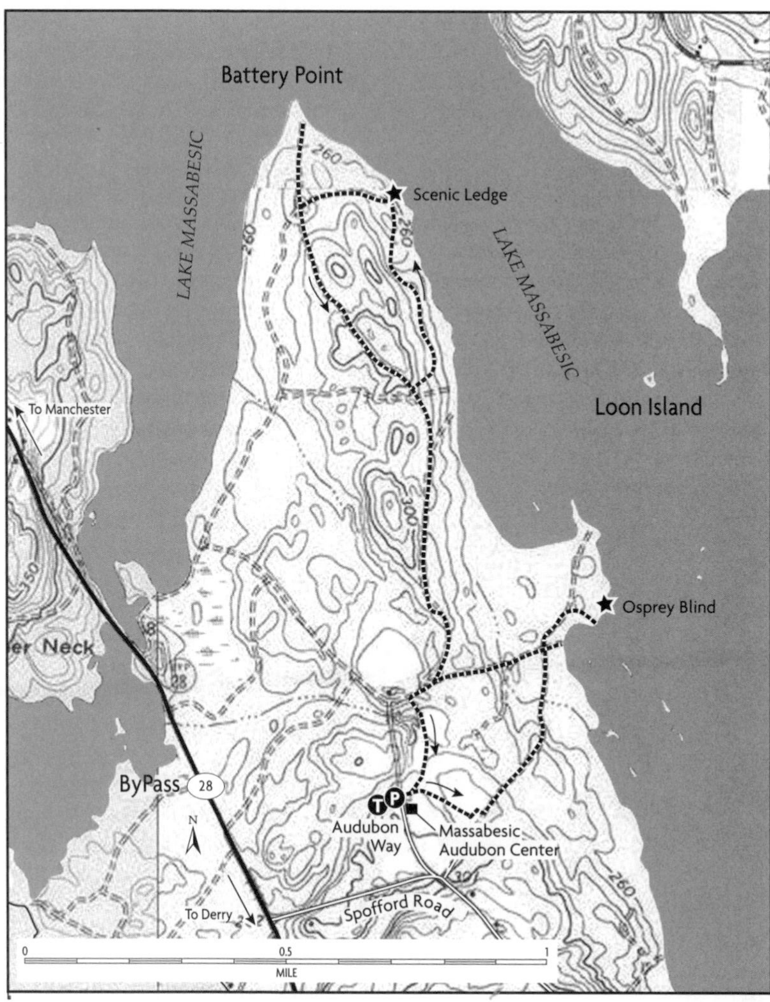

of New Hampshire Audubon. There are also restrooms, refreshments, and a nature store. Here signs describe a number of important rules associated with the sanctuary, among them: pets must be on leashes at all times and are not allowed in the open fields; do not pick flowers; stay on marked trails. There is also a brochure available that describes eighteen stops along the 1.5-mile trail.

From the nature center, head north to reach the trailhead at the edge of the field (ask in the center about the alternate dog-walking trail). With blue-and-white tree swallows circling around, continue straight to a trail junction. Veer right and head east across the field. Listen closely for the gurgling, bubbling call of the bobolink. Skunklike in appearance, these sparrow-sized, mostly black birds with white patches on their backs nest in tall grasses. As the open spaces of New England have developed and reforested, the number of bobolinks have declined. The careful management here continues to aid in their success.

The trail winds around the edge of the pasture, then bears right into a forest of oak, maple, and birch, immediately reaching an old road. Turn left on the road and make your way gradually down toward the shore of the lake, heading northeast. At a four-way intersection, turn right to reach the shoreline. Straight ahead are signs leading 0.1 mile to a blind where ospreys and loons are frequently sighted. The loop continues left away from the water.

From here the trail winds over the gently rolling terrain, where sandy soils support a forest of white pine. Keep your eyes open for signs from the past. Like much of the land in southern New Hampshire, this piece of property has many stories to tell. Previous landowners have farmed, harvested timber, and grazed livestock here. Evidence of previous activities can be seen throughout, including rock walls and stone bridges.

Calm waters of Lake Massabesic

At the next junction the 1.5-mile loop veers left and returns to the nature center. However, for now, stay right and continue north along a wide path that is occasionally used by mountain bikes. Take advantage of the flat terrain to scan the area for any of the numerous songbirds that nest and frequent this area. Many of the species are quite colorful, such as the northern oriole. No birds can be confused with the brilliant orange and black of the oriole, and few are as melodious.

Ahead, turn right at another trail junction and join a more rustic path that meanders and eventually reaches a scenic ledge on the water's edge. Here, at one of the preserve's quieter shorefront locations, the 2500-acre Lake Massabesic stands on display. Since the late 1800s this lake has served as Manchester's water supply, and while swimming is off limits, viewing its beauty is not. From the shore, the trail heads west, soon joining the main thoroughfare. Turn right and follow the route to the end of Battery Point, a small peninsula that provides sweeping views of the sparkling blue water.

For the return trek to the nature center, remain on the old road. Follow it back to the interpretive trail and turn right down a small hill. Here the trail passes a vernal pool, a small body of water that typically dries up by late summer. Vernal pools are critical for the survival of frogs and other amphibians. Be careful here, because a lot of poison ivy grows in this area. Through the last stand of white pines, the path soon emerges onto open fields. Make your way past the last few stops along the interpretive trail before reaching the nature center.

4 North Pawtuckaway Mountain

Round trip ■ 4.9 miles
Loop direction ■ Clockwise
Rating ■ Moderate
Hiking time ■ 3 hours
Starting elevation ■ 520 feet
High point ■ 1011 feet
Elevation gain ■ 900 feet
Best season ■ May through November
Map ■ USGS Mount Pawtuckaway
Contact ■ New Hampshire Division of Parks and Recreation

Driving directions: From Route 101 in Raymond, take Exit 5. Drive 0.6 mile north on Route 107 and turn left at the light. In 4 miles, stay right on Route 107 at the Route 27 intersection, and then 3.1 miles farther turn right onto Reservation Road. After passing under powerlines, turn sharply right at 1.2 miles. Follow the dirt road 0.6 mile down the hill to a small parking area on the left, located near a gated snowmobile trail.

The three rocky ridges of Pawtuckaway State Park are a stark contrast to the low, rolling hills and marshy wetlands of southeastern New Hampshire. Rising from 800 to 1000 feet above sea level, North, Middle, and South Pawtuckaway mountains are the remnants of an ancient caldera. Today they stand parallel and apart, separated by two deep valleys further carved by the retreating glaciers that shaped this landscape thousands of years ago. These three ridges and the state park in which they are located provide

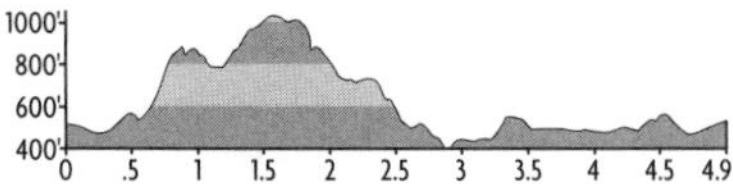

visitors a number of enjoyable hiking opportunities. The loop over North Pawtuckaway Mountain is especially attractive for the variety of habitats it traverses, the interesting geological features it passes, and the moderate challenge it offers.

The hike begins on a multi-use route used as a snowmobile trail. While trees are abundant now, it becomes apparent immediately that this landscape was once quite different. Beyond the gate, check out the large granite foundation slowly being consumed by the growing forest. The same processes that reclaimed the area following the last ice age are now shaping a land no longer valued for its limited agricultural potential.

Entering a shady pine grove, the trail wanders over the rolling landscape,

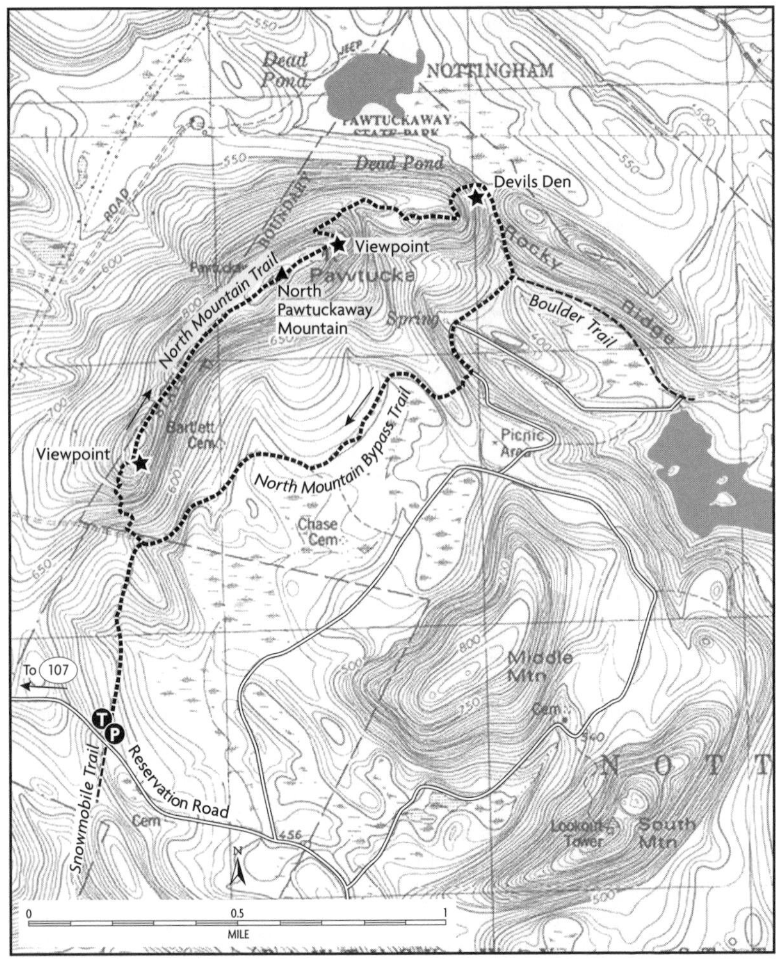

Exploring the North Mountain Trail

soon reaching an intersection at 0.5 mile. Stay straight (west) and ascend the short, steep slope. The trail quickly levels atop a rocky ridge of stunted oak trees. Here a thinner canopy allows for a carpet of green sedges, wildflowers, and ferns. The pleasant route reaches a scenic viewpoint on the right, then continues over moderate terrain while weaving between lichen-draped rocks and around small ledges.

After passing additional but more restricted viewpoints, climb over the wooded high point of North Pawtuckaway Mountain. The trail drops quickly down the other side to a utility tower and a nice view of the park.

Turn left and enter the dark hemlock forest. Swinging easily down the steep slope, the path levels across a low ridge, then descends more steeply while passing the Devils Den, a labyrinth of cliffs, caves, and ledges. At the bottom of the hill a small pond is visible through the trees.

From here the path becomes considerably wider and the terrain gradual. Enjoy the leisurely stroll that ends at the Boulder Trail, aptly named for the abundant number of large rocks sprinkled about. To the left the trail leads 0.5 mile one-way past the ledges of Rocky Ridge, often scaled by rock climbers, ending near Round Pond.

The loop continues right up the small incline and in 0.2 mile reaches a park road. Follow the road 0.1 mile south, and then turn right onto the North Mountain Bypass Trail. Follow this path down old roads for a relaxing end to the day's circuit. While passing through the young hardwood forests along the way, listen for the call of the many resident songbirds, including the vibrant rose-breasted grosbeak. This black-and-white bird with a bright red breast produces a melodious call reminiscent of a slightly congested robin. The final 0.5 mile to Reservation Road is a repeat of the hike's beginning.

On return trips to Pawtuckaway State Park, consider exploring the park's other features. In addition to trails up Middle and South Pawtuckaway mountains, the park includes a nice freshwater lake for swimming and canoeing, black gum and Atlantic white cedar swamps, and miles of four-season recreational trails. Pawtuckaway SP is also one of the few places in New Hampshire to see the cerulean warbler, a small bluish bird that is more common to swamplands in the southeastern United States than to wetlands in New England.

5 Mount Kearsarge

Round trip ■ 2.8 miles
Loop direction ■ Counterclockwise
Rating ■ Moderate
Hiking time ■ 2 hours
Starting elevation ■ 1840 feet
High point ■ 2937 feet
Elevation gain ■ 1100 feet
Best season ■ May through October
Map ■ USGS Andover
Contact/fee ■ New Hampshire Division of Parks and Recreation

Driving directions: From Concord, follow Route 89 to Exit 10. Turn right off the exit and then right at the T intersection. Travel 0.5 mile and turn left. Follow this road for 3.1 miles, turning right onto the Kearsarge

Mountain Road. Continue up the mountain, following Winslow State Park signs, until reaching the park entrance in 2.3 miles. A parking lot, picnic area, and small playground are located 0.3 mile beyond the entrance.

Believed to be named for a Native American word meaning "notch, pointed, mountain of pines," Mount Kearsarge is more noteworthy for the treeless summit that a 1796 fire has left behind. Today the mountain provides a hiking destination where the whole family can enjoy a big-mountain experience with a fraction of the effort needed to scale similar-sized mountains. Although not as difficult as other hikes, the climb is hardly easy. The elevation gain is in excess of 1000 feet in a little over a mile—just enough to a feel a strong sense of accomplishment when enjoying the summit's breathtaking views, whether you are four years old, seventy, or any age in between.

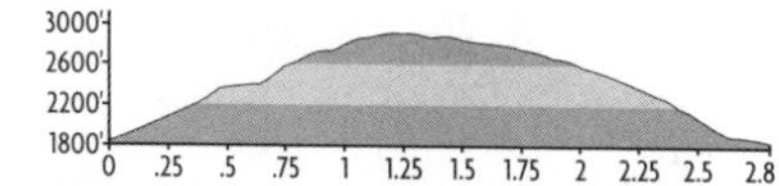

The loop begins on the 1.1-mile Winslow Trail, named for Admiral

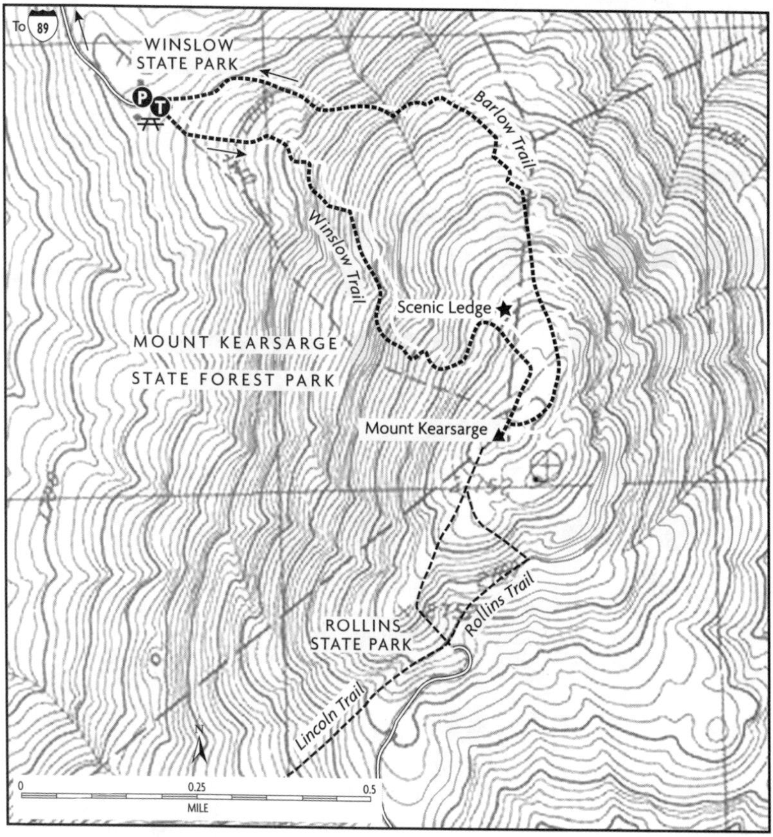

John Winslow, commander of the USS *Kearsarge*. Admiral Winslow became a Civil War hero by defeating a Confederate ship off the coast of France, helping to discourage European nations from entering the war. Paralleling a powerline, the trail soon crosses to the other side and wastes little time ascending the slope. Climbing over rocks and roots under the thick canopy of spruce and fir trees, the first half of the hike is straightforward. As you climb higher, the small individual rocks tend to give way to ledge. Watch your footing, but relax; there are enough safe places to step along the way.

Soon the trail veers left and levels off briefly before reaching a scenic ledge at 0.7 mile. Beyond the scenic ledge, with expansive views north and west, the

The summit towers

trail continues through a thinning canopy of trees and an expanding series of open ledges as the summit towers become visible. Swing right at an intersection with the Barlow Trail and complete the final few hundred yards to the treeless top. The only things blocking the 360-degree views are the two towers, including the fire tower that is open to the public and often staffed by the park service. Mount Washington and the White Mountains loom to the north, Mount Killington and the Green Mountains to the west, Mount Monadnock to the south, and the small hills and valleys of the Merrimack Valley to the east. On a clear day even the Boston skyline is visible on the southeastern horizon.

Sufficiently recharged by the cool winds, the warm sunshine, and the beauty that abounds in all directions, retrace your steps back to the Barlow Trail. This new 1.6-mile option, created in the 1990s, provides a slightly longer, more moderate, and less rocky alternative to the Winslow Trail. At first the route continues along the semi-open ridge with nice views of Ragged Mountain in the foreground. Swinging left, reenter the woods and meander along the moss and bunchberry-covered ground. Listen for the high-pitched whistles of golden- and ruby-crowned kinglets, chickadee-sized, gregarious birds that often bounce from branch to branch in high-elevation coniferous forests. While drab in color, the bright yellow top on the golden-crown and the small red spot on the ruby-crown can add a bit of bright color to the dark green surroundings.

Slowly the balsam-scented forest becomes replaced by taller birch and maple. The moderating descent quickly returns to the parking area, where the picnic facilities and playground offer additional diversions for those not eager for a return to civilization.

6 Mount Cardigan

Round trip ■ 7.6 miles
Loop direction ■ Counterclockwise
Rating ■ Moderate–Difficult
Hiking time ■ 4 to 5 hours
Starting elevation ■ 1390 feet
High point ■ 3155 feet
Elevation gain ■ 2350 feet
Best season ■ May through November
Map ■ USGS Mount Cardigan
Contact ■ New Hampshire Division of Parks and Recreation

Driving directions: From Bristol, take Route 3A north to the southern tip of Newfound Lake. Turn left near a stone church and follow West Shore

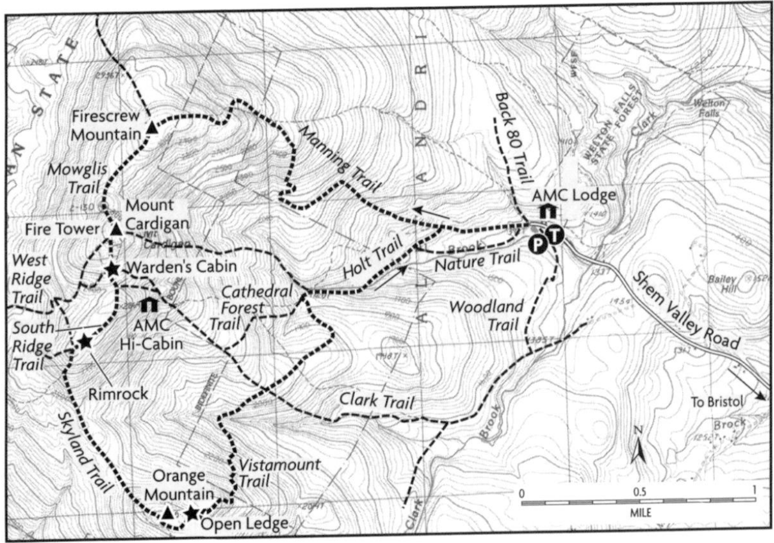

Road for 1.9 miles. Continue straight onto Fowler River Road. Turn right at an intersection in 1.2 miles, then 3.2 miles farther turn left onto Brook Road. Follow Brook Road 1.1 miles before turning right onto Shem Valley Road. Cross a bridge and turn right on the dirt road that leads 1.4 miles over a hill to the Appalachian Mountain Club's (AMC) Cardigan Lodge. Parking is available along the road's left side.

A shorter ride from the region's population centers than taller mountains to the north, Mount Cardigan offers some of the finest views of New Hampshire from its rocky summit, including the rugged White Mountains, the blue waters of the Lakes Region, and the rolling hills of the Connecticut River valley. Despite Mount Cardigan's lower elevation, its trails are as steep and challenging as many that scale the state's 4000-foot peaks. The mountain also has a tremendous variety of routes from which to choose. While most opt for the shorter, easier hikes from the west, the best of what Mount Cardigan has to offer can be found on its longer, quieter, and more scenic trails to the east.

Begin along the well-traveled path near the lodge, which is surrounded by 1200 acres of conservation land owned and managed by the AMC. The lodge and nearby campsites, as well as a rustic cabin high on the mountain, are available for overnight stays. Contact the AMC (see the appendix) for more information or to make reservations. The loop begins in 0.3 mile where the Holt and Manning

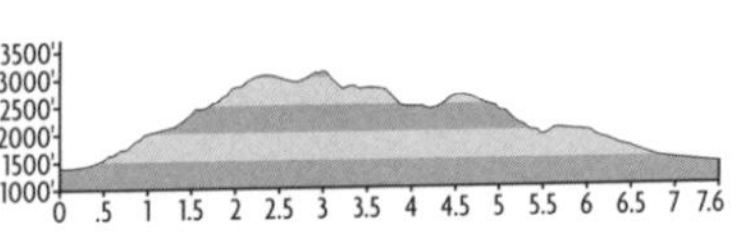

trails diverge. Stay right on the Manning Trail as it gradually winds through a classic northern hardwood forest. Swinging to the right the path climbs more quickly up rock and over pine needles.

After crossing a small, shady brook, emerge onto the first of many open ledges as the trail leaves AMC land and enters Cardigan State Park. A series of short, steep climbs leads to the top of a flat, scenic ridge, culminating upon the 3064-foot summit of Firescrew Mountain. With the fire tower and summit of Mount Cardigan in plain view, turn left onto the Mowglis Trail for the final 0.6 mile of the 3-mile ascent. The leisurely path reaches the base of the mountain, where a final scramble up open rock is all that stands in the way of the refreshing breezes and breathtaking views of the summit. When the trail is dry, only your stamina should be tested. If wet or icy, the final climb may be challenging.

The descent begins on the Clark Trail, which branches left off the West Ridge Trail a few hundred feet from the fire tower. A very steep 0.2-mile drop down the solid rock face ends at a small fire warden's cabin. Here the Clark Trail continues left and, combined with the Cathedral Forest and Holt trails,

Cardigan Mountain and Firescrew Mountain from the Vistamount Trail

provides the shortest and easiest return to the parking area. For a more adventurous and less crowded alternative, follow the South Ridge Trail straight towards the open ledges of Mount Cardigan's South Peak to an intersection at Rimrock. Turn left on the Skyland Trail for an enjoyable 1-mile trek across the gentle ridge. Along the way listen for the raucous call of the northern flicker, a large woodpecker that when seen in flight is easily identified by the bright yellow undersides of its wings and the large white patch on its rump. Look for flickers near or on large dead trees, a preferred nest location.

After the Skyland Trail ascends the 2684-foot summit of Orange Mountain, turn left onto the 1.6-mile Vistamount Trail. Quickly reach an open ledge where views of Mount Cardigan's summit and Firescrew Mountain stand in full view. This great resting spot is one few fellow hikers will share and a great place for lounging in the sun.

After a series of switchbacks ends in a narrow valley, cross the small brook and climb up to the Clark Trail intersection. Continue straight along the flat terrain until reaching the Cathedral Forest Trail. Turn right here and right again in 0.1 mile onto the Holt Trail. The final 1.1 miles is very gradual and becomes easier with each step—the perfect way to cap off a day on Mount Cardigan's majestic rocky ridges.

WHITE MOUNTAINS

1 Mount Whiteface

Round trip ■ 11.5 miles
Loop direction ■ Clockwise
Rating ■ Difficult
Hiking time ■ 8 hours
Starting elevation ■ 1200 feet
High point ■ 4010 feet
Elevation gain ■ 3800 feet
Best season ■ May through October
Maps ■ USGS Mount Tripyramid and Mount Chocorua
Contact/fee ■ White Mountain National Forest

Driving directions: Follow Route 113A to Wonalancet Village, 6.6 miles west from Route 113 in the center of Tamworth or 6.7 miles east from Route 113 north of Center Sandwich. Turn north onto Ferncroft Road. Follow this dirt road 0.5 mile and turn right—the parking area is a few hundred feet ahead.

Scenic ridges, wooded summits, gently sloping valleys, and short, steep ascents characterize many of the hikes in the southern White Mountains. Since the late 1800s, Wonalancet Village and members of the Wonalancet Out Door Club (WODC) have constructed and maintained trails throughout this area, while inviting guests to partake of the region's tranquil beauty. From the Ferncroft trailhead alone, no fewer than six loop hikes of varying lengths and degrees of difficulty can be completed. This recommended loop over Mount Whiteface, though long, includes many miles of peaceful ridge-walking where you are more apt to stumble upon a family of ruffed grouse foraging in the thick vegetation than fellow hikers following in your footsteps.

Follow the driveway back to Ferncroft Road and turn right. Pass a few private residences and then turn left across the Squirrel Bridge. Here the Blueberry Ledge Trail begins a 3.7-mile climb to Mount Whiteface's south summit. As the road dead-ends, the trail leads right into the forest. Beyond the Blueberry Ledge Cut-off Trail you enter the White Mountain National Forest and soon after the Sandwich Mountain Wilderness.

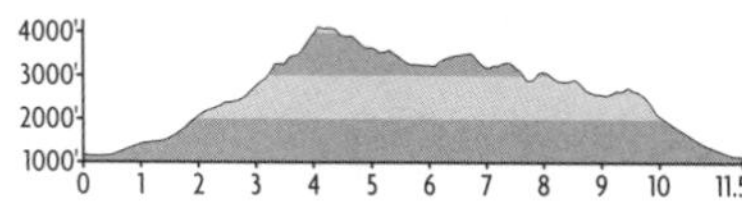

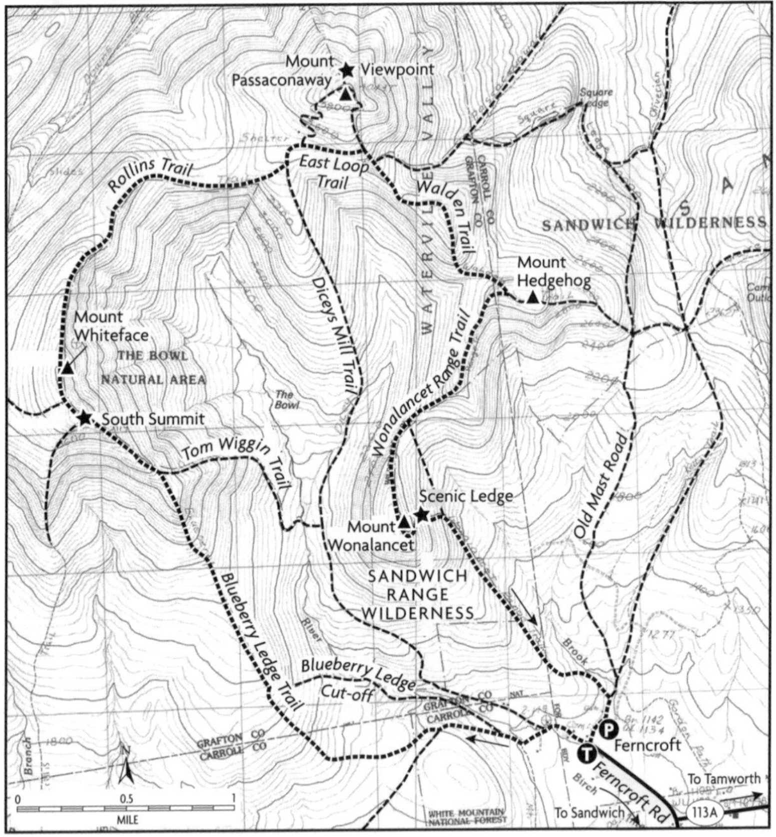

The gradual path eventually emerges onto exposed rock and passes through an open area with limited views south, before returning to the woods beyond the upper junction of the cut-off trail.

From this point a more aggressive climb ensues. After hiking through a small saddle where the Tom Wiggin Trail enters, you will reach an open ledge with views of the south peak and the white face that inspired the mountain's name. From here, scale a series of short, steep rock faces that are not ideal when wet or icy. Each scramble brings increasing views, culminating with a 180-degree vista from the south summit, where New Hampshire's Lakes Region stretches out before you.

A short drop along the Rollins Trail, followed by a slightly longer climb, ends at Mount Whiteface's wooded 4010-foot summit. Having reached this destination, most peak-baggers turn around here opting for the shortest way back; however, a longer more enjoyable alternative lies ahead. For nearly 2 miles the Rollins Trail meanders along the ridge, occasionally stopping briefly atop rocks perched high above the steep walls forming the Bowl, a protected natural area that includes 500 acres of old-growth forest that has never been logged.

The Rollins Trail ends, providing two options. To the right the Diceys Mill Trail leads 3.7 miles back to the parking area along moderate terrain that continues to ease along the way—a good choice for sore knees. For a more adventurous route, head left and climb 0.3 mile to the former site of Camp Rich (along with two other shelters on Mount Whiteface, the camp was recently removed due to deterioration and to comply with the Federal Wilderness Act). Again there are options. The first is to ascend more than 500 feet in 0.5 mile to the summit of 4060-foot Mount Passaconaway. From there follow the Walden Trail back down. While wooded, the summit has two accessible viewpoints: one along the way, and another on a spur trail that descends 0.3 mile to a spot above the Downes Brook Slide.

A second choice (featured route on the map accompanying this hike) is to veer right (east) on the East Loop Trail, which crosses over level ground 0.3 mile before intersecting the Walden Trail. Follow the Walden Trail 1.3 miles to the right along the gentle fern-covered ridge. The trail soon descends abruptly into a small notch, only to climb briefly up the other side onto the west shoulder of Mount Hedgehog (not to be confused with a similarly named peak in Hike 15). Turn right here onto the 3.2-mile Wonalancet Range Trail. An enjoyable walk begins along another gradual, wooded ridge with a couple of viewpoints along the way.

South Summit's "white face"

Before arriving atop Mount Wonalancet and reaching a scenic ledge with nice views of the countryside, a cut-off trail leads left, providing an easier alternative, especially if the ledge is likely to be wet or icy. After the trails rejoin, continue down a steep rocky slope that soon moderates. Under a stand of hemlocks, reenter private property and quickly reach the Old Mast Road. Turn right and hike 0.1 mile back to the parking area.

For a shorter, 8.2-mile loop on

Mount Whiteface, use the Blueberry Ledge Trail for the ascent but take the Tom Wiggin Trail to the Diceys Mill Trail for the return. If you are not concerned with bagging a 4000-footer, ascend the Wonalancet Range Trail to the Walden Trail, then turn right (east) onto the Walden Trail and climb up and over Mount Hedgehog. Pass a few viewpoints before descending to the Old Mast Road. Follow this trail back to the parking area to complete a quiet and more leisurely 6.2-mile loop.

With access all year long, this area is a nice location to snowshoe, but be leery of those trails with steep ledges.

8 Jennings Peak

Round trip ■ 6.5 miles
Loop direction ■ Counterclockwise
Rating ■ Moderate–Difficult
Hiking time ■ 4 hours
Starting elevation ■ 1400 feet
High point ■ 3460 feet
Elevation gain ■ 2100 feet
Best season ■ Year round
Maps ■ USGS Waterville Valley and Mount Tripyramid
Contact/fee ■ White Mountain National Forest

Driving directions: On Interstate 93, north of Plymouth, New Hampshire, take Exit 28. Head northeast on Route 49 toward Waterville Valley. The parking area is located on the right, exactly 10 miles from the highway. Look for trail signs indicating the Drakes Brook and the Sandwich Mountain trails.

Many people looking for a half-day hike in Waterville Valley make their way to the Welch and Dickey Loop. Located a few miles south on the opposite side of the Mad River Valley, the 4.4-mile Welch and Dickey Loop is an enjoyable excursion with nice views of the surrounding area. However, if you are in search of less company and don't mind a slightly harder workout, choose an equally scenic loop to nearby Jennings Peak. This 6.5-mile hike can also be extended 2.4 miles by including a side trip to the summit of 3980-foot Sandwich Dome, a New England Hundred Highest Peak.

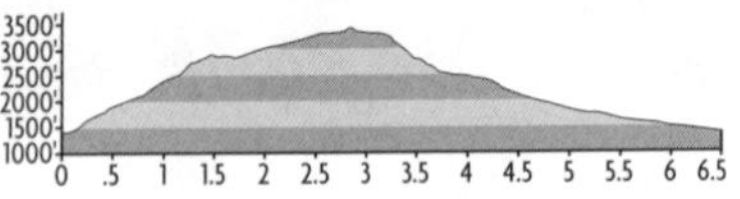

Leaving the parking area's south side, pick up the Sandwich Mountain Trail as it enters the woods past a fenced-in power station. Immediately

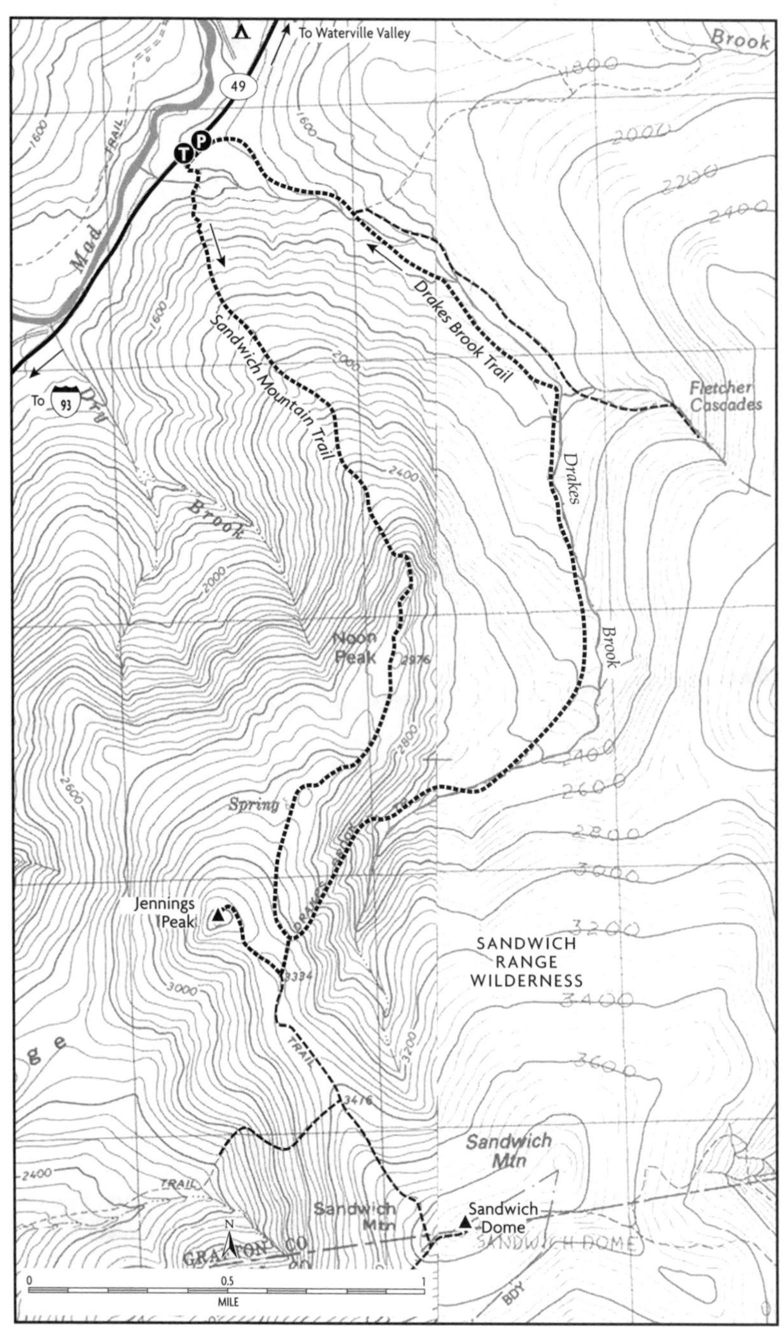
To Waterville Valley
49
Brook
Mad
TRAIL
To 93
Drakes Brook Trail
Sandwich Mountain Trail
Fletcher Cascades
Drakes
Brook
Noon Peak
2976
Spring
Jennings Peak
3334
3476
SANDWICH RANGE WILDERNESS
Sandwich Mtn
Sandwich Dome
TRAIL
0
0.5
1
MILE

Crossing Drakes Brook (photo by Craig Romano)

you arrive at Drakes Brook, where you should use caution crossing, especially during high water. Once on the other side, take a deep breath; if your heart is not pumping from the brook crossing, the next 1.5 miles will definitely speed up the blood flow. Wasting little time ascending Noon Peak, a ledge-covered bump on the ridge, the trail climbs an average of 100 feet per tenth of a mile. While the climb is straightforward, it may be slippery in spots if the ground is wet or icy. Rest assured your hard work will be rewarded as you step out on Noon Peak's first ledge, high above the steep sides of the Drakes Brook Valley. To the left, Waterville Valley lies surrounded by a ring of 4000-foot mountains including Tecumseh, Osceola, and the Tripyramids (from west to east). Oddly, the first two mountains are named for Native Americans with no connection to New England.

With most of the climb completed, you can enjoy the gently rolling ridge that lies ahead. The journey leads through shady moss-covered forest, across sunny open ledges, and over a series of small minor knolls. Entering from the left, 2.7 miles from the start, is the Drakes Brook Trail, the final leg of the day's loop. Before descending, continue straight for a few hundred yards where the 0.2-mile Jennings Peak spur trail leaves right. After a steep but brief climb the path emerges from the stunted trees onto an open ledge with 180-degree views to the south and west—a fine vantage point perched high above the slopes below.

The 3.2-mile descent down the Drakes Brook Trail begins quickly with the aid of switchbacks and soon reaches the edge of the brook. Paralleling the running water along the moderating terrain, the path's footing becomes easier as the valley floor broadens. Near the end, make your way across the brook and onto a woods road. After passing the site of some recent timber harvesting, the trail ends at the parking area.

Choose this hike from midsummer to early fall if you are uncomfortable with water crossings or if you like hikes with nice swimming holes for cooling off. This hike is also a good winter trip when snow is plentiful; however, you may want to do the hike in reverse for an enjoyable slide down Noon Peak. Also, consider remaining on the Sandwich Mountain Trail 1.2 miles past the Jennings Peak spur to the summit of Sandwich Dome. The trail climbs gradually at first and then more steadily before reaching the top where 180-degree views to the north await. The entirety of this longer option takes place in the Sandwich Mountain Wilderness area and traverses a thick spruce-fir forest that provides a good opportunity to see northern bird species like boreal chickadees, closely resembling the more common black-capped variety, with the exception of their brown caps and nasal calls.

9 Tripyramids

Round trip ■ 11.1 miles
Loop direction ■ Clockwise
Rating ■ Difficult
Hiking time ■ 8 hours
Starting elevation ■ 1580 feet
High point ■ 4180 feet
Elevation gain ■ 3000 feet
Best season ■ May to October
Map ■ USGS Mount Tripyramid
Contact/fee ■ White Mountain National Forest

Driving directions: Take Exit 28 off Interstate 93. Drive northeast on Route 49 toward Waterville Valley. Turn left off Route 49 at 10.5 miles onto Tripoli Road. Continue for another 1.2 miles, veering right at the fork, staying on Tripoli Road. Drive 0.6 miles and turn right and then immediately left into the Livermore Road parking area.

Not for the faint of heart, this loop scales two of New Hampshire's 4000-foot mountains up a long, rocky slide gaining nearly 1200 feet in a half mile and down a gravel slide dropping more than 800 feet in 0.4 mile. Apart from the spectacular scenery and the steep slopes along these two dramatic rock slides, much of the rest of the loop traverses easy to gradual terrain, along bubbling brooks and through serene forested surroundings. While not an acrophobic's preferred adventure, the Tripyramid loop is a must-visit for those yearning for the White Mountains' most spectacular landscapes.

With little elevation change follow the Livermore Trail past a number of side paths that lead to interesting natural features including Greeley Ponds, The Scaur, The Kettles, The Big Pines, and Norway Rapids. Each destination by itself is ideal for a half-day (or shorter) trip, while visiting a number of these locations in one day can make for an enjoyable longer adventure.

At 2.4 miles turn left on the narrowing Livermore Trail. Continue 1.2 miles past small cascades, the south branch of the Mount Tripyramid Trail, and the site of an old logging camp. At a sharp left turn, pick up the northern end of the Mount Tripyramid Trail on the right, 3.6 miles from the parking area.

Once across Avalanche Brook the trail proceeds moderately up the shrinking valley. Suddenly, the soils become shallower and the slope steeper. You have reached the bottom of the north slide. Take a deep breath—the most challenging (and fun) part of the hike is about to begin. The climb is trickiest on the wet and smooth rocks near the bottom. A few scrambles up ledges get the adrenaline flowing. Take advantage of the small trees; they provide nice handholds. Before you know it, the slide opens, the surface loosens, and the climb becomes less intimidating. A number of unofficial paths lead up the slide. For the best route, look for small cairns in the middle. Slowly the dramatic scenery unfolds with Mount Washington, Mount Carrigain, and the Franconia Range in the distance, and Mounts Tecumseh and Osceola nearby. Take your time—these are the best views of the day.

In approaching the top, stay right and look for the trail as it reenters the forest to the left of the second of two large cairns. Hike up the slope 0.1 mile before turning right at the intersection with the Pine Bend Brook Trail. The wooded 4140-foot summit of the North Peak lies a few dozen feet beyond.

A welcome, gradual trek across Tripyramid Ridge follows. While not teeming with an abundant diversity of wildlife, the ridge, by midsummer, is a perfect location for finding Swainson's thrushes. A bit smaller than robins, these olive-brown birds are more often heard than seen. Listen for their rising flutelike song and their shorter "whit" call.

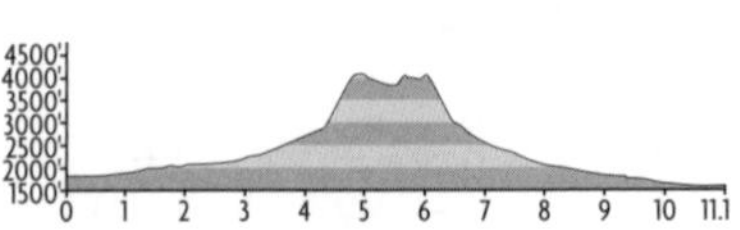

Descend past the Sabbaday Falls

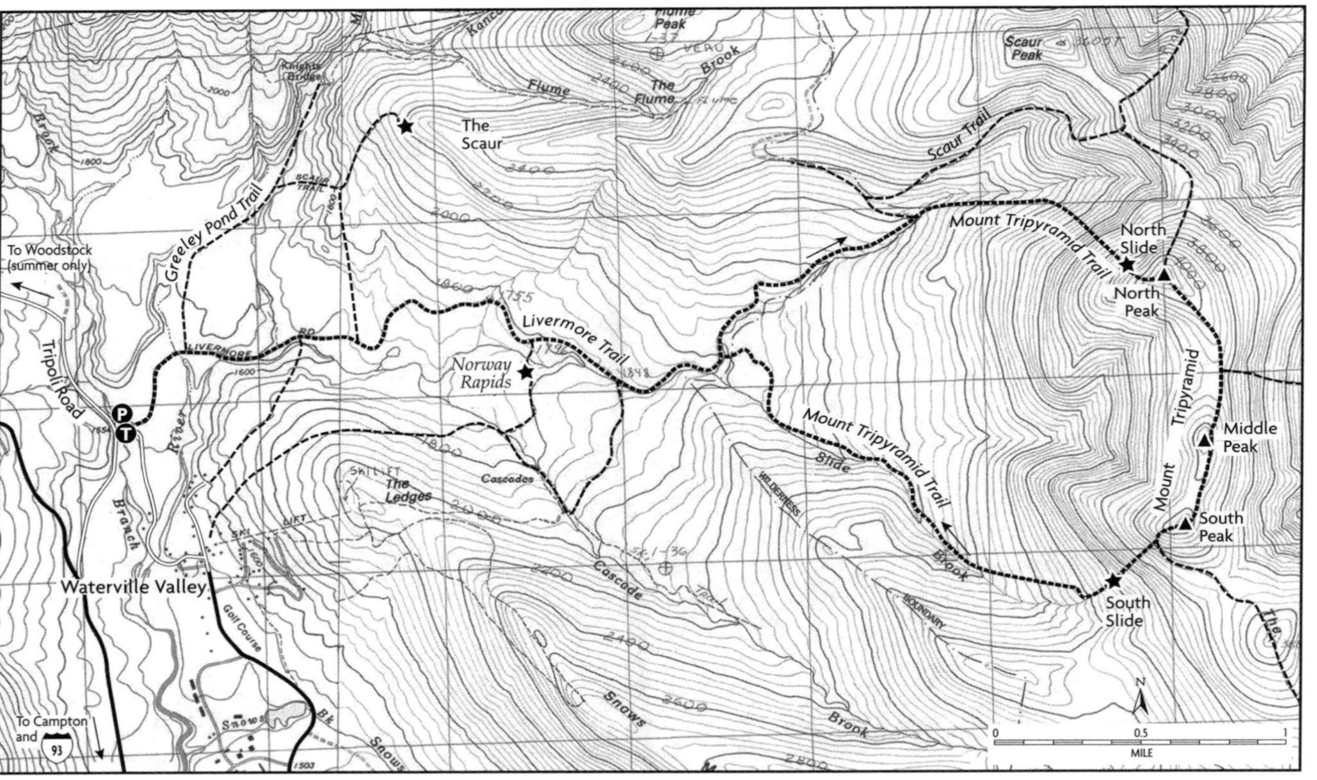
The Scaur
Scaur Peak
Scaur Trail
Flume Peak
The Flume
Flume
Brook
Knights Bridge
Greeley Pond Trail
To Woodstock (summer only)
Tripoli Road
Livermore Trail
Norway Rapids
Mount Tripyramid Trail
North Slide
North Peak
Mount Tripyramid
Middle Peak
South Peak
South Slide
Slide
The Ledges
Cascades
Cascade
Snows
Brook
Waterville Valley
Golf Course
Branch
River
To Campton and 93
0
0.5
1
MILE

View from North Slide

Trail and begin the short 0.4-mile climb to the narrow summit of the 4100-foot Middle Peak. Near the top, you will pass a small but expansive western view. From the highest point there are also limited views east and north.

The trail drops quickly down a small ledge and meanders across the ridge to the wooded South Peak. Here the descent begins in earnest. For 0.6 mile the trail drops steeply, at first in the forest, but soon it joins the South Slide. While not as big or daunting as its northern counterpart, the hike down the south slide definitely requires care. The footing is mostly loose rock, so the possibility for slipping is great. As the slide peters out, the forest envelops the trail. Here the path heads sharply right and moderately descends while crossing a number of small streams. Once across Avalanche Brook, you reach the Livermore Road 1.9 miles from the base of the slide. Turn left for the final 2.6-mile haul to the parking area.

A good alternative in the winter or for those wary of heights is to use the Scaur Trail instead of scaling the North Slide. Located a few tenths of a mile farther north along the Livermore Road, the Scaur Trail in combination with the Pine Bend Brook Trail extends the loop about a mile.

10 Mount Moosilauke

Round trip ■ 11 miles
Loop direction ■ Counterclockwise
Rating ■ Difficult
Hiking time ■ 7 hours
Starting elevation ■ 2460 feet
High point ■ 4802 feet
Elevation gain ■ 2750 feet
Best season ■ May through October
Maps ■ USGS Mount Moosilauke and Mount Kineo
Contact/fee ■ Dartmouth Outing Club

Driving directions: Follow Route 118 north 5.8 miles from Route 25 in Warren or 7.3 miles south from Route 112 in Woodstock. From the south, turn left (right from the north) onto Ravine Road (open from May 1 to December)—look for signs indicating Dartmouth College's Moosilauke Ravine Lodge. Travel up the dirt road 1.6 miles to a turnaround area. After turning around, park along the right (west) side of the road, heading out. Do not park in the turnaround area.

Standing prominently over the Connecticut River Valley, 4802-foot Mount Moosilauke is the highest mountain in western New Hampshire. Beginning as early as 1685, when Abenaki Chief Waternomee was believed to have stood upon its summit, this mountain has lured us to its flowing ridges and deep ravines. Dartmouth College faithful have long visited its heights in search of outdoor adventure. And with numerous routes leading to the peak Native Americans once called the "Bald Place," Mount Moosilauke continues to be a popular destination for hikers today. Well before you reach the top to gaze upon the expansive views or enjoy its invigorating winds, you will come to understand why so many before you have been attracted to Mount Moosilauke.

Beginning on an old woods road beyond the turnaround area, you quickly reach the start of the loop where a trail leads left toward the Baker River. Continue straight on the Ridge Trail, which begins its 3.9-mile northerly course along a flat road. Proceed past the Al Merrill Loop (which branches right) to a bridge that leads to the other side of the river. The relaxing grade continues to loosen muscles, while the bubbling river helps clear the mind. After crossing a second bridge and veering right (southeast), the trail begins to climb more moderately away from the river and in about a

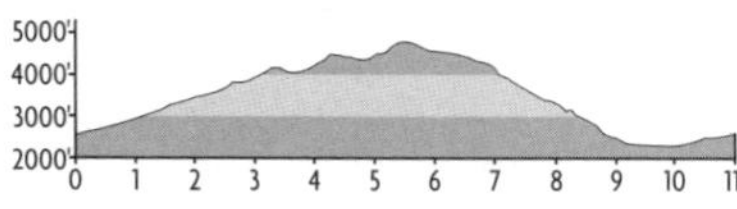

quarter-mile reaches another intersection with the Al Merrill Loop. Stay on the Ridge Trail, which turns sharply left (north). The moderate climb continues to a small saddle on the ridge, where a more aggressive ascent begins up and over the wooded summit of Mount Jim.

Upon reaching the Beaver Brook Trail 1.9 miles from the top, turn left and prepare for the most demanding part of the hike. The trail soon winds

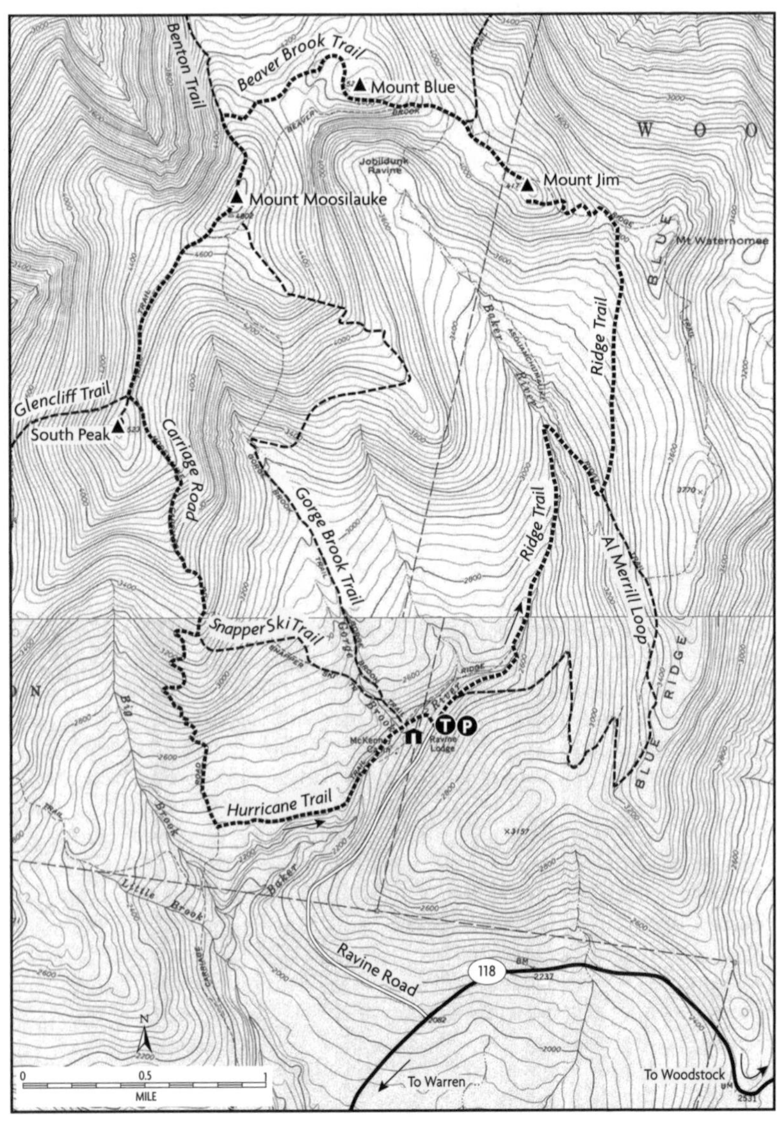

Beaver Brook Trail ascends alpine summit

around the side of Mount Blue. Fortunately, the rough footing and strenuous climb are surpassed by the views south into the steep walls of nearby Jobildunk Ravine and the headwaters of the Baker River. Continuing up the mountain, the trees become shorter and, once past the Benton Trail, give way altogether.

The route through Mount Moosilauke's alpine zone is laid out beautifully, with a rock border separating the barren trail from the fragile alpine flowers that abound. Equally impressive are the views of countless peaks and ridges in all directions. The summit is definitely a place to savor the fruits of your labor. If the wind whips up, take advantage of the many structures offering protection, including the eroded foundations of buildings that stood here from 1860 until 1942.

The journey down begins on the Carriage Road, which leaves the summit to the south. After a gradual descent, leave the alpine zone and follow the flat, narrowing ridge line. The spruce-fir forest here is an ideal place for spotting blackpoll warblers, small black-and-white birds frequently seen singing from the tops of trees. At the Glencliff Trail intersection a path leads

0.1 mile to the South Peak—a good side trip to an open and quiet summit. Stay left on the Carriage Road, where the footing remains good but the slope becomes steeper.

After passing the Snapper Ski Trail the path turns sharply right, descends with the aid of switchbacks, and enters a stand of maturing maples, beeches, and birches—a nice change of scenery. Arriving at the Hurricane Trail, 3.6 miles from the summit, turn left for an easy 1-mile trek to the banks of the Baker River. Turn right upon reaching the Gorge Brook Trail and right again across the bridge. Follow the trail up the hill and past the lodge to the parking area. You should have plenty of fond memories on your drive home.

By taking advantage of the Gorge Brook and/or the Snapper Ski Trails, shorter loop hikes of Mount Moosilauke are also available. Both trails will get you to the summit in 3.8 miles but are steeper and more crowded. Together the two trails complete a 7.6-mile loop; or alternatively, hike up either one and down the Ridge Trail for a 9.6-mile loop.

The trails that begin from the Moosilauke Ravine Lodge travel through 4600 acres of land owned and managed by Dartmouth College. The Ravine Lodge is open to the public from mid-May to mid-October (as a rule). People are welcome to make arrangements to stay overnight, or stop by for a snack and to fill water bottles. For more information, contact the Dartmouth Outing Club (see the appendix).

11 Franconia Notch

Round trip ■ 6.2 miles
Loop direction ■ Clockwise
Rating ■ Moderate
Hiking time ■ 3.5 hours
Starting elevation ■ 1520 feet
High point ■ 2750 feet
Elevation gain ■ 1300 feet
Best season ■ Year round
Maps ■ USGS Lincoln and Franconia
Contact/fee ■ New Hampshire Division of Parks and Recreation

Driving directions: From the south, follow Interstate 93 north of Lincoln, past Exit 34A. Continue on Route 93 to the Basin parking area on the right. From the north, take Interstate 93 through Franconia Notch State Park. Take Exit 34A, follow the exit under the highway, and turn left. Drive onto Interstate 93 north and continue ahead to the Basin parking area.

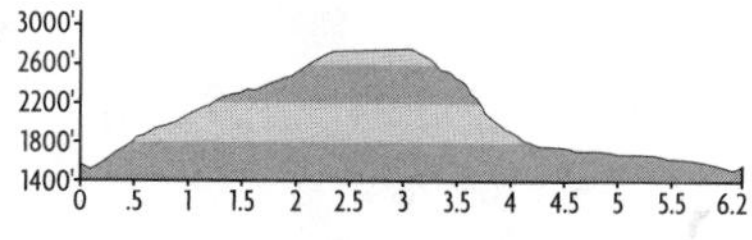

Finding solitude in Franconia Notch can be difficult. Its beauty and accessibility have resulted in many well-trodden trails. Fortunately, there are still less-traveled locations in the Notch to explore. This loop visits popular destinations. However, it also passes through Franconia Notch's quieter places, where thick spruce forests cast shadows over cascading mountain streams and darting critters escape to dark cavities hidden in gnarled yellow birches.

From the parking area, follow the signs leading to the Basin, a smooth, round rock the river continues to carve on its journey to the sea. The loop begins a few hundred feet west of the Basin, at the intersection of the Pemi and Basin–Cascades trails. Begin on the Basin–Cascades Trail for a 1-mile journey up the side of a scenic mountain brook. Initially very popular, the trail quickly becomes less crowded as the incline increases and the footing roughens. Along the way, many interesting features are displayed, including Kinsman Falls at 0.4 mile and Rocky Glen Falls at 0.9 mile. Near the trail's halfway point, a brook crossing provides a small challenge, but rocks are present for assistance.

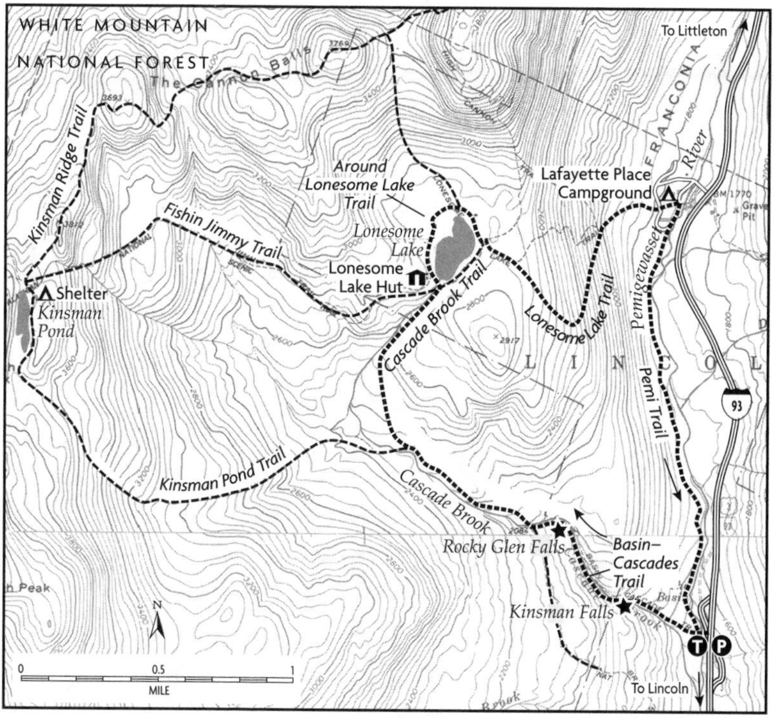

Upon reaching the Cascade Brook Trail, turn right and immediately arrive at the final bridgeless water crossing of the day. With minimal effort, hop across the rocks; you will be rewarded with a pleasant path along the other side. After passing the Kinsman Pond Trail, you briefly leave the noisy yet tranquil proximity of the running water. Take this opportunity to scan the dense forest for winter wrens, tiny bent-tailed birds with long, flutelike calls. They are more often heard than seen. In so doing, you will certainly see many of the large rocks scattered about, including a large lichen- and moss-covered boulder on the left.

Returning to the brook's side once again, the trail climbs more aggressively until reaching the shores of Lonesome Lake. Turn left and cross the small bridge. While the lake's name is rarely applicable, it quickly becomes evident why so many are drawn to its shore. With Cannon Mountain and the Franconia Ridge standing as a spectacular backdrop, few lakes this size and at this elevation can boast of a finer view.

Just beneath the hilltop where the Appalachian Mountain Club's Lonesome Lake Hut is perched, pick up the Around Lonesome Lake Trail. This flat trail skirts the shore of the lake, crosses boardwalks, and leads through marshy areas providing optimum wildlife viewing opportunities. Upon reaching the Lonesome Lake Trail, turn right and travel nearly a quarter mile to another trail junction. Here a short path leads to the east shore of the lake and views of Kinsman Mountain. Stay on the Lonesome Lake Trail, which heads east away from the lake. Over a small hill the frequently used trail descends south along moderate grades, but eventually swings north toward the Lafayette Campground.

Once in the campground, turn right onto the Pemi Trail, following the road to where the route enters the forest between sites 67 and 68. The quiet 2-mile stroll along the shores of the Pemigewasset River is easy on the legs. Surrounded by tall, mature trees, a carpet of wildflowers, and the soothing sound of the rushing water, the Pemi Trail is a perfect way to cap off the day's journey. Before heading back to your car, check out the many displays, cascades, and natural features exhibited around the Basin.

If you are looking for a harder workout and the closest thing to solitude in Franconia Notch, extend this hike as described by turning off the Cascade Brook Trail onto the Kinsman Pond Trail. Follow this lesser-used route up to scenic Kinsman Pond. Just beyond the pond, pick up the Kinsman Ridge Trail and head northeast over the Cannon Balls. Following a steep descent from the third Cannon Ball, turn right on the Lonesome Lake Trail, following it back to the Lafayette Campground, the Pemi Trail, and the Basin—a 10.6-mile loop.

Opposite: View along the Basin-Cascades Trail

12 Flume and Liberty

Round trip	9.9 miles
Loop direction	Counterclockwise
Rating	Difficult
Hiking time	7 hours
Starting elevation	1520 feet
High point	4460 feet
Elevation gain	3500 feet
Best season	Year round
Map	USGS Lincoln
Contact/fee	New Hampshire Division of Parks and Recreation

Driving directions: From the south, follow Interstate 93 north from Lincoln. Take Exit 34A onto Route 3. Drive 0.3 mile, pass the entrance to the Flume, to a parking lot up a hill to the right. From the north, follow Interstate 93 through Franconia Notch State Park. Follow Exit 34A under the highway to a stop sign. Turn right, then left in 0.3 mile into the parking lot.

Like most destinations in Franconia Notch, Mounts Flume and Liberty are very popular and very scenic. Some visitors surprisingly choose to scale these two peaks via the Liberty Spring Trail only, but the best option is a loop that includes a scramble up the Flume Slide Trail. Varying terrain along the way pleasantly shifts from bubbling mountain brooks to changing forest scenery. The views from both summits are quite impressive, each peak showcasing the higher summits to the north as well as the deep valleys and notches far below. With year-round access, this hike is possible any time of year. For the more adventurous, complete the described loop in reverse when snow levels are high for an enjoyable ride down the Flume Slide.

Begin the hike along the Whitehouse Trail. Created in the 1980s when the highway through the Notch was widened, this route travels 0.5 mile slightly downhill before reaching a paved bicycle path. Follow the path 0.2 miles farther across a small bridge to where the Liberty Spring Trail heads right up the slope. This well-used footway, a section of the Appalachian Trail, moderately ascends through a maturing hardwood forest. With large yellow birch trees providing ample cover, continue in a northerly direction.

Soon the trail veers right and upon joining an old woods road reaches the start of the Flume Slide Trail. Turn right and begin the loop. Over the next 1.5 miles the trail gains modest elevation, but there are a number of

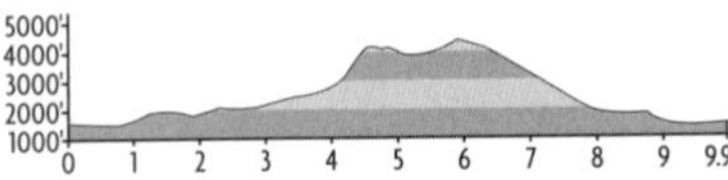

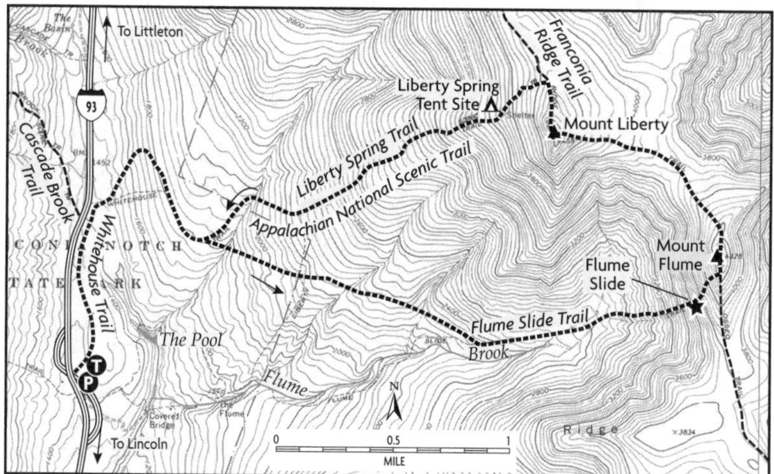

small ups and downs while crossing a series of mountain streams. The wet and forested landscape provides ideal habitat for a number of birds, including the Canada warbler. This small yellow bird with a black necklace is often heard and less frequently seen within the low vegetation that thrives in wetlands in the lower elevations of the White Mountains.

Upon reaching Flume Brook, the trail turns left and heads toward the base of the slide. While much of the Flume's west face is exposed rock, the trail ascends sections of the slide that are largely forested. The path is steep and crosses exposed rock, but there are plenty of places to hold on as you climb. While this is the hardest section of the hike, it is a section that ensures significantly more people will continue visiting the deep gorge located a few miles downhill, rather than scaling the higher elevations of the mountain named for it.

At the end of the trail, turn left onto the narrow prism-shaped ridge for the final 0.2 mile to the top. There are a number of impressive views along the way, especially looking down the steep slides below. From the mostly open 4326-foot summit, the pointy tops of Mount Lincoln and Lafayette stand prominently to the north. The hike, continuing along the Franconia Ridge Trail, travels 1.2 miles past standing and blown-over spruce and fir trees. The final 0.1 mile is a bit steep as the path scales the rocky and open 4460-foot summit of Mount Liberty. Like many peaks in the area, this pointy mountain was once known as Haystack. Fortunately, creativity eventually set in and bestowed a name more fitting. Surrounded by 360 degrees of beauty atop a rocky outcrop, it is hard to think of a finer place to contemplate and appreciate liberty.

Begin the descent by following the ridge north for 0.2 mile. At first crossing over rock and passing by interesting formations of ledge, the path reenters the forest just before reaching the top of the Liberty Spring Trail. Turn

Rocky summit of Mount Liberty

left and head down the rocky trail. While it wastes little time descending, the trail is not difficult. In 0.4 mile reach the Liberty Spring tent site area, an overnight facility managed by the Appalachian Mountain Club ($8 per person per night). Past the camping area, the trail stays relatively straight, dropping at a consistent and steady rate. After the hardwood forest returns, veer right onto an old road. The remaining stretch is relatively level until reaching the intersection with the Flume Slide Trail. Stay right, retracing your steps back to the Whitehouse Trail and the parking area.

13 Franconia Ridge

Round trip ■ 8.8 miles
Loop direction ■ Counterclockwise
Rating ■ Strenuous
Hiking time ■ 8 hours
Starting elevation ■ 1780 feet
High point ■ 5260 feet
Elevation gain ■ 4000 feet
Best season ■ Year round
Map ■ USGS Franconia
Contact/fee ■ New Hampshire Division of Parks and Recreation

Driving directions: Follow Route 93 north of Lincoln into Franconia Notch. Drive 2.3 miles north of the Pemigewasset River crossing and turn right into the parking area across from Lafayette Place Campground. From the north, follow Route 93 south. Turn right into Lafayette Place Campground. Two

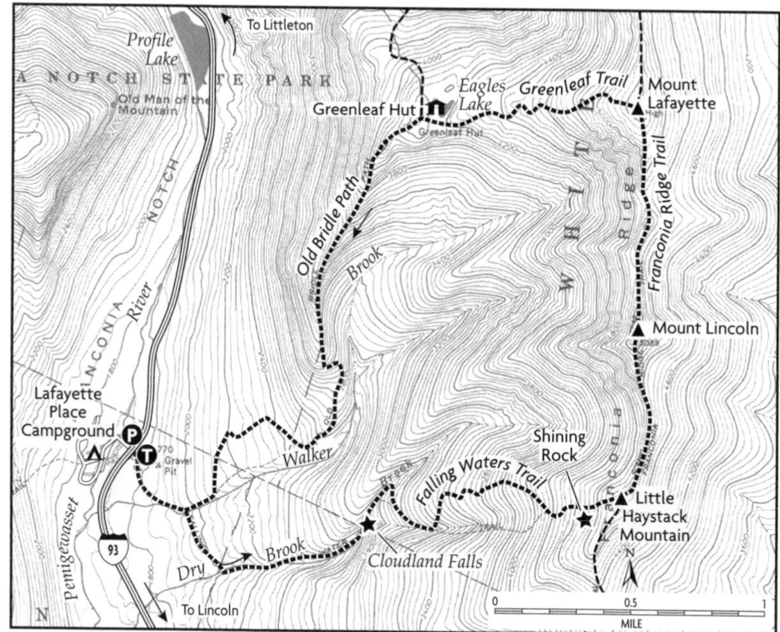

right turns lead to a small parking area near the side of the highway. Follow the pedestrian tunnel under the road to the trailhead.

Probably the most popular high-elevation loop hike in the White Mountains, the Franconia Range is not a destination for solitude, especially on summer weekends, but it is a place of spectacular beauty. While its popularity may suggest otherwise, the loop over Mounts Lincoln and Lafayette is strenuous and very demanding. The hike's rewards, however, greatly exceed its challenge. In addition to a series of scenic mountain cascades, the summits of two towering 5000-foot mountains, and panoramic views throughout the day, this excursion in Franconia Notch State Park includes one of the finest alpine ridges in all of New England.

Pick up the Old Bridle Path and hike 0.2 mile to the loop's beginning. Turn right onto the Falling Waters Trail and across a short wooden bridge. The trail gradually leads south to Dry Brook, which it quickly crosses before beginning a more moderate climb. Pass two delightful cascades, Stairs Falls and Swiftwater Falls, and continue the ascent after crossing the brook a second time. Now along the north bank, the trail reaches the largest and most picturesque cascade, Cloudland Falls. Ahead, cross Dry Brook a last time and proceed up along the side of a steep slope.

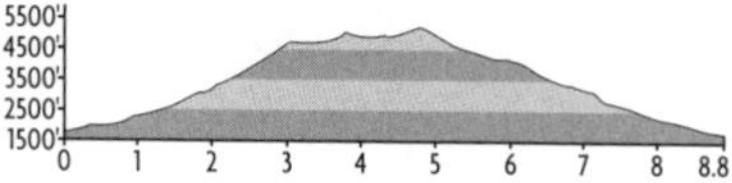

Near a small stream, the route veers left and begins the hardest part of the hike, gaining more than 1600 feet in less than 1.5 miles. Aided by switchbacks, the trail winds up the ridge. In between breaths, listen for the low-pitched "chebunk" call of the yellow-bellied flycatcher, a small, rarely seen bird that nests in high elevation spruce-fir forests. One of the few birds you will hear above 4000 feet, yellow-bellied flycatchers are voracious insect eaters.

Just below tree line, a small spur leads right to the base of Shining Rock, a nearly 1600-square-foot ledge that is almost always wet and very dangerous to climb. The barren summit of Little Haystack Mountain is just ahead, at an intersection with the Franconia Ridge Trail.

The 1.6-mile trek over Mount Lincoln to the summit of Mount Lafayette is a glorious stretch of alpine hiking. However, with no safe means of escape, you should attempt it only under good weather conditions; in the past, some have died here from exposure and lightning.

Now completely in the open, with views stretching in all directions, begin the traverse north across the ridge. To avoid damaging fragile alpine flowers, hikers are asked to remain on the trail, which is bordered by rocks throughout. While the abundant beauty can be distracting, do your best to stay on rocky surfaces. A short climb ends at the 5089-foot summit of Mount Lincoln, named in honor of the nation's sixteenth president, the "Great Emancipator." Fittingly, the peak stands perilously, uniting the northern Franconia Ridge with the south; there is no place to go but forward.

Scenic Franconia Ridge

Continuing north, a short descent into a grove of tiny trees is followed by the final push to the seventh highest peak in New England. Named for the French national who played a critical role in America's independence, Mount Lafayette stands high above western New Hampshire. The views from the summit are incredible and the wind in the face invigorating. It is 4 miles and all downhill from here.

Pick up the Greenleaf Trail, which leaves the summit in a westerly direction. The path meanders down the barren landscape, eventually reaching the thin forest. Past a small pond, hike up to the Appalachian Mountain Club's Greenleaf Hut before turning left onto the Old Bridle Path. Descending what many refer to as Agony Ridge, the steep trail can be agonizing on the knees, but certainly not on the eyes. There are a number of exceptional vistas into Walker Ravine and up to the towering pinnacles above.

Following the last viewpoint, the trail drops quickly off the ridge. Entering the shade of the tall hardwood forest, the trail slowly moderates over the remaining 1.5 miles. Sufficiently drained, your mind is left to wander, happily recalling the sweeping views and boundless splendor that is New Hampshire's Franconia Ridge.

14 Pemigewasset Wilderness

Round trip ■ 25.5 miles
Loop direction ■ Clockwise
Rating ■ Difficult–Strenuous
Hiking time ■ 2 to 3 days
Starting elevation ■ 1160 feet
High point ■ 4902 feet
Elevation gain ■ 4750 feet
Best season ■ May through October
Maps ■ USGS Mount Osceola and South Twin Mountain
Contact/fee ■ White Mountain National Forest

Driving directions: Follow Interstate 93 into Lincoln to Exit 32. Travel east on Route 112 toward Conway. Drive 5.3 miles and turn left into a large parking area.

With many roads dissecting the White Mountains, there are few areas where one can go and feel a strong sense of isolation. The heart of the 45,000-acre Pemigewasset Wilderness, the state's largest wilderness area, is one such place. The Pemigewasset is a region of roaring rivers, cascading falls, rugged landscapes, and scenic mountaintops. This loop offers the adventurer

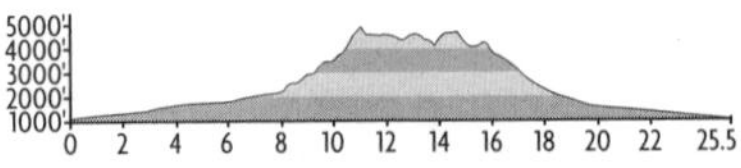

an opportunity to scale five New Hampshire 4000-foot mountains, traverse breathtaking scenery, and pass through forests teeming with wildlife. While more than 25 miles in length, much of the loop follows easy to moderate terrain. With a number of developed overnight destinations, this route provides an ideal opportunity for two- to three-day adventures.

Begin by crossing the large suspension bridge that spans the East Branch of the Pemigewasset River. Turn right onto the Lincoln Woods Trail, an old abandoned railbed that follows the banks of the rushing river for 2.9 miles, gaining little elevation. After a second bridge leads across Franconia Brook, the Lincoln Woods Trail ends at a three-way intersection. This is also the Pemigewasset Wilderness boundary. It is hard to believe, but from the late 1890s to the 1940s much of this land was heavily harvested and burned.

Turn left onto the Franconia Brook Trail. It quickly joins another abandoned railroad bed and follows it for most of the next 5.2 miles. The route passes a number of wetlands and beaver ponds along the way. While large rodents and a growing forest continue to erase many signs of the area's logging history, a number of abandoned camps and artifacts still remain, all protected from disturbance by federal law.

The growing forests also showcase the whirling, flutelike calls of resident thrushes. At this relatively low elevation, look for hermit thrushes and veeries, both slightly smaller than robins. Hermit thrushes have distinct breast spots, olive-colored backs, and rusty tails that frequently move up and down. Veeries exhibit fainter breast markings and cinnamon-colored backs.

The trail slowly climbs to the Thirteen Falls tent site 8.1 miles from the start, but just barely 1000 feet higher in elevation. Located near a series of scenic falls in the heart of the wilderness, this location, managed by the Appalachian Mountain Club (AMC), provides a perfect, secluded overnight location. It offers nine tent sites, for $8 a person, on a first-come, first-served basis.

The loop continues on the Twin Brook Trail. Climbing gradually but steadily, the path leads 2.7 miles up the quiet valley before reaching the Frost Trail. To the left, the mostly wooded summit of 4024-foot Galehead Mountain can be reached in 0.4 mile. Veer right, quickly arriving at AMC's Galehead Hut, which provides bunks and meals (reservations are required).

From here, the steepest section of the loop begins—a 1100-foot climb up the Twinway to the 4902-foot summit of South Twin Mountain. The 0.8-mile climb is not technically difficult but saps the energy with its steepness and rocky surface. Fortunately, the reward is tremendous. South Twin is the highest peak between the Franconia Ridge and the Presidential Range, and it provides excellent views of both from its barren summit.

Gradually descending the ridge, the Twinway proceeds south for 2 miles to the start of the Bondcliff Trail, 0.1 mile below the top of Mount Guyot. While unheralded, as it is not officially recognized as a 4000-footer, Mount Guyot provides one of the finest views in the White Mountains.

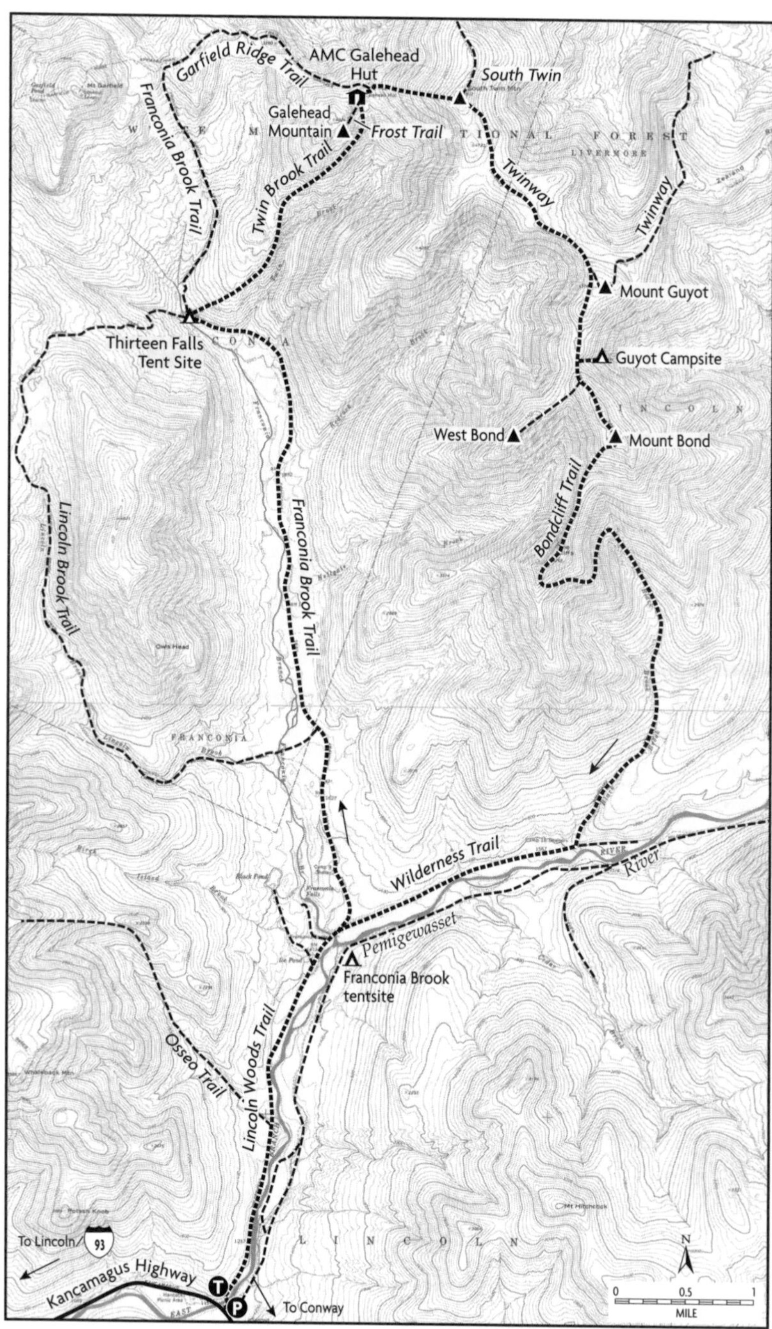
Garfield Ridge Trail
AMC Galehead Hut
South Twin
Galehead Mountain
Frost Trail
Franconia Brook Trail
Twin Brook Trail
Twinway
Twinway
Mount Guyot
Thirteen Falls Tent Site
Guyot Campsite
West Bond
Mount Bond
Bondcliff Trail
Lincoln Brook Trail
Franconia Brook Trail
Wilderness Trail
River
Pemigewasset
Franconia Brook tentsite
Osseo Trail
Lincoln Woods Trail
To Lincoln
93
Kancamagus Highway
To Conway
N
0
0.5
1
MILE

East Branch of the Pemigewasset River

Follow the Bondcliff Trail over the scenic south summit of Guyot 0.8 mile into a saddle where a 0.2-mile spur leads left to the AMC's Mount Guyot campsite. Only 6.3 miles from Thirteen Falls, this campsite, which includes a shelter and tent platforms, is an excellent location to spend the evening. This is a popular destination that is also available for $8 a person on a first-come, first-served basis. If you are able to set up camp early for the evening, consider a trip to West Bond Mountain. To reach West Bond, return to the Bondcliff Trail and turn left 0.2 mile to the West Bond Trail. This path leads 0.5 mile along a narrow ridgeline to an open and very scenic 4540-foot summit.

The loop's 11-mile conclusion leads south past the West Bond Trail. Quickly climbing out of the forest, arrive atop the 4698-foot Mount Bond. With views in all directions, this picturesque location is the perfect place to usher in a new day. The barren rocky ridge below is Bondcliff, the next stop on the journey. Descending to the southwest, the trail drops steeply into a thin forest of trees, but not for long. Near the low point on the ridge, a nearly 1-mile section across the wide-open landscape begins. The trail slowly climbs across the open ridge above the edge of the cliff. While not an ideal place in bad weather, there are few places in the White Mountains more dramatic. After reaching the high point on the ridge, take some time to savor the view, the last one on the hike.

Reenter the forest and begin a slow and steady 4.4-mile descent, eventually crossing and following the banks of the Black Brook. The relaxing hike down ends at the Wilderness Trail. Turn right here and follow the flat, old railroad bed 1.8 miles to the Lincoln Woods Trail, 2.9 miles from the hike's conclusion.

15 Hedgehog Mountain

Round trip ■ 4.8 miles
Loop direction ■ Counterclockwise
Rating ■ Moderate
Hiking time ■ 2.5 hours
Starting elevation ■ 1100 feet
High point ■ 2535 feet
Elevation gain ■ 1350 feet
Best season ■ Year round
Map ■ USGS Mount Chocorua
Contact/fee ■ White Mountain National Forest

Driving directions: The trailhead is located on the Kancamagus Highway 14.2 miles west of Route 16 in Conway and 21.2 miles east of Interstate 93 in Lincoln. Look for signs indicating the UNH, Potash Mountain, and Downes Brook trails. Directly across from the Passaconaway Campground, turn south on a dirt road that quickly leads to a parking area.

Within walking distance of one national forest campground and near two others, the Hedgehog Mountain loop is a pleasant half-day hike in the heart of the White Mountains. Primarily along moderate terrain, the route traverses changing forests before arriving at countless open ledges. Hedgehog Mountain is a perfect introductory hike to the region's wildlife, plants, and geology, and reminds us all that beautiful views can exist well below tree line.

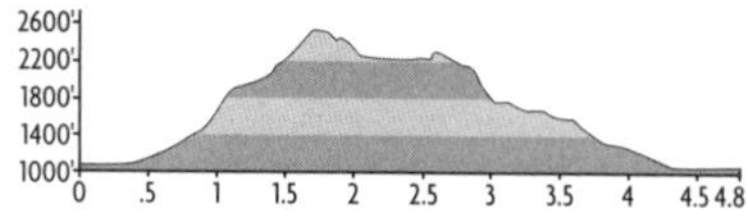

Immediately beyond the information kiosk, turn left on the UNH Trail and head up the sandy hillside.

Proceed under the tall pine forest until reaching a four-way intersection—the start of the loop. Turn right along the flat terrain, quickly arriving at a second intersection. The sign mentions the West Loop, a cross-country ski trail that leads right, but the trail up Hedgehog Mountain continues straight where the footing remains easy and the climb moderate. The lower slopes are a perfect location to scan the trees for songbirds such as the red-eyed vireo, a small but loud inhabitant of northern hardwood forests. Its repetitive whistle like call demands your attention over and over again. After the trail veers left, the climb accelerates along the crest of a narrow spruce-covered ridge, and at 1.1 miles from the parking area you reach a short spur trail leading to Allens

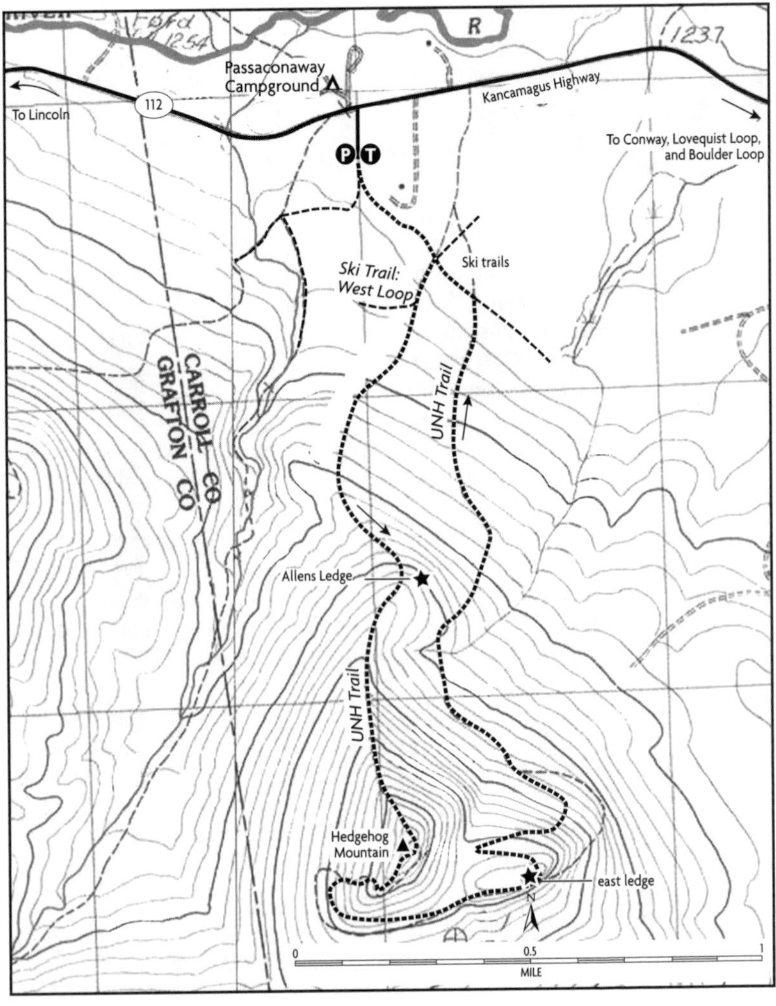

Gnarly yellow birch

Ledge—a good vantage point to scan for moose in the marshes below.

Above Allens Ledge the steepest section of the hike awaits you, but it does not last long. With 1.9 miles completed, you reach the summit where a number of ledges provide resting spots and views in most directions. From the summit, the trail winds south, dropping steadily. After passing through a field of boulders, a short climb brings you to the wide-open east ledge. While a few hundred feet lower than the summit, the east ledge offers views that are more impressive, especially of Passaconaway Mountain, the 4060-foot peak whose rocky slopes rise steeply above.

The 2-mile journey back from the east ledge begins by passing a small eastern viewpoint. A moderate descent at first, the path soon levels off while crossing a number of small streams. Beyond the last crossing, briefly climb up and over a low ridge before returning once again to a gradual descent down the mountain. The thick hardwood forest is carpeted throughout with blue-bead lily, Indian cucumber, and other common wildflowers. As the terrain flattens, reach another junction with a cross-country ski trail. Turn left and follow the old woods road straight back to the parking area.

Not ready to call it a day? Take the Kancamagus Highway east toward Conway to access the Lovequist and/or Boulder Loop trails. The Lovequist Loop begins at the Rocky Gorge parking area, crosses the river on a bridge, and leads 1 mile through the woods and around a scenic lake. The Boulder Loop Trail is located a few miles farther east near the Covered Bridge Campground. This 3.1-mile loop, which includes an interpretive brochure explaining the natural history in the area, is very informative, but also includes a climb of nearly 1000 feet. Both trailheads are well marked and easy to locate.

16 Mount Chocorua and the Three Sisters

Round trip	9.8 miles
Loop direction	Counterclockwise
Rating	Difficult
Hiking time	7 to 8 hours
Starting elevation	780 feet
High point	3500 feet
Elevation gain	2950 feet
Best season	Year round
Maps	USGS Chocorua and Silver Lake
Contact/fee	White Mountain National Forest

Driving directions: From Chocorua Village, at the junction of routes 113 and 16, follow Route 16 north for 5 miles and then turn left into the parking area for the Piper Trail. Beginning from the eastern terminus of the Kancamagus Highway in Conway, follow Route 16 south. In 5 miles pass the USFS White Ledge Campground on the right. Continue another 1.2 miles before turning right into the Piper Trail parking lot.

Chocorua is one of New Hampshire's most hiked, most known, and most easily recognizable mountains. Standing prominently in the southeast corner of the White Mountains, its pointy, rocky summit appears to change shape depending on one's location, yet remains alluring from all perspectives.

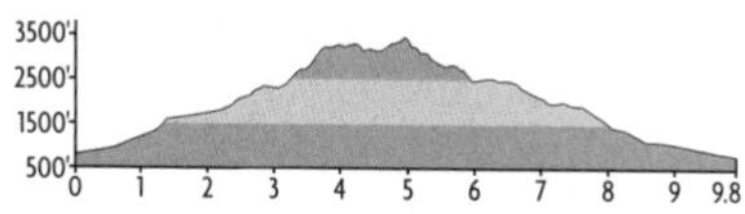

There are many different trails that lead to the peak's sweeping views; the most scenic, and conveniently less-traveled option traverses Carter Ledge and journeys over the wide-open knobs known as the Three Sisters. With panoramic views throughout the day, this hike is one you will remember for years to come.

The hike begins on the Piper Trail and easily leads through the Chocorua River Valley. Pass the Weetamoo Trail in little more than a half-mile, continue right, and moderately climb 0.6 mile to the start of the Nickerson Ledge Trail. Turn right up the short, steep slope to the mostly wooded ledge. The route levels off significantly before ending at the Carter Ledge Trail.

Stay left and quickly wind up the ridge. Soon the path emerges onto a series of open ledges that provide tremendous views of Mount Chocorua's uniquely shaped summit. Like much of the day's loop, the trail passes over exposed rock that can be tricky when wet or icy. The hike is straightforward, but in a few locations extra caution is required to avoid slipping.

After tunneling through a dark evergreen forest, carefully ascend a steep rocky slope before reaching the Middle Sister Trail. Follow this trail left for 0.3 mile to the summit of Middle Sister, where the foundation of an old tower stands surrounded by 360 degrees of views. This is a great place to inhale the beauty of the White Mountains with few distractions, save a broad-winged

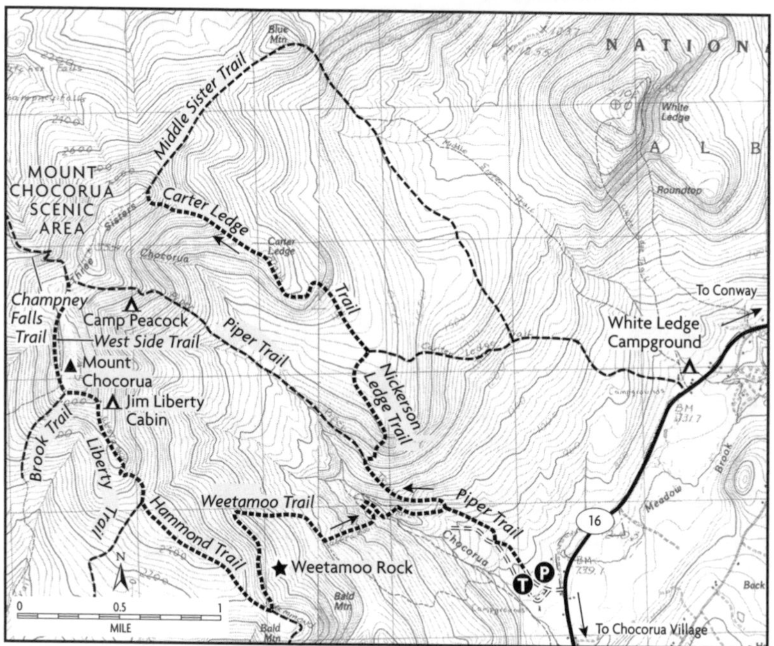

hawk soaring above in the cool mountain breezes. With rounded wings and a fanned-out, banded tail, this medium-sized bird of prey provides graceful and welcome entertainment.

The trail resumes by dropping into a small saddle and then quickly climbing to the wide-open summit of the First Sister—the last of the loop's quiet vistas. Descend to the Champney Falls Trail, turn left, and in 0.1 mile rejoin the Piper Trail. Follow the trail to the right and traverse through the spruce-fir forests. In 0.2 mile pass the West Side Trail, a poor-weather option that avoids the open summit. Ahead, the Piper Trail exits the forest and makes its way around the west side of the mountain. Upon intersecting the Brook Trail, a short scramble leads a few hundred feet up open rocks to the spectacular summit of Mount Chocorua. While you are likely to have company, there are many locations to spread out.

Descend the Brook Trail as it drops quickly past the southern end of the West Side Trail. Soon after, turn left onto the Liberty Trail. Slowly moderating in difficulty, the route passes over a few ledges before reaching the Jim Liberty Cabin. Located beneath Mount Chocorua's east face, the cabin, maintained by the White Mountain National Forest, provides shelter on a first-come, first-served basis (Note: water may not be available during dry times, and fires are not permitted).

After hiking another 0.6 mile, stay straight and join the Hammond Trail. Considered the oldest path on the mountain, the Hammond Trail, many believe, was used by Native Americans centuries ago. Who knows, perhaps this was the route chosen by Chief Chocorua for his one-way journey up the mountain in the 1700s. Did he fall to his death, or perish at the hands of European settlers? As you ponder this age-old question, before you know it

Chocorua from the Three Sisters (photo by Doug Romano)

you arrive at a junction with the Weetamoo Trail. Named for the daughter of Passaconaway, a Penacook chief in the 1600s, this 1.9-mile leg of the loop passes the massive Weetamoo Rock near its upper reaches, and then moderately makes its way through the mostly mixed hardwood forest to the banks of the Chocorua River. Follow the running water to a crossing that leads to the Piper Trail. Turn right for the final 0.6 mile.

Looking for other loop opportunities? Choose the Piper Trail, avoiding the section over the Three Sisters, and then descend using the Brook, Liberty, Hammond, and Weetamoo trails to complete an 8.9-mile hike. To maximize solitude, avoid the crowded summit of Mount Chocorua altogether and use the Piper, Middle Sister, Carter Ledge, and Nickerson Ledge trails for an enjoyable 8.1-mile circuit.

17 North Moat Mountain

Round trip ■ 10 miles
Loop direction ■ Clockwise
Rating ■ Difficult
Hiking time ■ 6 to 7 hours
Starting elevation ■ 550 feet
High point ■ 3195 feet
Elevation gain ■ 2750 feet
Best season ■ Year round
Map ■ USGS North Conway West
Contact/fee ■ White Mountain National Forest

Driving directions: Starting from Route 16 in downtown North Conway, travel north and turn left at the second set of lights north of the train station onto River Road. Continue straight over the Saco River and veer right (north) onto West Side Road. Turn left, 2.4 miles from Route 16, into a large parking area for Diana's Baths.

Leveling out at less than 3200 feet, North Moat Mountain often is overlooked by those seeking to scale the forty-eight mountains that rise higher than 4000 feet in New Hampshire. While not high enough for some, North Moat's ridges and views are far more beautiful and expansive than many of the peaks that tower above it. Along the way, encounter cascading brooks, pass imposing rock formations, climb barren ridges, and tunnel through picturesque forests. While neighboring 4000-foot mountains attract larger crowds, North Moat Mountain awaits those seeking places where the White Mountains' quiet beauty is on display.

Beginning under the shade of tall white pines and lofty red oaks, follow

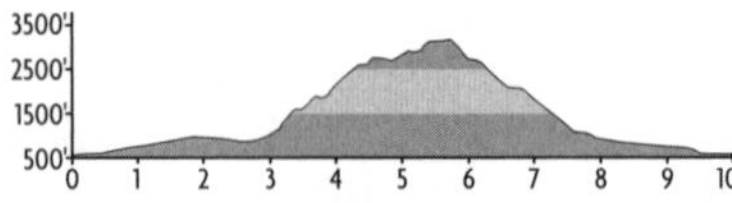

the Moat Mountain Trail 0.6 mile over flat, well-manicured ground. The trail's condition is maintained to serve the many people who visit Diana's Baths, an old mill site that has become an increasingly popular swimming area. Upon reaching Diana's Baths, turn right for a 0.5-mile walk along an old woods road, which briefly swings away from the brook before returning to its banks. After crossing a small tributary, you arrive at the Red Ridge Trail—the start of the day's loop.

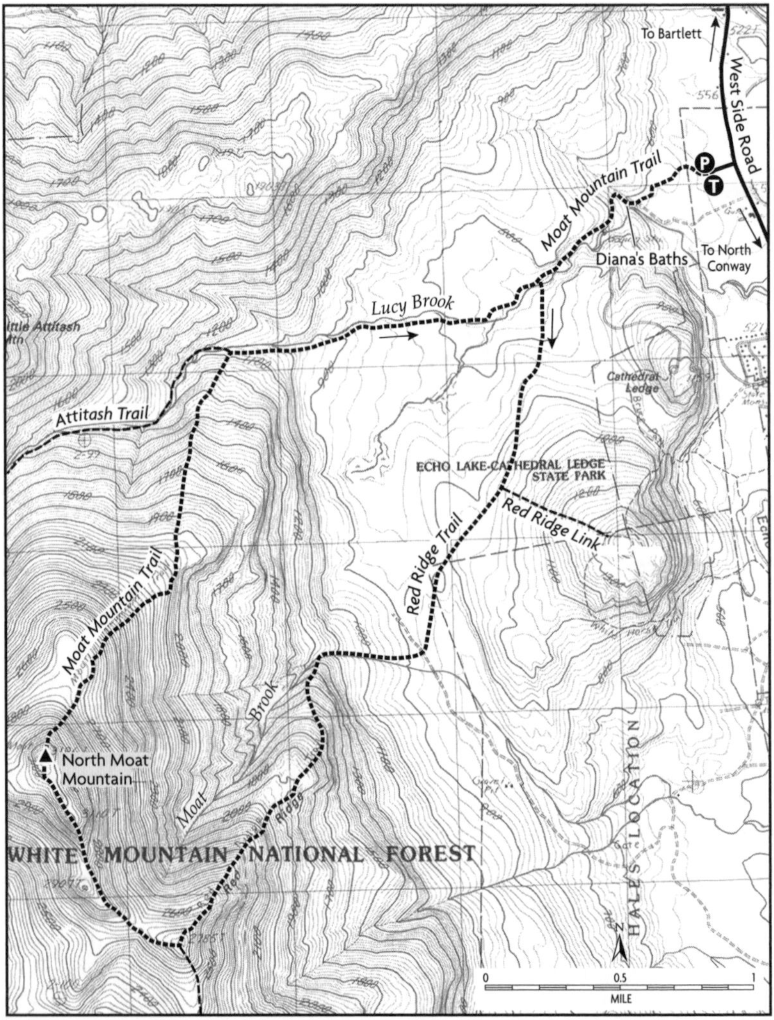

Take the trail south across Lucy Brook. You may get a little wet if the water is high, but there are rocks offering assistance and the current is slow. On the other side, begin a relaxing 2-mile journey that ends at the base of Red Ridge. The footing may be wet in spots; however, with little elevation change, the going is easy. Soon you reach Moat Brook, which is easily crossed, followed by a steady climb up the ridge.

Towering pines

From the edge of an eroded hillside, the first views of the summit appear. The slope remains fairly steep, but as the forest thins the terrain moderates. Passing occasional views, you arrive at the base of a half-mile section of bare ledge. The small trees and bushes that have found life within the seams of the solid rock do little to obstruct the spectacular views across the fertile valley that unfolds below.

Above the barren ridge, rejoin the Moat Mountain Trail near some large rocks, which provide excellent views and sunny resting spots. Initially wandering through a thick and maturing spruce-fir forest, the 1.1-mile route to North Moat Mountain ascends over and skirts around a number of small ledges and rock outcroppings. The short scrambles are not too difficult, unless wet or icy, and with each climb an increasing number of views opens up, including glimpses toward the Swift River and the Kancamagus Highway. Throughout, the forest provides excellent habitat for diminutive dark-eyed juncos which dart here and there, fanning out the white edges of their slate-colored tails. The final scramble leads to 360-degree views from the wide-open summit, the views of Mount Washington being especially impressive.

The 1.9-mile descent from North Moat Mountain can be steep and rocky in places, but the use of hands is not often required. The path quickly drops beneath the trees, levels off, and reaches the top of a long series of scenic ledges. Take your time and enjoy the views; the dry, sunny soil is a preferred location for many wildflowers such as bunchberry, Labrador tea, and pink lady's slippers.

The final descent traverses a hemlock and mixed-pine forest where the footing is fine, but your knees will definitely be under pressure until arriving at the banks of Lucy Brook. Here, where the Attitash Trail leaves left, turn right for a leisurely 2.5-mile hike back to the parking area. Take your time to enjoy the brook and the handful of cascades along the way. Feel free to cool off in the refreshing waters of Diana's Baths, but be prepared to have company.

18 Green Hills Preserve

Round trip ■ 5.6 miles
Loop direction ■ Clockwise
Rating ■ Moderate–Difficult
Hiking time ■ 3 hours
Starting elevation ■ 550 feet
High point ■ 1857 feet
Elevation gain ■ 1600 feet
Best season ■ Year round
Map ■ USGS North Conway East
Contact/fee ■ The Nature Conservancy, New Hampshire Chapter

Driving directions: Starting in downtown North Conway near the train station, follow Route 16 south for 0.5 mile and turn left onto Artist Falls Road. Travel for 0.4 mile, passing under a bridge, and then turn right onto Thompson Road. Follow Thompson Road 0.3 mile to a small parking lot on the right. Look for signs indicating Conway Municipal Land and Pudding Pond.

Tired of outlet shopping in North Conway? I get tired just thinking about it. A half-day outing in the Green Hills Preserve is the answer to your prayers—not to mention a reprieve for your credit cards. Established in 1990 through a generous donation to the New Hampshire Chapter of The Nature Conservancy, this nearly 5000-acre oasis contains several options for exploring. The loop to Peaked and Middle mountains is a great introduction to the area, as it provides panoramic views of the Mount Washington Valley, pleasant paths along streams and through nicely forested landscapes, and ample exposure to many of the rare plants, natural communities, and wildlife species that call this place home.

From the parking area, follow the woods road straight 0.2 mile to the information kiosk. To the right is a flat 1.6-mile loop that goes to Pudding Pond, a relaxing hike if you are interested in extending your trip for an hour or so. Turn left and follow the signs pointing toward Middle

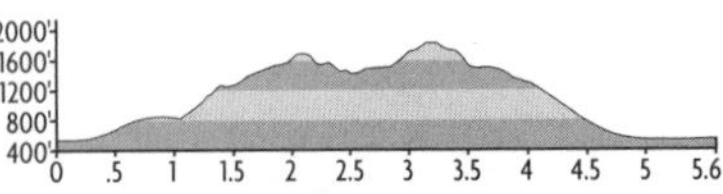

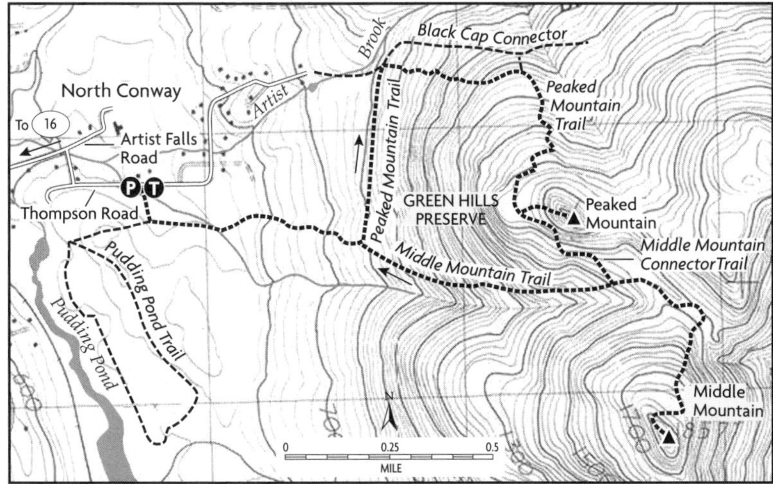

and Peaked mountains. At the top of a small incline, you quickly reach another trail junction; this is where the Green Hills Preserve begins and the Conway municipal property ends. It is also the start of the loop.

Stay left, picking up the Peaked Mountain Trail as it ascends a short gully and passes a wooden fence. Through a nice stand of northern hardwoods, the route remains relatively level over the next 0.8 mile with only minor elevation changes. Here is a perfect opportunity to get out your binoculars and scan the forest undergrowth for ovenbirds, small, spotted-breasted birds that frequently bellow out a chorus of "teacher, teacher, teacher."

At a second information kiosk and four-way intersection, turn right and head up the steeper slope. The trail that heads straight leads to Black Cap Mountain, the highest point in the preserve—a longer hike for another day. The climb up Peaked Mountain slowly levels off as the trail hugs the north side of the mountain. After passing a trail junction that leads left, the path veers sharply to the right. Suddenly, the soils become shallower and rockier, more amenable to the white, red, and pitch pines that thrive here.

With only 0.6 mile left to reach the 1739-foot summit, the remaining climb, although moderately steep, offers many nice spots to catch your breath and enjoy the views of Mount Washington standing majestically to the north, the Moats stretching gracefully across the valley, and the walls of Crawford Notch looming impressively in the distance. Upon reaching the Middle Mountain Connector Trail, turn left onto a 0.2-mile spur trail that leads to Peaked Mountain. The trail, with a few steep, rocky sections, is lined with rare plants, including silverling, a small plant that grows in the cracks of the exposed granite. Be sure to stay on the trail to protect the fragile vegetation. Peaked Mountain is a great place to enjoy lunch and distant views before heading to the next destination.

Return to the Middle Mountain Connector Trail and turn left. Follow the blazes down through a series of small switchbacks that conclude at the Middle Mountain Trail. Veering left, work your way gradually up the trail looking for signs of deer—the tall hemlocks in the area provide good winter habitat and the many short plants are perfect for browsing. Climbing past a limited viewpoint, follow the trail as it curls up the rock to the narrow summit of Middle Mountain. Drop down to an excellent view toward Chocorua Mountain from the south side of the peak.

The final 2.1-mile leg of the journey begins by returning to the Middle Mountain Connector Trail junction. Stay left and head through a charming, narrow ravine where a small stream runs parallel to the footpath. You will soon reach the junction with the Peaked Mountain Trail and the start of the hike's 0.7-mile conclusion.

Winter's sun casting shadows on Middle Mountain

19 Mount Carrigain

Round trip ■ 13.5 miles
Loop direction ■ Counterclockwise
Rating ■ Strenuous
Hiking time ■ 8 to 10 hours
Starting elevation ■ 1380 feet
High point ■ 4700 feet
Elevation gain ■ 3900 feet
Best season ■ Late May through October
Map ■ USGS Mount Carrigain
Contact/fee ■ White Mountain National Forest

Driving directions: From the junction of Route 302 and Bear Notch Road in Bartlett, head west 4 miles on Route 302. Turn left onto the dirt surface of Sawyer River Road—not maintained in the winter. Continue 2 miles to a parking lot on the left.

Atop the 4700-foot summit of Mount Carrigain, one stands at the center of the White Mountain National Forest. With more than forty of New Hampshire's highest peaks in view, the large expanse of the Pemigewasset Wilderness spreading out below, and most signs of civilization nowhere to be seen, there are few spots more alluring. However, even more enjoyable than the summit of Mount Carrigain is the journey there, a tour of rushing water, rugged mountainsides, bountiful wildlife, and peaceful isolation.

The hike begins on the Signal Ridge Trail in Livermore, New Hampshire. Incorporated in 1876, Livermore was once a bustling timber industry community of nearly two hundred citizens with a sawmill employing more than fifty people. In 1927, after a November storm damaged the railway that served the mill, the town faded away. By 1935, all traces of the town were removed, and in 1949 the last resident departed. Today all but twelve acres of Livermore are managed by the White Mountain National Forest, with little more than the remnants of old roads to show for the not-so-distant past. The hike to Mount Carrigain begins down the corridor of one such road as it hugs the side of a rushing brook. Quickly, the trail turns left and crosses a small tributary then the main branch. These crossings and others along the hike may be difficult during high water. Once across, the path winds gradually up a scenic valley passing large pools and crashing falls. The terrain levels near a trail junction and the start of the loop.

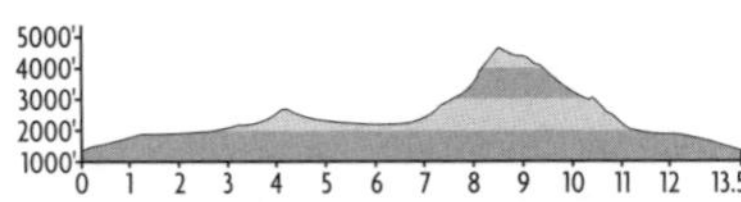

Turn right (north) onto the Carrigain Notch Trail, immediately reaching a brook crossing. Beyond the crossing, gradually climb into the narrow notch between the steep, rocky sides of Mount Lowell and Vose Spur. Through the notch and into the Pemigewasset Wilderness the trail follows Notch Brook, dropping 600 feet in 1.5 miles before reaching an old railroad bed. Turn left at a junction with the Nancy Pond Trail and follow the flat path above deep green mossy bogs for 0.8 mile to the banks of a small brook.

To the right a trail leads northwest into the heart of the wilderness, a great area for future backcountry adventures. Turn left onto the Desolation Trail, and upon crossing the small brook begin the arduous 1.9-mile ascent to the summit of Mount Carrigain. While it begins quite gradually, the slope steadily increases and eventually concludes with a half-mile, very steep and rocky pitch that cuts through a section of old-growth spruce-fir forest before arriving at the base of the summit tower.

While the top is thickly wooded, the renovated fire tower rises well above the trees and provides spectacular 360-degree views, and due to Mount Carrigain's central location the tower offers one of the most comprehensive panoramas of the White Mountain National Forest. Take your time and enjoy the scenery; it is mostly downhill from here.

The 5-mile journey back begins through the balsam-scented slopes below the summit. Pass the site of the old fire warden's cabin, where a small spring provides fresh water (to be safe, the water should be treated). The descent

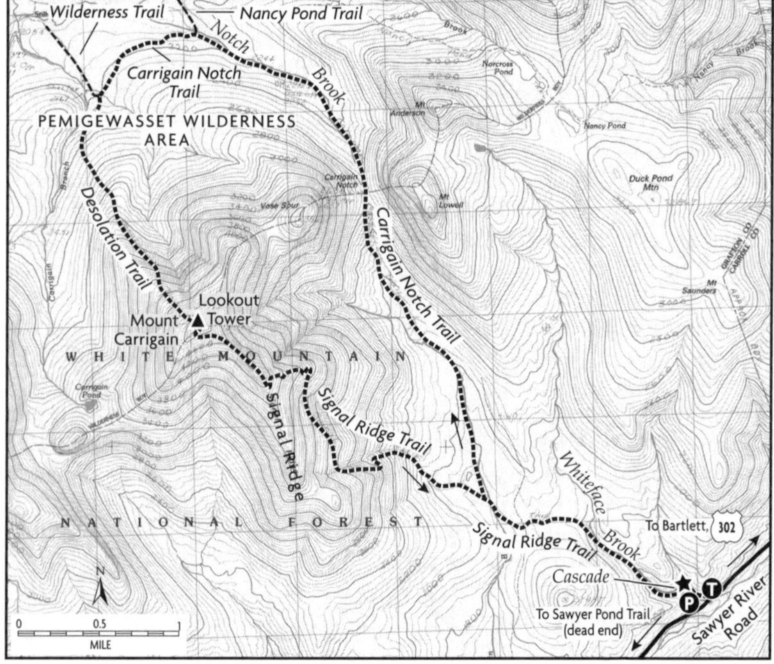

Brook crossing on the Desolation Trail

is pleasantly interrupted by a short climb over the wide-open and narrow spine of Signal Ridge. Dropping off steeply on both sides, the ridge provides excellent views and is also a prime location for spotting hawks cruising in the mountain winds. Look for the sharp-shinned hawk, a small bird of prey with a long, rectangular tail and less rounded wings than other raptors. Rather than soaring, this bird prefers to flap its wings, glide, flap its wings, and glide.

After passing over the high point on the ridge, the trail drops into the woods and slowly winds down the mountain. Aided at first by switchbacks, the path soon eases aside a steep slope through an attractive birch forest where young spruce trees are slowly taking over. Down the ridge the trail eventually levels off, passes some small wetlands, and reaches Carrigain Brook. The end of the loop and the junction with the Carrigain Notch Trail are a few hundred feet ahead. This crossing, while not dangerous, often results in wet boots. For a drier option, walk through the woods a few hundred feet to the left to where the Carrigain Notch Trail crosses. From the junction, the trail leads 1.8 miles to the end.

20 Arethusa Falls and Frankenstein Cliff

Round trip ■ 5 miles
Loop direction ■ Counterclockwise
Rating ■ Moderate–Difficult
Hiking time ■ 2.5 hours
Starting elevation ■ 1170 feet
High point ■ 2530 feet
Elevation gain ■ 1600 feet
Best season ■ May through November
Maps ■ USGS Crawford Notch and Stairs Mountain
Contact/fee ■ New Hampshire Division of Parks and Recreation

Driving directions: Starting from the center of Bartlett where Bear Notch Road meets Route 302, head west on 302 toward Crawford Notch. Travel 8.2 miles and turn left near a large sign for Arethusa Falls. There are two parking areas: a large area at the base of the hill and a second smaller spot 0.1 mile up the road.

This enjoyable half-day adventure leads to the cool, refreshing mist at the base of New Hampshire's highest falls and to the precarious edge of a 600-foot cliff with breathtaking views of the Saco River Valley. Generally along easy to moderate terrain, the hike's one steep section becomes a faded memory as wildflowers, moss-covered forests, and choruses of songbirds quickly instill more lasting memories. Complete this hike in conjunction with nearby trails to enjoy a full day of Crawford Notch State Park's scenic and rugged beauty.

Leaving the lower parking area, the trail climbs 0.1 mile to the start of the loop. Turn right and hike along the flat terrain for a half-mile to the Frankenstein Trestle. This impressive bridge spans a small stream along the historic railroad line that leads through Crawford Notch. Swing under the trestle, and begin the steep climb up the loose and rocky soil. Gaining more than 800 feet in less than three-quarters of a mile, the trail passes under sheer rock faces, ascends a small ledge, and enters a dark evergreen forest before suddenly emerging atop the impressive Frankenstein Cliff. Named for a German-born artist, not the infamous monster, the cliffs are an excellent vantage point to gaze upon Arethusa Falls plummeting into the Bemis Brook Valley in the distance, but more impressively, the nearby views of the Saco River far below.

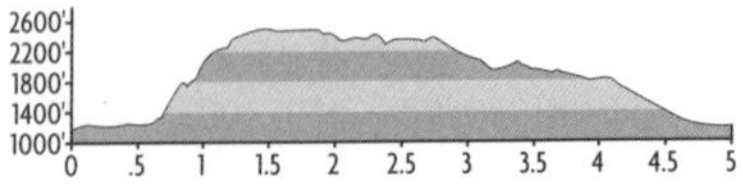

Return to the forest and follow the trail near the edge of the cliff. Leaving the rim, the route passes

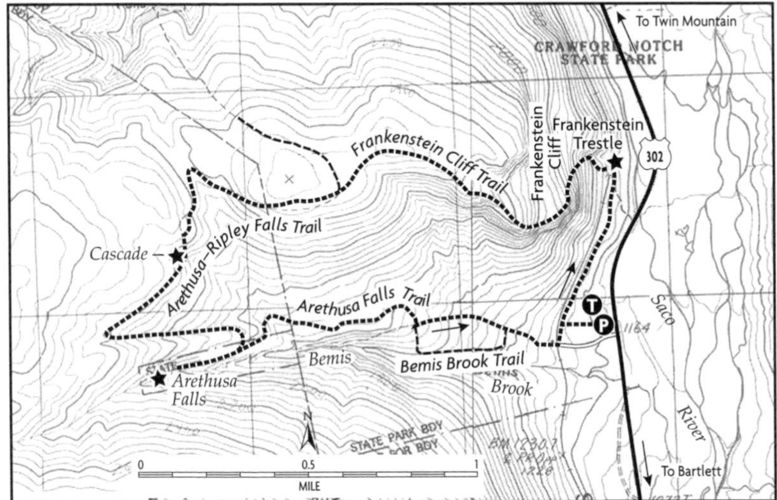

on the right a little-used and overgrown path that leads 0.7 mile to Falcon Cliff. Here, begin a steady climb that culminates at a viewpoint of Mount Washington near the highest point of the hike. Past the viewpoint, the path gently meanders along the pleasant ridge, reaching the Arethusa–Ripley Falls Trail 2.1 miles from the parking area. Stay straight, joining a 1-mile trek down the ridge, past a small cascade, and into a dark evergreen forest that teems with flowering pink and white lady-slippers from late May through June.

Upon reaching the Arethusa Falls Trail, turn right, dropping 0.2 mile to the edge of Bemis Brook and the base of the falls. With water crashing over open ledge before taking a final plunge to the pool below, this spot is an ideal location to soak in the cool damp air, especially on hot summer days.

The 1.5-mile return trip from this popular destination follows on the rerouted Arethusa Falls Trail. The new route, which now remains exclusively on the brook's north side, has better footing and is easier to follow, improvements that allow for maximum viewing of the forest's tamer inhabitants. For example, look for hairy woodpeckers foraging among the many decaying trees. Their black-and-white, ladder-design backs can only be confused with the slightly smaller but identical-looking downy woodpecker. The males of both also exhibit a small red spot on the backs of their heads.

Wind back to a junction with the Bemis Brook Trail, a slightly more difficult route that drops down to the water's edge and past additional waterfalls. To the left the Arethusa Falls Trail continues in the woods high above the water. Both options meet up in a half-mile near the trail's end. Upon reaching the trailhead, cross the railroad tracks—they are still actively used—and pass a private residence. Walk through the upper parking area and pick up the trail that points toward Frankenstein Cliff. Once in the

woods, you will quickly arrive at the junction where the loop began. Turn right to return to the lower parking area.

Looking for a second loop to enjoy in the afternoon? Drive west on Route 302 to the head of Crawford Notch. Behind the Appalachian Mountain Club's Highland Center, the Around the Lake Loop heads down an old road and continues for 1.2 miles around Ammonoosuc Lake. There is also a 0.3-mile extension to a fine viewpoint of the Presidential Range. Parking is available on Route 302 opposite Saco Lake, as well as on the Clinton Road, a paved road 0.1 mile past the AMC buildings.

21 Zealand Notch

Round trip	17 miles
Loop direction	Counterclockwise
Rating	Difficult
Hiking time	10 hours or 2 days
Starting elevation	2000 feet
High point	4320 feet
Elevation gain	3300 feet
Best season	May through October
Map	USGS Crawford Notch
Contact/fee	White Mountain National Forest

Driving directions: Beginning at the intersection of Routes 302 and 3 in Twin Mountain, drive east on Route 302. Travel 2.1 miles and turn right onto Zealand Road. Follow the road 3.2 miles where it dead-ends at a parking area.

As a long day hike or an overnight backpacking trip, the loop through Zealand Notch and over the Willey Range showcases the best of what the White Mountain National Forest has to offer. The 17-mile adventure travels through numerous forest and wetland habitats, passes rugged landscapes scoured during the last ice age, visits roaring waterfalls and serene mountain streams, and traverses long, rolling mountain ridges. As an added bonus, with the exception of 1 mile of heart-pumping steepness, the route follows easy to moderate terrain.

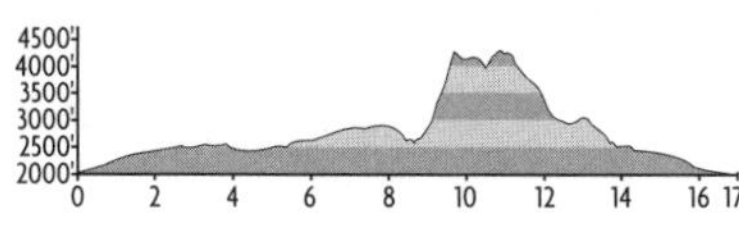

Begin along the 2.5-mile Zealand Trail. The rock-covered path quickly gives way to a sandy old railroad bed. Passing a series of beaver ponds,

Opposite: Arethusa Falls

a chorus welcomes the morning sun. A number of small songbirds are typically present. Listen for the loud call of the "neighborhood lush," the olive-sided flycatcher. This drab-colored bird prefers to shout out its "quick . . . three beers" call from the pointy tops of trees in wetland areas.

The loop begins upon reaching a junction with the A–Z Trail. Continue straight 0.2 mile toward the Zealand Falls Hut and the start of the Ethan Pond Trail. To the right the Twinway leads to roaring falls in a few hundred feet.

Picking up the Ethan Pond Trail, head south, still on the old railroad bed, surrounded by a young but growing birch forest. The area still shows the impact caused by the many fires that roared here a century ago. Attributable largely to poor forest management, the fires ironically played a significant role in the creation of the White Mountain National Forest in 1911, and the rebirth of the degraded ecosystem followed soon after. Ahead, further evidence of the past fury becomes clear as the trail emerges onto the open talus

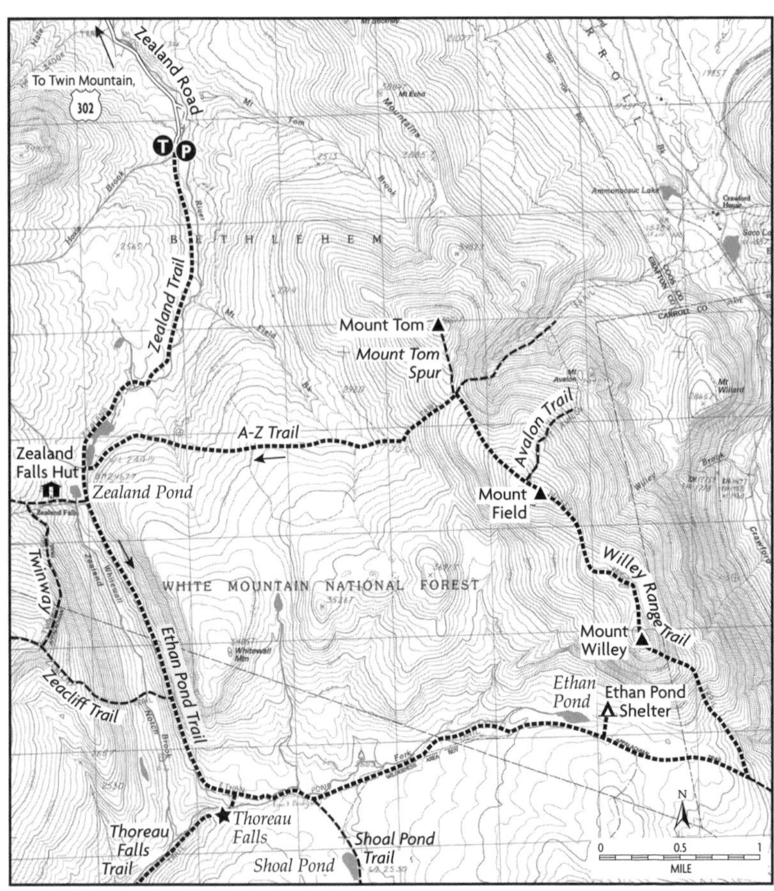

Ethan Pond

slopes of Whitewall Mountain. The exposed soil from these steep slopes has long since eroded. The lack of vegetation today allows for excellent views of the notch and Mount Carrigain in the distance.

The next stop on the journey is Thoreau Falls. Located on the edge of the Pemigewasset Wilderness, the roaring falls are 0.1 mile down a side trail to the right. Surrounded by forests and mountains, the falls are an ideal location to reflect on the writer for whom they are named. In 1854, Henry David Thoreau wrote in *Walden*, "I went to the woods because I wished to live deliberately, to front only the essential facts of life, and see if I could learn what it had to teach, and not, when I came to die, discover, that I had not lived."

Eager to learn more of what the woods have to teach, retrace your steps back to the Ethan Pond Trail and head right. Across the river and through an assortment of wetlands, the trail makes great use of boardwalks to ease the passage. Roughly 2.5 miles from the falls, turn left onto a spur trail that ends at the shore of Ethan Pond. Here the Appalachian Mountain Club maintains a shelter and tent sites ($8 per person) available on a first-come, first-served basis. This picturesque pond provides a serene setting to watch the sunset or to gaze upon the nighttime sky.

Returning once again to the Ethan Pond Trail, continue east 1 mile to the start of the Willey Range Trail on the left. The trail climbs slowly at first, before beginning a relentless pursuit of Mount Willey. Recent trail work has replaced many of the ladders and has added rock steps, but you will feel your leg muscles burning while gaining 1600 feet of elevation in a little more than a mile. Before reaching the summit, a path leads right to a spectacular reward. Perched above the slide-covered sides of Crawford Notch, the Southern Presidentials and Mount Washington loom to the northeast. With the day's hard work completed, savoring the view is in order.

After passing the 4285-foot summit of Mount Willey, continue along the ridge. Occasional views south and west will appear, as the path winds pleasantly through the spruce-fir forests to the wooded summit of Mount Field. Named for Darby Field, the first person of European descent to reach the summit of Mount Washington, the mountain has limited views. A relaxing descent to the A–Z Trail follows.

If 4000-footers are an objective, turn right and hike a hundred feet to pick up the 0.7-mile Mount Tom Spur on the left. Otherwise turn left and begin a short drop below the ridge. After crossing a small stream the trail levels off, resulting in a nice stroll through the forest. The reemergence of birch trees signals the approaching end of the trail. Passing wetlands, you soon arrive at the Zealand Trail, where a right turn leads 2.3 miles to the journey's end.

22 Crawford Notch

Round trip ■ 10 miles
Loop direction ■ Clockwise
Rating ■ Difficult
Hiking time ■ 7 hours
Starting elevation ■ 1900 feet
High point ■ 4312 feet
Elevation gain ■ 3100 feet
Best season ■ Year round
Maps ■ USGS Crawford Notch and Stairs Mountain
Contact/fee ■ White Mountain National Forest

Driving directions: Follow Route 302 to the top of Crawford Notch—8.8 miles east of the junction with Route 3 in Twin Mountain and 14.3 miles west of Bear Notch Road in Bartlett. The parking area is located near the railroad tracks just south of Saco Lake.

This classic loop hike contains a splash of many things people associate with the White Mountains: history, waterfalls, panoramic views, dizzying heights, a relaxing ridge walk, and two 4000-foot mountains. Mounts Pierce,

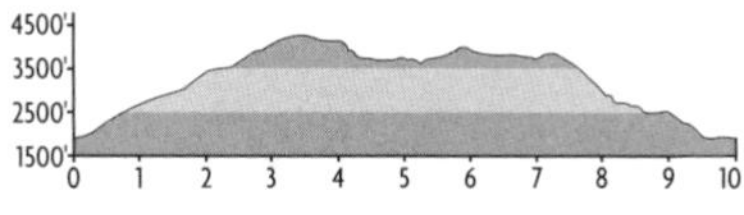

Jackson, and Webster have been favorite destinations for nearly two centuries. Choose this hike and you will quickly understand why people continue to be drawn to this area twelve months a year.

Begin the hike on the Saco Lake Trail, which enters the woods at the lake's south outlet. Cross the bridge and hike along the eastern shore 0.3 mile before arriving at Route 302. Turn right and follow the paved road briefly to the start of the Crawford Path, the oldest continuously hiked trail in the country. Established by New Hampshire hiking legend Abel Crawford, the path leads 8.5 miles from the head of Crawford Notch to the summit of Mount Washington. Today's loop will include 3.1 miles of this historic trail.

Climbing past the Crawford Cut-off, the Crawford Path soon passes Gibbs Falls—a nice stopping point and photo opportunity. Continue the moderate ascent, pass the Mizpah Cut-off at 1.9 miles, and begin to climb along the side of Mount Pierce. As the trees become smaller and the views uninhibited, you will reach the Webster Cliff Trail.

Turn right onto the Webster Cliff Trail to easily reach the summit of Mount Pierce, which enjoys sweeping views of the southern ridges emanating from Mount Washington. Originally named Mount Clinton in honor of a former governor of New York, the mountain was renamed in 1913 for the nation's only New Hampshire–born president. While President Pierce tends

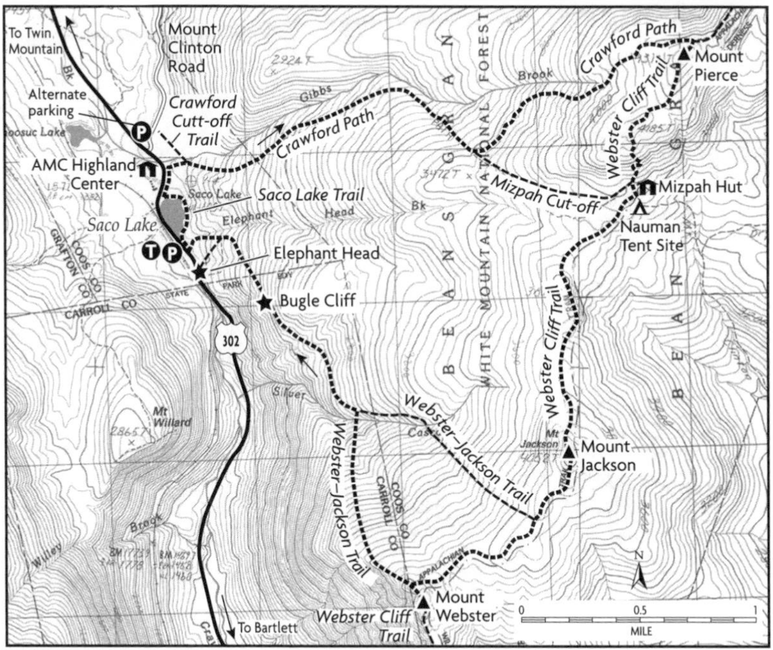

to be on the list of forgotten leaders unable to solve the slavery issue, it was during his administration that the United States completed its final land acquisition in the lower forty-eight states—the Gadsden Purchase, which today is southern New Mexico and Arizona.

Continue south along the ridge. Following a short descent the trail arrives at the Mizpah Hut and the Nauman tent site, overnight accommodations managed by the Appalachain Mountain Club, by reservation and on a first-come, first-served basis, respectively.

The Webster Cliff Trail follows a relatively flat and quiet ridge 1.7 miles to the summit of Mount Jackson. Meandering through the boreal forest, the haunting call of the white-throated sparrow echoes through the air: "Old Sam Peabody, Peabody, Peabody, Old Sam Peabody. . . . " Suddenly you emerge upon some high-elevation bogs. While crossing the boardwalks, turn back to enjoy the views of Mount Washington, but also look down to see vegetation more common to the tundra of northern Canada, including cotton grass. Once through the bogs, a final climb up exposed rock, not difficult unless wet or icy, ends at the summit and its 360-degree views.

From Mount Jackson two options are available. The Webster–Jackson Trail leads 2.6 miles back to the parking lot. However, if the sky is clear and daylight is plenty, continue on the gently rolling Webster Cliff Trail 1.4 miles to a second branch of the Webster–Jackson Trail. Proceed 0.1 mile past the intersection to the summit of Mount Webster. From the open rocks perched

Webster Cliff Trail

more than 2000 feet above Crawford Notch, there are few views in the White Mountains more impressive. Looking down at the steep slopes and rock-slides that have inspired such writers as Nathanial Hawthorne, you could easily spend the rest of the day gazing in wonder—but alas.

Returning to the Webster–Jackson Trail, quickly descend to the top of Silver Cascade. After a short climb the two trail branches converge. For 1.4 miles the trail descends in a staircase-like fashion, alternating moderate drops with flat terrain. After passing the second of two side trails, each offering good views of the notch, the trail ends at Route 302.

An added attraction of this loop hike is that it contains two shorter loops that provide a similar adventure with less effort. Using the Mizpah Cut-off, try the 6.6-mile loop over Mount Pierce, starting on the Crawford Path. The best place to access this shorter loop is from a parking area located on the Clinton Road. The Clinton Road is located 0.1 mile west of the Crawford Path's start. Use the Crawford Cut-off Trail to begin the hike. For a similar excursion, use both branches of the Webster–Jackson Trail along with the Webster Cliff Trail to complete a 6.5-mile loop. Both hikes are also good introductions to 4000-foot mountains in the winter.

23 Mount Washington

Round trip ■ 10.5 miles
Rating ■ Strenuous
Loop direction ■ Clockwise
Hiking time ■ 8 to 9 hours
Starting elevation ■ 2030 feet
High point ■ 6288 feet
Elevation gain ■ 4600 feet
Best season ■ May through October*
Map ■ USGS Mount Washington
Contact/fee ■ White Mountain National Forest

* Early in the season, you may need to use Lion Head Trail around Tuckerman Ravine.

Driving directions: From the junction of Routes 2 and 16 in Gorham, drive 10.5 miles south on Route 16. (Beginning at the junctions of Routes 302 and 16 in Glen, drive 11.9 miles north on Route 16.) The parking area is on the western side of the road near the Appalachian Mountain Club Pinkham Notch Visitor Center.

The highest mountain in New England and the location where some of the world's most severe weather has been recorded, Mount Washington can

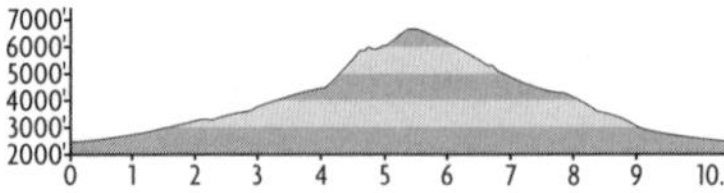

punish the ill-prepared as well as dazzle those who come in respect and awe. With large, steep-walled basins carved by glaciers now receded, windswept ridges barren of all but the heartiest of plants, and breathtaking views that can stretch from the Atlantic Ocean to the Province of Québec, the 6288-foot mountain is a massive pile of rocks with an abundant supply of trails to entertain those lured to its slopes. While the hike will pound your knees and sap your energy, choose this adventure when the weather is right and you are guaranteed a day to remember for the rest of your life.

Start on the Tuckerman Ravine Trail behind the visitor center where signs and bulletin boards provide information on the day's weather and warnings to be prepared. Quickly reach a small bridge that crosses over the Cutler River. Beyond, a short trail leads right to Crystal Cascade, a pleasant stopping point on the journey. At a bend in the path, stay straight and join the Boott Spur Trail, which immediately crosses over the Sherburne Ski Trail.

Wasting little time, the route aggressively heads up the increasingly steep slope, occasionally providing limited views toward Huntington Ravine. In 1.7 miles, a short spur leads right to Harvard Rock. This is one of the finest vantage points to look into Tuckerman Ravine, which lies hidden from most of the surrounding area. The trail begins to swing south and upon reaching appropriately named "split-rock," rises above tree line for good. The final 1.2-mile trek up the barren ridge is demanding, but surrounded by the unsurpassed beauty, one hardly notices. More and more of the mountain's features become visible as you crest the ridge and arrive atop the 5500-foot Boott Spur.

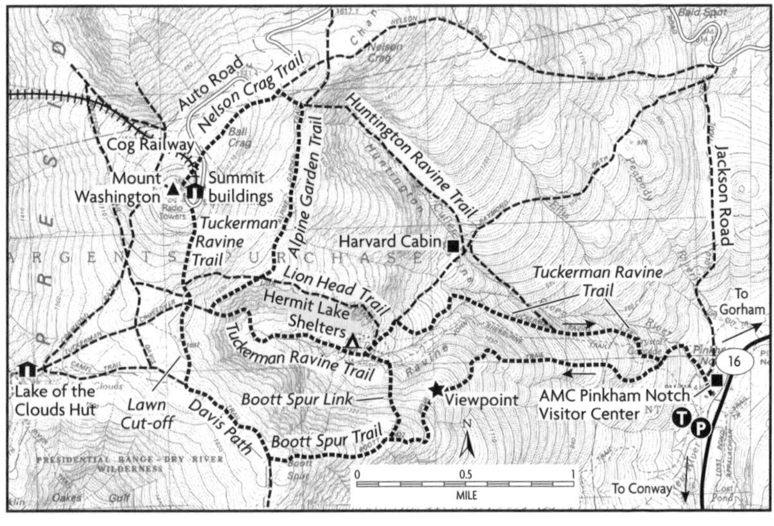

Tuckerman Ravine from the Boott Spur Trail

With most of the climb over, the loop continues right on the Davis Path. Crossing over a large, flat section of alpine terrain, the Davis Path provides a relaxing reprieve for tired legs and allows for maximum viewing of the area, including the now visible Dry River Wilderness.

In 0.6 mile turn right onto the Lawn Cut-off and head across the open landscape in a straight line toward the summit. In less than a half-mile, the trail ends at Tuckerman Junction, a popular resting spot. Catch your breath, and have a drink and a small snack in preparation for the last 0.6 mile and 900-foot climb to the top of New England. On a clear day the views from Mount Washington appear endless; however, so too does the number of people arriving up the auto road.

When ready to leave the hordes behind, pick up the Nelson Crag Trail, which leaves to the left of the Cog Railway. It quickly crosses the tracks and the auto road, and then climbs to the small knob of Ball Crag. This area provides a good perspective of the Northern Presidential Mountains and the Great Gulf Wilderness.

Drop down and turn right onto the Huntington Ravine Trail, following it for 0.2 mile. Turn right again, this time onto the Alpine Garden Trail. Famous for the abundant small alpine flowers that bloom here, particularly from late May to early July, this trail is both scenic and relaxing. In 0.9 mile arrive at an intersection with the Lion Head Trail. If Tuckerman Ravine's headwall is closed because of snow, follow this path left 1.1 miles to the lower section of the Tuckerman Ravine Trail. Otherwise, proceed straight for 0.3 mile before turning left into the ravine.

Despite its reputation and steep walls, when free of snow the Tuckerman Ravine Trail is not an extremely difficult route. Follow it past the headwall where small cascades tumble down the mountain. Returning to the high-elevation forest, wildlife diversity slowly increases. One of the few birds that ventures at this elevation is the yellow-rumped warbler. Appropriately named, this small bird also has streaks of yellow on its head and wings, as well as black and white facial marks. The path quickly moderates and arrives at the Hermit Lake Shelters, a popular overnight destination maintained by the AMC. The final 2.4 miles back to Pinkham Notch are rocky but straightforward and usually teeming with hikers.

24 Mount Jefferson

Round trip ■ 10.5 miles
Loop direction ■ Clockwise
Rating ■ Strenuous
Hiking time ■ 8 hours
Starting elevation ■ 1500 feet
High point ■ 5716 feet
Elevation gain ■ 4250 feet
Best season ■ June through October
Maps ■ USGS Mount Washington
Contact/fee ■ White Mountain National Forest

Driving directions: Following Route 2, drive 8.3 miles west of Route 16 in Gorham or 4.2 miles east of Route 115 in Jefferson. Turn south onto a dirt road to a sign and small parking area on the right.

When Thomas Jefferson drafted the Declaration of Independence, he spoke of three inalienable rights: life, liberty, and the pursuit of happiness. When climbing to the summit of the mountain in New Hampshire that now bears his name, it is hard not to have a greater appreciation for these important principles that form the foundation of our nation. Standing atop the third highest peak in New England, the wind in your face, warmed by

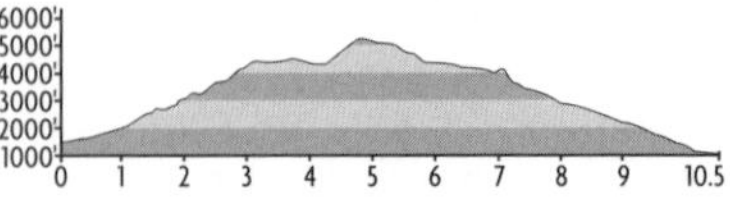

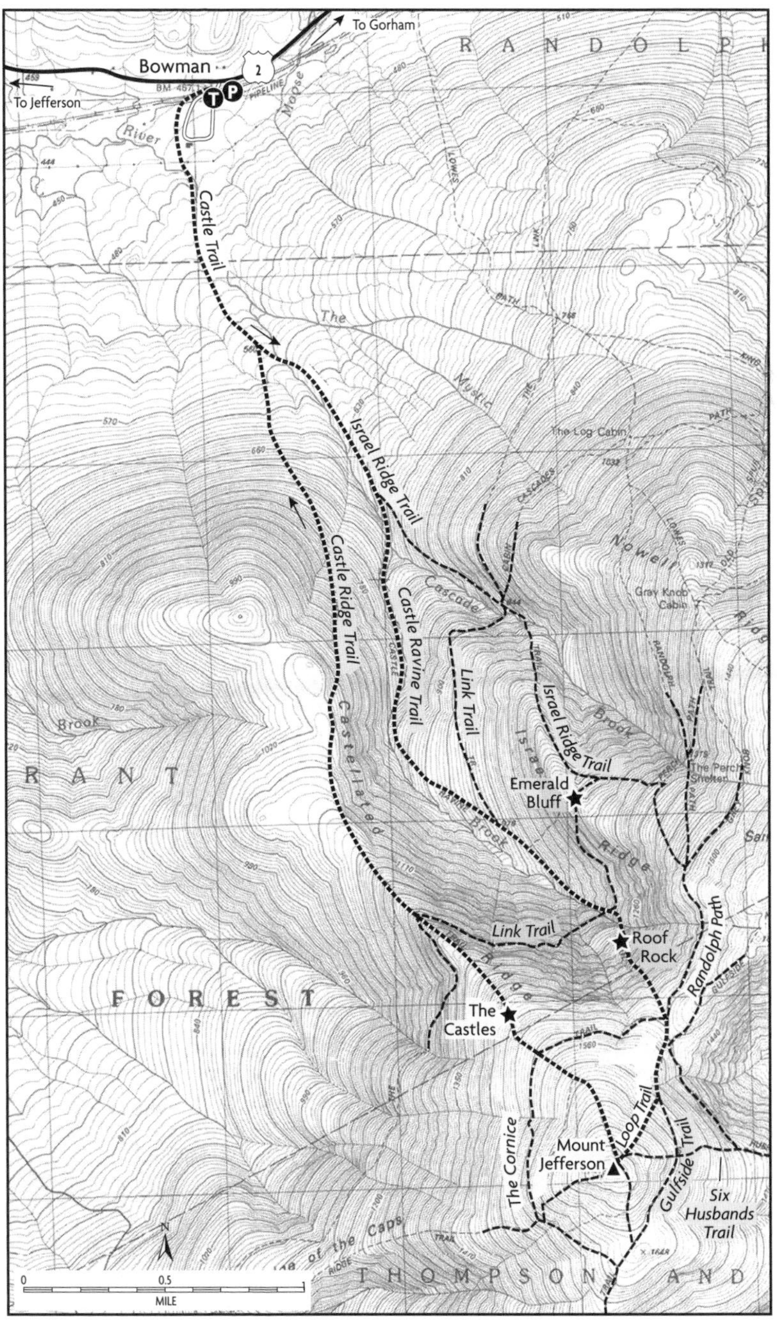

To Gorham
Bowman
2
To Jefferson
Castle Trail
Israel Ridge Trail
Castle Ridge Trail
Castle Ravine Trail
Link Trail
Emerald Bluff
Israel Ridge Trail
Roof Rock
Randolph Path
Link Trail
The Castles
The Cornice
Mount Jefferson
Loop Trail
Gulfside Trail
Six Husbands Trail
The Log Cabin
Gray Knob Cabin
The Perch Shelter
R A N D O L P H
R A N T
F O R E S T
T H O M P S O N A N D
0
0.5
1
MILE
N

Castle Ridge

the sun above, where could one feel more alive? Scaling the steep face of Castle Ravine, heart pumping and muscles flexing, where could one feel more liberated? Descending a barren ridge, views in all directions and recalling the day's accomplishment, how can one feel any happier?

With Mount Jefferson looming nearly 4500 feet above, pick up the Castle Trail along the old railroad bed. Quickly you are serenaded by the sound of chestnut-sided warblers. These small singing birds, common in very young forests, are identified by their chestnut sides and bright yellow patch on the top of their heads.

At a gate turn left, soon passing under a powerline where you leave private property and enter the White Mountain National Forest. The trail veers left and follows the Israel River a few hundred feet before reaching a crossing. Jumping from stone to stone, make your way to the other side and continue the gradual ascent aside the river once again. At 1.3 miles you reach a trail junction and the start of the loop.

Follow the Israel Ridge Trail left for 0.4 mile, then turn right onto the Castle Ravine Trail. For 2.1 miles enjoy the pleasant hike up through the narrowing valley. The footing is good and the incline remains moderate; however, a number of short brook crossings, while not extremely difficult, demand some attention.

With each step the steep walls and the serrated crest of Castle Ridge become more striking. Hike through a thick, moss-covered spruce-fir forest and pass three intersections before reaching Roof Rock, a large boulder that forms a natural tunnel on the trail. Beyond lies the most difficult stretch, where the route climbs 1300 feet in 0.7 mile. The trail also begins to rise above tree line, making this the best place to turn around if the weather is uncooperative.

If clear skies abound, begin the ascent, stepping from boulder to boulder on the wide-open slope. Take your time and enjoy the tremendous views; few trails in the White Mountains are harder, less crowded, or more beautiful. Upon reaching the headwall, pass a small wetland before arriving at the Randolph Path. Continue straight to Edmands Col, where a small plaque in the rock honors J. Rayner Edmands, a pioneer trail maker and hiking enthusiast who left his mark on this region in the late 1800s.

The final 0.7-mile climb to the summit of Mount Jefferson begins right on the Gulfside Trail and concludes on the Jefferson Loop Trail. The climb is steady but straightforward. Past the Six Husbands Trail you arrive at a junction just below the summit. Follow the Caps Ridge Trail a few dozen feet to the high point. With Mounts Washington and Adams, and the Great Gulf in front of you, and countless ridges and mountains in the distance, enjoy the well-earned scenery, but remember, while it is all downhill from here, your work is not done.

The 5-mile Castle Ridge Trail has many personalities. The first third of the hike follows an open ridge—a wonderful distraction from the pounding of foot to rock. Before dropping below tree line, the trail passes over and around a number of small knobs that look like a castle's turrets. Each provides nice views, especially into the ravine.

Take a few last glimpses to the horizon before entering the forest; the final views of the day are followed by a short, steep descent, culminating at a junction with the Link Trail. Here the trail moderates along a nicely forested ridge. Gone are the rocks and the steepness; present are needles and fern fronds. Eventually the trail veers right and begins to drop more aggressively to the valley floor. Small switchbacks ease the incline a bit and as the Israel River becomes louder the trail becomes more gradual.

After reaching the start of the loop, complete the final 1.3 miles to the end. While difficult, this loop's challenges are greatly outweighed by the rewards—a perfect tribute to the nation's third president.

A good alternative route, to bypass Castle Ravine, is to continue on the Israel Ridge Trail to where it joins the Randolph Path. This route in combination with the Randolph Path adds 0.3 mile to the loop, but provides an option that is available twelve months a year.

25 Mount Madison

Round trip ■ 9.6 miles
Loop direction ■ Clockwise
Rating ■ Strenuous
Hiking time ■ 8 hours
Starting elevation ■ 1225 feet
High point ■ 5367 feet
Elevation gain ■ 4300 feet
Best season ■ May through October
Map ■ USGS Mount Washington
Contact/fee ■ White Mountain National Forest

Driving directions: Beginning at the intersection of Routes 16 and 2 in Gorham, travel west on Route 2. At the bottom of a large hill, 4.6 miles from Gorham, turn left onto Pinkham B Road. The parking area is 0.2 mile on the right. From the junction of Routes 2 and 115 in Jefferson, travel east for 8 miles, and then turn right onto Pinkham B Road.

At the end of a ridge stretching north of Mount Washington, the pointy summit of Mount Madison stands a few hundred feet lower than its neighbors. Consequently, like the fourth president of the United States for whom the peak is named, Mount Madison's prominence tends to be overlooked. However, just as President Madison's role in the drafting of the U.S. Constitution and the creation of America was as important as the role played by more noteworthy founding fathers, a hike to the summit of Mount Madison is as awe-inspiring and exhilarating as scaling any of the nearby mountains that rise above it.

Initially crossing private property, the loop begins on the opposite side of an abandoned railroad bed where the Randolph Path enters on the right.

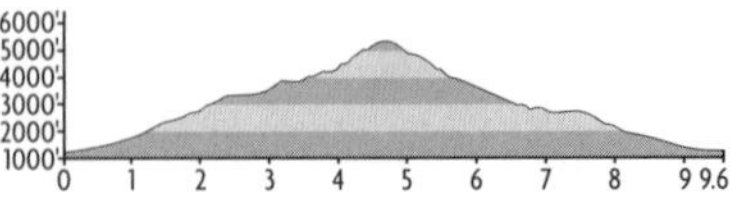

In 2004 the Society for the Protection of New Hampshire Forests acquired a conservation easement on this private property, helping to protect

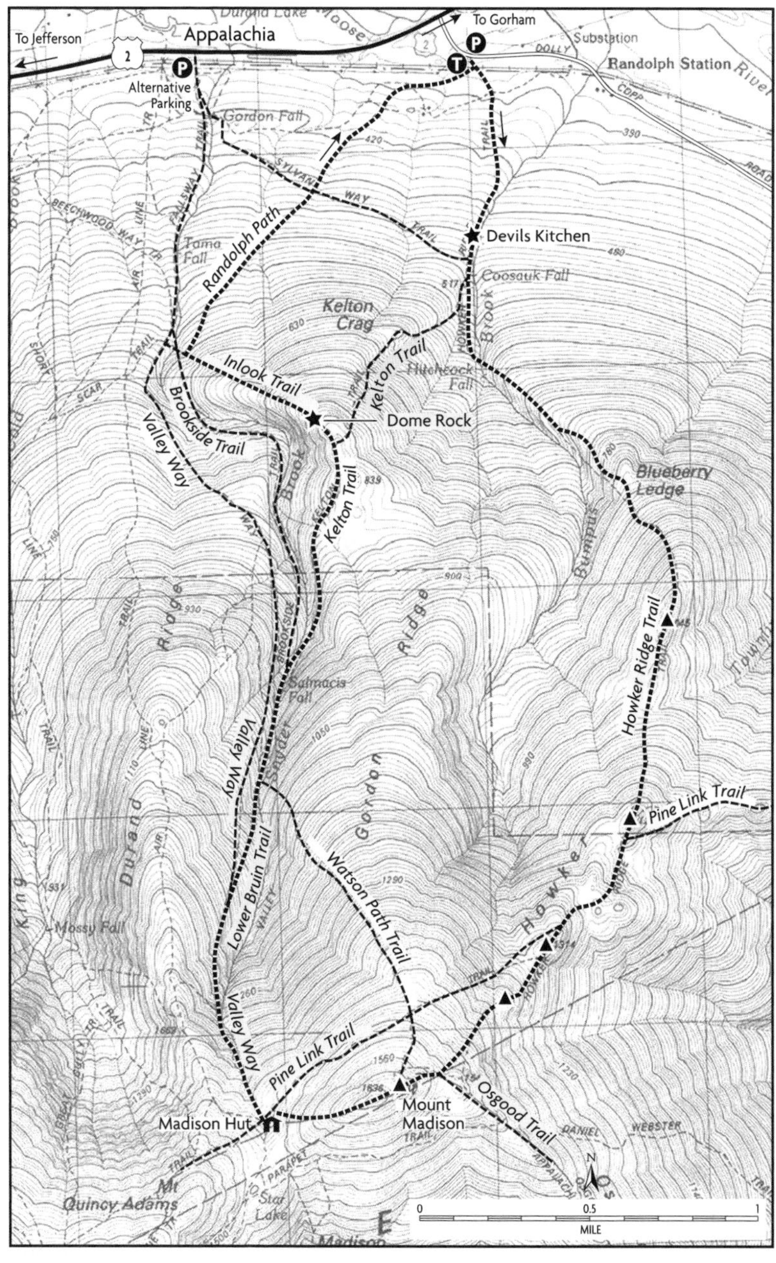
To Jefferson
Appalachia
To Gorham
Alternative Parking
Substation
Randolph Station
Gordon Fall
Randolph Path
Devils Kitchen
Coosauk Fall
Kelton Crag
Inlook Trail
Kelton Trail
Hitchcock Fall
Dome Rock
Brookside Trail
Valley Way
Blueberry Ledge
Salmacis Fall
Howker Ridge Trail
Pine Link Trail
Lower Bruin Trail
Watson Path Trail
Mossy Fall
Madison Hut
Mount Madison
Osgood Trail
Star Lake
MILE

access and ensure continued sustainable use of the natural resources.

Stay left on the Howker Ridge Trail and begin a gradual ascent. The trail soon reaches the side of Bumpus Brook, home to a number of small cascades as well as the Devils Kitchen—a gorge with steep rock walls dozens of feet high. After entering the White Mountain National Forest and passing two trail junctions, arrive at the steep valley that frames Hitchcock Fall. Cross the brook and climb a few hundred feet up to a short trail that leads right to the Bear Pit, an interesting gap in the rock. Continue the steady climb up the steep slope. After passing a limited northern outlook, the trail traverses a narrow ridge, culminating at the first howk (the name given to the series of small peaks on the ridge). From here enjoy restricted views of Madison's rock-covered summit.

The trail descends briefly before climbing to a more open ledge on the second howk. Down the slope the path converges with the Pine Link Trail and for a quarter mile the two coincide. Turn left, remaining on the Howker Ridge Trail, and scramble up to a wide-open peak with impressive views north and east. A short descent and another steep climb later ends at the fourth and final howk. Rise out of the stunted forest and across the rocky terrain, reaching the Osgood Trail 4.2 miles from the start.

Turn right for the final 0.3 mile to the top and prepare to sit back and enjoy the fruits of your labor, including glorious views of Mount Washington, Mount Adams, and countless mountains in every direction. Looking into the chasm of the Great Gulf is especially impressive; in fact, if you stare long enough, it is possible to see the massive sheet of ice that carved and sculpted the steep walls not that long ago.

While it can be hard to leave such beauty, descent eventually becomes a necessity. Continue west on the Osgood Trail and drop 0.5 mile, among boulders, to the grassy, protected saddle where the Appalachian Mountain Club's Madison Hut is located. There are a number of interesting places to explore nearby, including the Parapet and a small tarn.

Hike down the Valley Way, the most moderate and safest trail to use, especially during bad weather or in the winter. The most straightforward journey is to stay on the Valley Way 3 miles, then turn right, following the Randolph Path 1.5 miles to your car. However, a more scenic alternative is to follow the Valley Way 1 mile and instead turn right onto the Lower Bruin Trail. Continue down 0.2 mile and pick up the Brookside Trail, a path that passes a series of scenic cascades and waterfalls. After passing Salmacis Fall, turn right onto the relatively level Kelton Trail. Upon reaching the Inlook Trail, turn left, following the route down the ridge past a number of scenic ledges until reaching the Randolph Path.

Turn sharply right here for a relaxing conclusion to the day. After crossing the Sylvan Way you will once again enter private property. Look for signs near a small clearing where the trail bends left before reentering the

Opposite: Duck Fall

woods. The poplar growing in this recent timber harvest area provides good habitat for yellow-bellied sapsuckers, a red-crested and red-throated woodpecker that drills rings of small holes in the bark of trees to facilitate the oozing of sap.

If you are looking for a half-day excursion, then combine the Howker Ridge, Kelton, and Inlook trails with the Randolph Path for a 4.5-mile loop with great views, a scenic brook, and quiet trails where you are not likely to have much company. Similarly, if you are looking for a less crowded (but steeper) descent of Madison, skip the Valley Way and follow the Watson Path directly from the summit; turn right upon reaching the Brookside Trail.

26 Carter Dome

Round trip ■ 11.9 miles
Loop direction ■ Clockwise
Rating ■ Difficult
Hiking time ■ 8 hours
Starting elevation ■ 1810 feet
High point ■ 4832 feet
Elevation gain ■ 3160 feet
Best season ■ May through October
Maps ■ USGS Jackson and Carter Dome
Contact/fee ■ White Mountain National Forest

Driving directions: From Route 16A in Jackson Village, turn north onto the Carter Notch Road. Past Jackson Falls, travel 2.1 miles to the junction of Route 16B. Continue straight. After the pavement ends, follow the dirt road down a short hill to a parking lot on the right and a sign for the Bog Brook Trail, 3 miles from Route 16B.

Not only does this loop ascend the tenth highest peak in New England, it does so by following two trails that are far less traveled than others reaching the same destination. Throw in some quiet mountain streams, an unnamed bald summit south of Carter Dome, and breathtaking views above the cliffs of Carter Notch to complete a rewarding day-long adventure in the White Mountains. For fewer bugs, easier river crossings, and optimum daylight, choose this hike midsummer through early fall.

The first 0.7 mile traverses level terrain; however, you will also encounter three river crossings that require some attention to avoid saturating your boots early in the hike. After the third crossing the trail veers

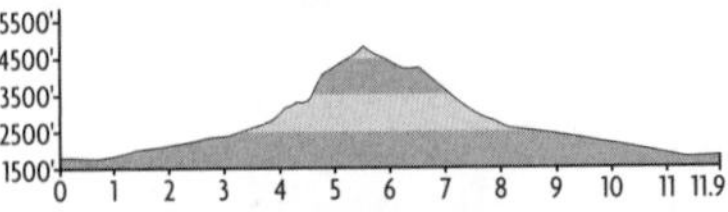

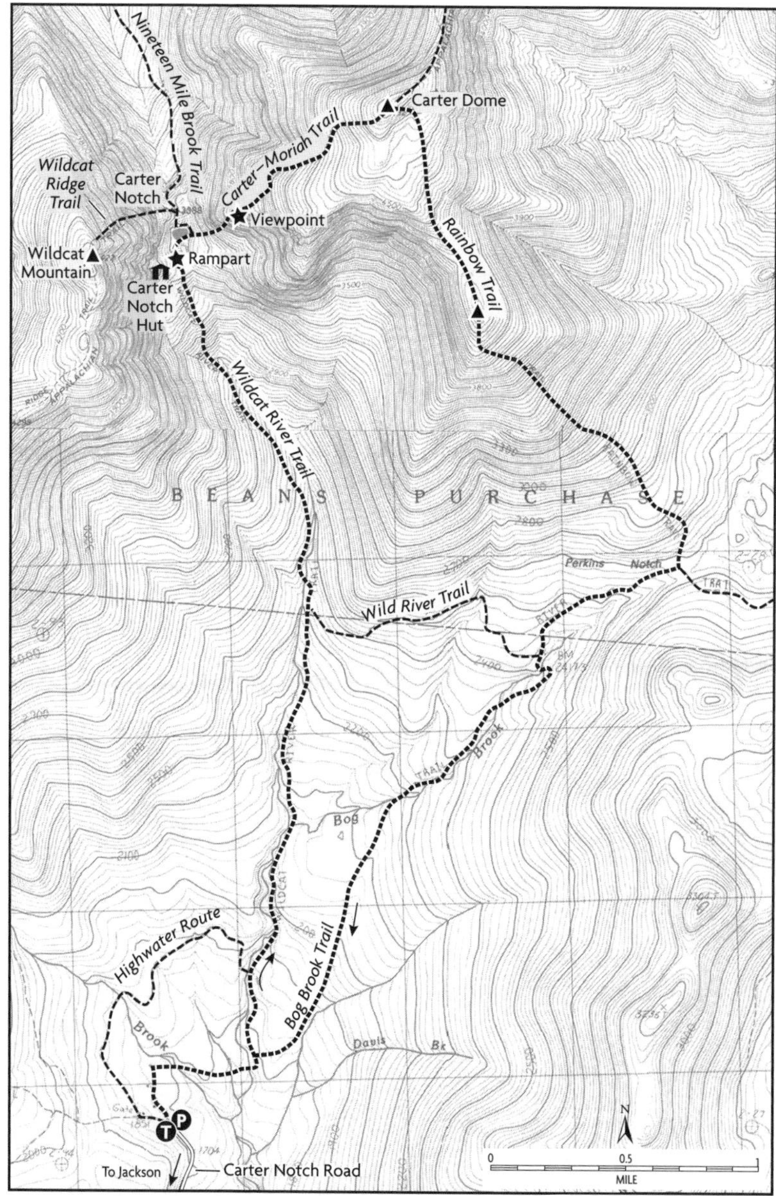

sharply to the left and arrives at a junction with the Wildcat River Trail and the start of the loop. Staying to the left, you will soon reach a woods road that can be used as an alternative high-water route from the parking area.

Continue straight, climbing gradually along the banks of the running water, past the Wild River Trail, to a final crossing.

Beyond this crossing the climb becomes more rigorous, ascending 1.6 miles to the base of Carter Notch. As the ground levels, a short path leads right to the Rampart, a boulder field with excellent views of the notch and the ridge leading up to Carter Dome. From here, the summit is within reach.

Just ahead, the Appalachian Mountain Club's Carter Notch Hut sits above a number of small ponds. Hike to the start of the Carter–Moriah Trail near the shore of the second pond. This is an ideal location to grab a snack and a drink of water, because the next 1.2 miles will consume a lot of energy as you ascend more than 1600 feet.

While climbing the steep ridge be sure to pause occasionally to catch your breath as you observe the Presidential Range to your left and the steep slopes of Wildcat Mountain behind. Push on until you reach a viewpoint sign on the right. The short climb required to reach the reward is well worth the effort. From atop the ledge, enjoy the truly awesome view of the notch. Scan the area for crested cedar waxwings whistling and gracefully flying across the open landscape, but remember to watch your step—it's a long way to the rocks below.

Back on the main trail the remaining climb to the summit moderates but remains steady. A few dozen feet beyond the site of the old fire tower, Carter Dome provides nice views of Mount Washington, the Carter Range, and north to the Mahoosucs. Sit back and relax; the climb is over.

From the summit, pick up the Rainbow Trail as it heads east into the woods.

Bunchberries

For 1 mile the path pleasantly wanders through the spruce-fir forest to a bald summit on the ridge. This little-known and infrequently visited peak offers grand views of the Wild River Valley and the hills and lakes of western Maine. These are the last views of the day, so savor them before departing.

Once in the woods, a steady 1.5-mile descent begins. At this point in the hike the legs begin to feel the pressure, but fortunately it does not last long. Before you know it the ground levels and you reach the trail's end. Rather than a pot of gold, at the end of this rainbow you are more likely to encounter a pile of moose nuggets, since the large mammals are frequent visitors to the many boggy wetlands in the area.

Turn right and follow the Wild River Trail 0.7 mile along flat terrain until joining the Bog Brook Trail on the left. The hike's gradual 2.8-mile conclusion begins along the shady banks of the brook, passes the start of the loop, and crosses the three rivers before ending at the parking lot. You will feel this one tomorrow, but it is a hike you will remember long after your muscles have recovered.

If 11.9 miles is a bit more than what you are looking for, a shorter 6.5-mile loop is possible by using the 1-mile stretch of the Wild River Trail that connects the Wildcat River and Bog Brook trails. This quiet hike along mountain streams provides ample wildlife viewing opportunities and is especially nice during the autumn when the foliage is most vibrant.

27 Imp Face

Round trip	6.5 miles
Loop direction	Clockwise
Rating	Moderate–Difficult
Hiking time	4 hours
Starting elevation	1270 feet
High point	3350 feet
Elevation gain	2125 feet
Best season	Year round
Map	USGS Carter Dome
Contact/fee	White Mountain National Forest

Driving directions: There are two trailheads for this hike, located 0.2 mile apart. Follow Route 16 south of Gorham for 5.2 miles, or north of Pinkham Notch for 5.3 miles to the northernmost trailhead. Traveling from Gorham, the trailhead is located on the left shortly past Dolly Copp Campground. There is ample room for parking on the roadside.

Suppose during the night, a strong high-pressure system has blown in from northern Canada. There is not a cloud in the sky. While the Presidential

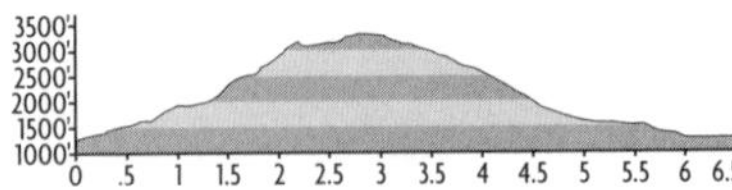

Range is tempting, venturing that high above tree line would require dealing with unrelenting winds. A perfect solution is a nearby hike to a more protected location that offers one of the region's most impressive views. With an option to scale a 4000-foot mountain and the opportunity to view raptors soaring in the mountain air, choosing this pleasant loop and saving the Presidential hike for a calmer day is a decision few would regret.

The path begins under a dark forest of tall hemlock trees high above a bubbling mountain stream. The gradual grade remains until the trail reaches the confluence of two small streams, before crossing both of them. Since the stream valley is quite narrow, the second crossing can be a bit tricky with heavy rainfall or abundant snowmelt.

Once across, the forest brightens as the trail ascends to a hardwood-covered plateau. Up the slight incline, the trail veers left and the climb becomes steadier. Make your way along the side of the slope. Turning sharply to the right, the route uses a series of short switchbacks to reach the rocky, wide-open Imp Face. From this vantage point—roughly half the elevation of Mount Washington—the ravines, gulfs, and rock summits of the Presidential Range stand impressively before you. This spot is also a great place to scan the sky, above and below, for hawks, falcons, and ravens circling in the cool mountain air.

The hike continues near the side of the ledge, but soon reenters the forest for good. Around the rim of a deep valley, the trail crosses a number of small and seasonal brooks. There is not much overall elevation change, but the terrain is uneven in places. After joining an old woods road, briefly descend

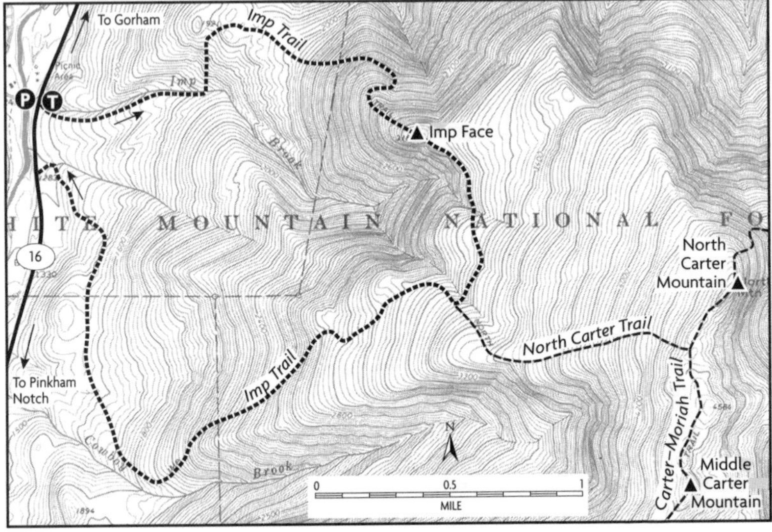

The Presidentials from the Imp Face

to a junction with the North Carter Trail. This is roughly the halfway point. Stay to the right on the Imp Trail.

At first the trail parallels a small stream, and occasionally both become one and the same. Heading in a southerly direction, the trail gradually winds down the ridge, soon skirting down a fairly steep slope. Swing north along the increasingly level terrain. Hike over a dirt road and across the small stream that soon appears. The trail follows relaxing grades while modestly descending to Route 16. Follow the paved road 0.2 mile right to your car.

If you are looking for a little longer workout or are interested in conquering a 4000-foot mountain, extend this loop by ascending the North Carter Trail. This path leads 1.2 miles steadily up the mountain through nice, high-elevation forests. Once on the ridge, turn right on the Carter–Moriah Trail and head 0.5 mile to the summit of Middle Carter. The views from Mount Lethe, a small open knoll just north of the summit, are impressive in all but the southerly direction.

Return to the Imp Trail the same way. As you do, be sure to scan the forest for the yellow crown of the black-backed woodpecker. This relatively rare and highly specialized species prefers to forage in diseased spruce-fir forests and is the only woodpecker other than the much larger pileated woodpecker to have a solid black back.

28 Wild River

Round trip	16.4 miles
Loop direction	Clockwise
Rating	Difficult
Hiking time	8 to 10 hours (or 2 days)
Starting elevation	1150 feet
High point	4049 feet
Elevation gain	3550 feet
Best season	May through October
Maps	USGS Carter Dome and Wild River
Contact/fee	White Mountain National Forest

Driving directions: Starting at the Junction of Routes 113 and 2 in Gilead, Maine, travel south on Route 113 for 3.1 miles, then turn right onto a dirt road. Follow the road 5.6 miles to the Wild River Campground and the parking area on the left for hikers.

Proposed to be New Hampshire's newest wilderness area, the Wild River watershed forms the largest roadless non-wilderness area in the White Mountain National Forest. Surrounded by mountains and dissected by footpaths, this area has ample opportunities for a variety of different loop hiking experiences, from half-day nature walks to multiple-day backpacking trips. This recommended hike provides a sampling of everything the area has to offer—long, gradual trails, excellent wildlife-viewing opportunities, scenic ridges, and plenty of solitude. Try this loop as an overnight hike, or get an early start and make a long day of it; either way, you will not go home disappointed.

From the parking area, hike across the road and follow the river upstream. At 0.3 mile turn right onto the Moriah Brook Trail, where a long suspension bridge leads to the other side of the river and an intersection with the Highwater Trail. Stay left as the two routes coincide. At the next intersection continue right on the Moriah Brook Trail as it ascends modestly through a delightful birch forest. With little elevation change, the biggest obstacles are brook crossings, the first occurring upstream from the steep-walled Moriah Gorge. Each crossing becomes easier and the river becomes smaller as you make your way up the valley. Blessed with a number of small cascades and large pools, the brook provides a constant soothing chorus of background music.

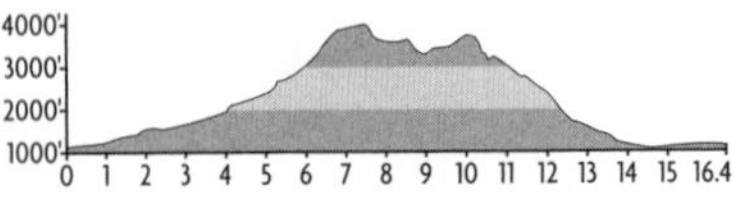

After the trail crosses a small tributary, the soil becomes rockier, the birches less prevalent, and the trail narrower. The path snakes its

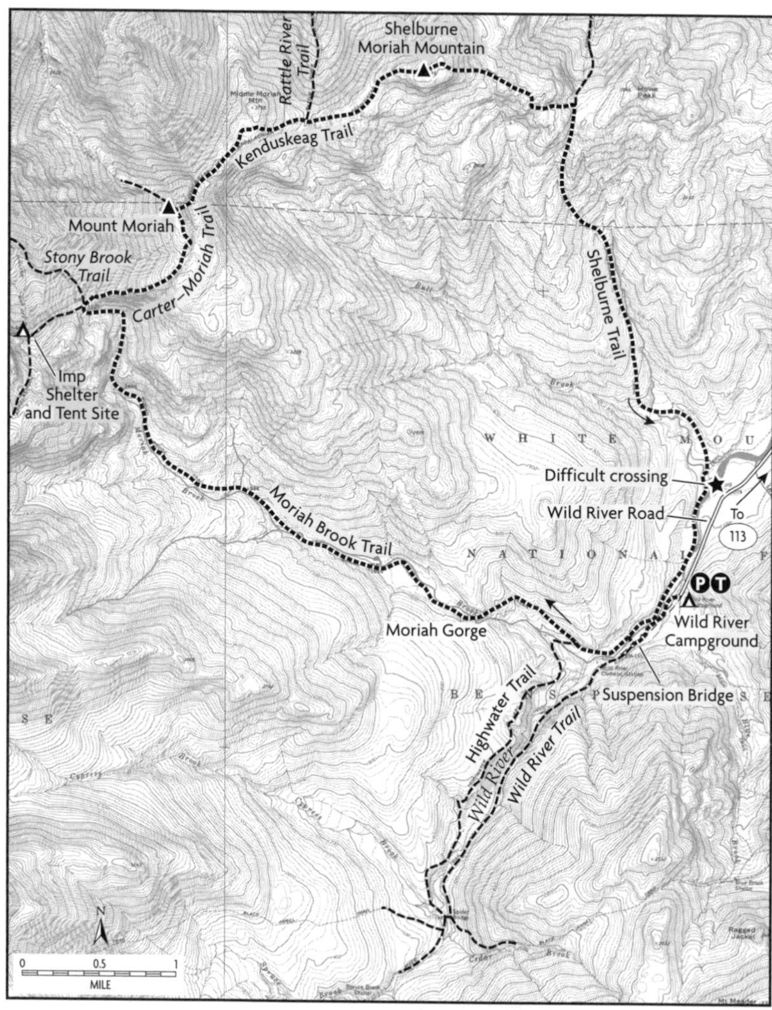

way through the valley, ascending more aggressively, but levels off once again before a short climb ends on the ridge and the Carter–Moriah Trail. The Appalachian Mountain Club's Imp Face Shelter and tent site ($8 per person) is located 0.6 mile south along the Carter–Moriah Trail. This campsite provides an ideal spot for hikers interested in completing this journey in two days.

A scenic 5.5-mile ridge walk begins with a challenging 1.4-mile climb to the summit of Mount Moriah; however, with plentiful and ever-increasing views you will hardly notice the effort. Soon the flat summit becomes visible on the left. Over a couple of small rises, follow the short boardwalk that ends at a three-way intersection. The Carter–Moriah Trail leads left 0.1 mile to the summit—worth the effort, although the first 50 feet is quite steep. Mount Moriah is also a popular destination for gray jays. Closely related to the blue jay, gray jays, or Canada jays, are friendlier than their more raucous cousins.

The loop continues right along the Kenduskeag Trail. After a short rise the trail descends fairly quickly, only to climb again over the southern shoulder of Middle Moriah Mountain. One more drop and across an extensive boardwalk system, and you arrive at a soggy trail junction where the Rattle River Trail veers left. Continue straight, climbing gradually over picturesque ledges and past the high elevation bogs of Shelburne Moriah. More scenic, Shelburne Moriah is also not as popular as its 4000-foot neighbor.

From the summit the trail descends the steepest part of the loop, requiring a little extra care. Upon moderating, the trail passes over a series of open knolls and cuts through a narrow notch in the ridge. After the last viewpoint, follow the path under a large rock face before turning right onto the Shelburne Trail. Through the pass the path drops steadily alongside a small stream, eventually turning sharply left to join an old woods road. At this point the bulk of the descent is complete.

Boardwalk on Kenduskeag Trail

Cross a branch of Bull Brook and make your way to the Highwater Trail. If the water is low, you can continue straight here and cross the Wild River, making your way back to the parking area by walking a little over a mile on the Wild River Road. However, the recommended choice is to turn right onto the Highwater Trail. This side of the river is very nice, with a number of large white pines and red oaks. Although generally flat, the trail does go up and over a few small hills before reaching the Moriah Brook Trail and the suspension bridge that started the day's journey.

For a shorter half-day loop, follow the Highwater Trail southwest of the Moriah Brook Trail. Upon reaching the Black Angel Trail, turn left across the water and return along the Wild River Trail. This 5.5-mile hike is fairly level and especially scenic during fall foliage.

29 BALDFACES

Round trip	9.7 miles
Loop direction	Clockwise
Rating	Difficult
Hiking time	7 to 8 hours
Starting elevation	520 feet
High point	3610 feet
Elevation gain	3450 feet
Best season	April through November
Maps	USGS Chatham and Wild River
Contact/fee	White Mountain National Forest

Driving directions: Follow Route 113 north of Route 302 in Fryeburg for 17.4 miles or south from Route 2 in Gilead for 12.7 miles (access in the winter is only from the south). The parking lot is on the eastern side of the road. Note: Route 113 is winding with many unusual intersections, but clearly marked.

The Baldfaces, which rise over 3600 feet in elevation, lie along a ridge nestled between higher and more rugged White Mountain summits and a landscape of farms, lakes, and low, rolling hills. Ravaged by fire in 1903, the mountains' open ridges provide countless vantage points from which to gaze upon this scenic corner of northern New England and marvel at its many diverse natural features. This full-day hike has significant elevation gain and can be challenging, but for those completing the circuit the rewards are great, and with many trails and potential loops available, the greatest challenge will be scheduling a return trip.

The hike begins easily across private property. In 0.7 mile enter the White Mountain National Forest and reach the start of the loop. To the right a 0.1-mile spur leads to Emerald Pool, a popular swimming spot beneath a small cascade.

Turn left onto the Baldface Circle Trail toward South Baldface. In 0.2 mile the Slippery Brook Trail branches left. Along with the Baldface Knob Trail, this route is a mile longer and a bit less spectacular; however, this option is less traveled and safer during wet, snowy, or icy conditions. Continuing up the Baldface Circle Trail the route passes two ends of a half-mile loop that leads left to Chandler Gorge, a flume with small falls and cascades. At this point the trail begins a more moderate climb and in 1.3 miles reaches the popular South Baldface Shelter where a lean-to and tent sites are available for overnight use.

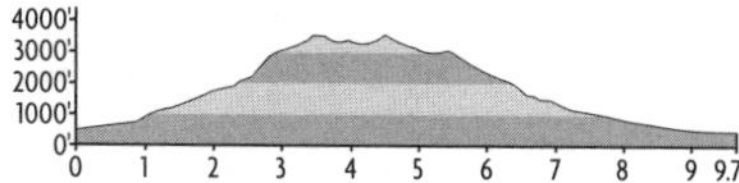

Leaving the shelter, ascend the

most difficult section of the loop. Climbing more than 1000 feet in 0.7mile, the trail aggressively scales up smooth rock and exposed ledges. As you reach the crest of the ridge the trail slowly moderates. Here enjoy the first spectacular vista of the day, including views of the two Baldface peaks. As you cross a flat section, the Baldface Knob Trail enters from the left. Beyond, the final half-mile climb is mostly in the open but is not very difficult. The scenes from South Baldface are expansive, including the towering summit of Mount Washington and the blue waters of Kezar Lake.

Reembarking on the day's journey, continue along the Baldface Circle Trail for 1.2 miles to the summit of North Baldface. Meandering in and out of thin forests, the trail provides views in all directions and offers great opportunity to spot high-elevation bird life. During fall migration the Baldface ridge is particularly welcoming to a number of sparrow-sized birds that nest in northern Canada, including snow buntings and horned larks. Snow buntings, while black and white during breeding season, often appear yellowish while traveling through New England. The mostly brown-horned larks can be identified by their black and yellow facial marks. Both birds remain close to the ground, foraging and reenergizing during long migratory travels. The final push to the wide-open North Peak ends with impressive views in all directions.

In the trees and out onto open ledges, the path tumbles 0.9 mile down and occasionally up small inclines until reaching a small open bump on the ridge. Pick up the Bicknell Ridge Trail here on the right. (For a less exposed but slightly longer option stay straight on the Baldface Circle Trail.) The Bicknell Ridge Trail drops moderately down a semi-exposed ledge where views of

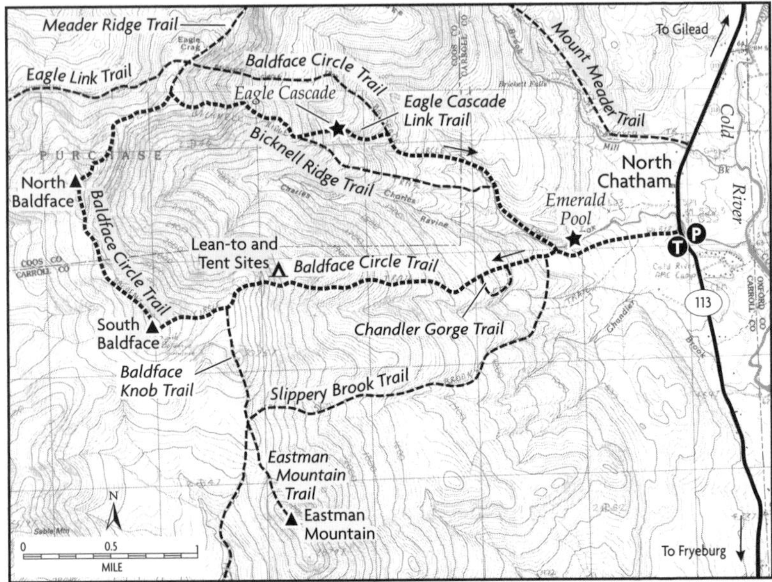

Evan's Notch from Bicknell Ridge

the large, glacially cut basin are noteworthy. Follow this path for 1.1 miles to the final open spot on the ridge before joining the Eagle Cascade Link Trail on the left. (The Bicknell Ridge Trail continues straight through nice, shady forests before reaching the Baldface Circle Trail at a brook crossing.)

Roughly halfway along its 0.7-mile course, the Eagle Cascade Link Trail crosses a stream above a small cascade. Upon returning to the Baldface Circle Trail, veer right down the moderating terrain. Beyond the intersection with the Bicknell Ridge Trail the path arrives at the banks of the rushing brook where large rocks lead to the other side and the final 0.7-mile stretch to the parking area.

If you are looking for a very quiet 9-mile hike, consider taking the north branch of the Baldface Circle Trail to the Meader Ridge Trail. Follow this 2-mile trail north over scenic Eagle Crag and down the peaceful, undulating ridge. (Personal note: My brother and I have helped maintain this trail for more than ten years through the Appalachian Mountain Club's Adopt-a-Trail Program.) Descend down the Mount Meader Trail and return to the parking area by walking 0.4 mile south along Route 113.

30 Speckled Mountain

Round trip ■ 8.6 miles
Loop direction ■ Counterclockwise
Rating ■ Moderate–Difficult
Hiking time ■ 6 hours
Starting elevation ■ 600 feet
High point ■ 2906 feet
Elevation gain ■ 2550 feet
Best season ■ Year round
Maps ■ USGS Wild River and Speckled Mountain
Contact/fee ■ White Mountain National Forest

Driving directions: Follow Route 113 north of Route 302 in Fryeburg for 19.8 miles, or south from Route 2 in Gilead for 10.3 miles (access in the winter is only from the south). The trailhead is located at the Old Brickett Place, located on the east side of the road 0.3 mile north of Cold River Campground. The campground entrance is plowed for winter parking.

For years Speckled Mountain, a large but unassuming peak on Maine's western border, has been one of the best-kept secrets in the White Mountains. Each year, however, more and more people are discovering the subtle beauty of its long, open ridges, its thickly forested slopes, and its cool, cascading brooks. This loop visits the most scenic of Speckled Mountain's features, including the rocky summit of Blueberry Mountain, and, with one brief exception, traverses gradual terrain to complete a great circuit any time of the year.

Begin on the Bickford Brook Trail. After a short climb, turn right onto the route fire wardens once used to access the former summit tower. Shrouded by a canopy of large oaks, maples, and yellow birches, the path quickly enters the Caribou-Speckled Mountain Wilderness and, soon after, reaches a trail intersection. Turn right onto the Blueberry Ridge Trail, briefly descending to the top of the cascading Lower Bickford Slides. Across the brook a path leads left a few tenths of a mile to the picturesque Upper Bickford Slides.

The loop continues across the slippery surface of Bickford Brook before climbing steeply 0.7 mile up to scenic Blueberry Mountain. Near the crest of the ridge, 0.1 mile beyond the White Cairn Trail, a short loop leaves right to an impressive southerly view above a large rock face. This optional route returns to the main trail 0.1 mile ahead at the junction with the Stone House Trail.

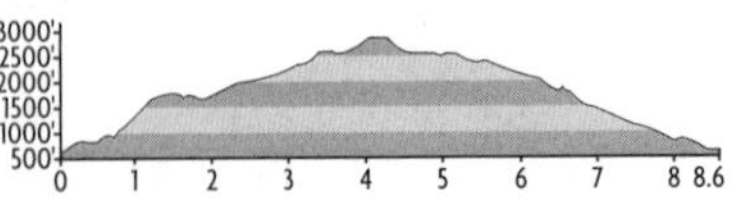

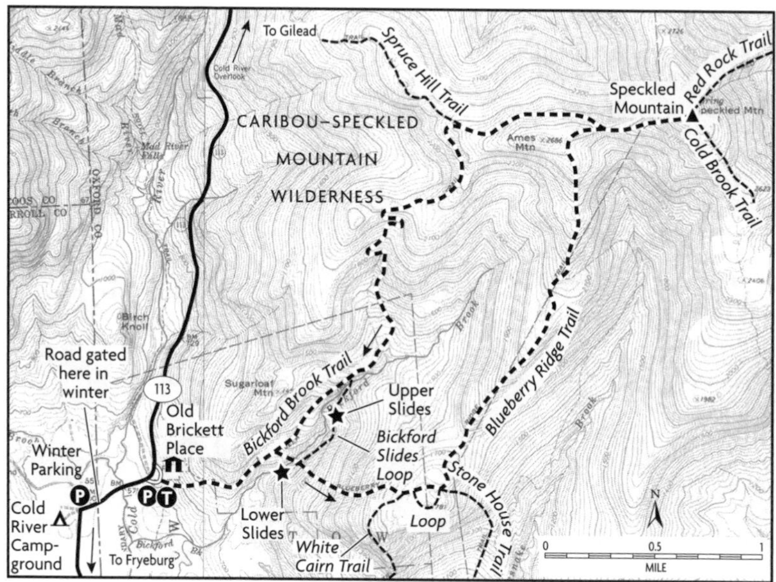

The remaining 2.5-mile hike along Blueberry Ridge is a steady, gradual climb mostly over open and semi-open ledges. There are a number of nice places to take a break, taste the blueberries in late summer, and enjoy the beautiful views of the Evans Notch area.

After entering a spruce-fir forest the trail climbs aggressively before rejoining the Bickford Brook Trail. Turn right for the final half-mile climb to the Speckled Mountain summit where views north toward the Mahoosucs and Saddleback Mountain provide a fine complement to the southerly vistas previously enjoyed.

The hike down the Bickford Brook Trail is very gradual, offers good footing, and is refreshingly easy on the legs. Once past the Blueberry Ridge Trail, the path circles around a small peak, Ames Mountain, before veering south. As you leave the evergreens behind, enter a series of short switchbacks that conclude at a small streambed. From here the path widens and remains so for the duration. If you skipped the Upper Bickford Slides on the ascent, for a small diversion consider turning left onto the Bickford Slides Loop. Blazed in yellow, but lacking a sign, the route leads left as the Bickford Brook Trail nears the rushing water in the steep valley below.

Upon returning to the parking area, check out the Old Brickett Place, a former homestead that is now the site of a wilderness information center. Behind the building in the apple orchard, listen for the loud call of the indigo bunting, a small, deep-blue bird that is often heard melodiously singing along forest edges.

Old Bricket Place

31 Caribou Mountain

Round trip	6.9 miles
Loop direction	Counterclockwise
Rating	Moderate–Difficult
Hiking time	4 hours
Starting elevation	960 feet
High point	2850 feet
Elevation gain	1950 feet
Best season	May through October
Map	USGS Speckled Mountain
Contact/fee	White Mountain National Forest

Driving directions: The trailhead is located on Route 113, 4.7 miles south of the junction of Route 2 in Gilead and 5.8 miles north of the New Hampshire border. Access to the trailhead is not maintained during the winter.

Caribou Mountain, with its indistinct profile and modest elevation, is a summit often overlooked by observers from nearby destinations. While

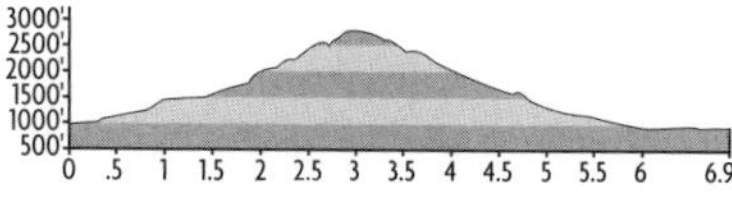

easily overlooked from a distance, the mountain begs your attention up close. From the open summit tremendous views spread out in all directions, and wildlife abounds throughout the forests that blanket its slopes. Each spring, while higher peaks remain buried in snow and ice, Caribou Mountain is carpeted with wildflowers, its waterfalls crashing with fury. By late September the hardwood-laden forest is a rainbow of yellows, purples, reds, and oranges. Between seasons, the beauty of the mountain is more subtle but no less impressive.

The 3.3-mile ascent to the summit begins on the Mud Brook Trail, which enters the forest right of the information kiosk. The hike begins gradually, affording ample opportunity to loosen any tight muscles. Approaching the banks of Mud Brook, steer left and parallel its course through a small, widening valley. The trail crosses the brook occasionally, without much difficulty, and soon enters the Caribou–Speckled Mountain Wilderness. Established in 1990, this wilderness area includes more than 12,000 acres and nearly 25 percent of the White Mountain National Forest that lies in Maine.

Beyond the boundary, bounce over the rocks of Mud Brook for the last time and begin the moderate climb out of the valley. With every step the soil becomes rockier and shallower. Continue through the increasingly shady forest, now dominated by spruce and fir, eventually arriving onto an open ledge that affords views of Speckled Mountain, Kezar Lake, and the Oxford Hills. The ledge is also a good location to spot the large silhouettes of ravens circling in the wind. The gurgling calls of these graceful birds eerily penetrates the thin mountain air.

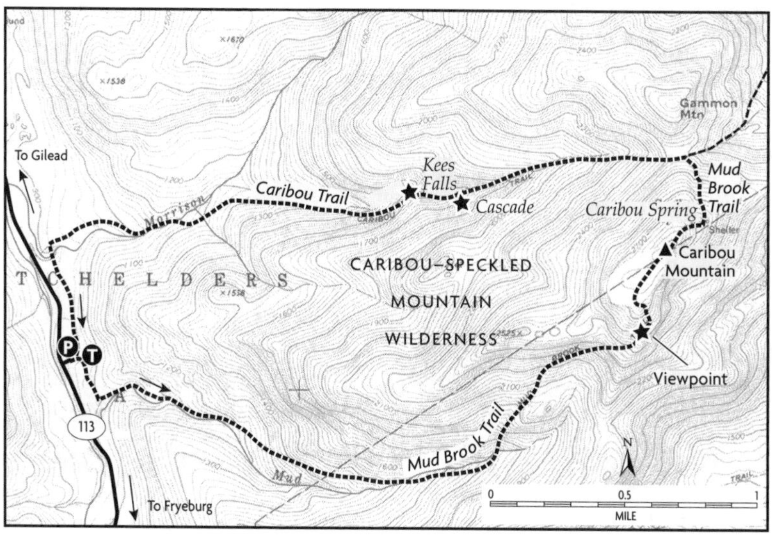

The final half-mile to the top includes small scrambles up the rising slope. Watch your step, as the trail winds around fragile and sensitive plants clinging to life within the rock. The Caribou Mountain summit consists of two open peaks, the second one slightly higher, but both offer expansive views in all directions. Even on days when hikers are plentiful, there are more than enough places to find serenity and to soak in the sun.

The 3.6-mile hike down joins the wooded north ridge. Descending to an old road, make your way through a gully past interesting rock formations and gnarly birch trees. Turn left onto the Caribou Trail, which soon descends rock steps into the Morrison Brook valley. Gradual at first, the trail eventually drops more rapidly near the first of many easy brook crossings. Two crossings of note include one that passes the base of a fairly large cascade on the left and another that occurs near the top of Kees Falls, where Morrison Brook drops a few dozen feet to a large pool below. Beyond the falls the trail exits the wilderness and levels off considerably. The relaxing grade and the tranquility of the hemlock-shaded brook make for a soothing end to the day's journey.

Before reaching Route 113 (the old trail continued straight), the trail turns left and makes one final crossing of Morrison Brook. A short climb and half-mile later, the circuit is complete.

Crossing Morrison Brook

NORTHERN MAINE

32 Goose Eye Mountain

Round trip ■ 9.5 miles
Rating ■ Difficult
Loop direction ■ Counterclockwise
Hiking time ■ 6 to 7 hours
Starting elevation ■ 1225 feet
High point ■ 3790 feet
Elevation gain ■ 2800 feet
Best season ■ May through October
Map ■ USGS Old Speck Mountain
Contact/fee ■ Maine Bureau of Parks and Lands

Driving directions: Driving north from Bethel on Route 2, turn left toward the Sunday River Ski Area. At 2.1 miles turn right, and right again in another 1.2 miles. Drive 4.3 miles up the Sunday River valley. Turn left over a bridge and then make an immediate right before a small cabin. Follow this road 1.8 miles past a MAHOOSUC PUBLIC RESERVE sign to the trailhead on the left. Parking is available on the right, just beyond the trailhead.

Straddling the Maine–New Hampshire border along the wild and rugged Mahoosuc Range, Goose Eye Mountain's barren summit has lured hikers for many years. From atop this 3790-foot peak there are few views in western Maine that are finer. Traditionally reached via two enjoyable trails located on the Success Pond Road (a logging road that begins in Berlin, New Hampshire), this destination now has a third and more scenic option, constructed by the state of Maine in the 1990s. With two branches, the Wright Trail journeys across many diverse and dramatic landscapes, including an old-growth spruce-fir forest, an outstanding rocky ridge, a cascading mountain stream, and a glacier-scoured cirque.

From the boulder that marks the trail's beginning, the route leads left away from the old road and toward the edge of Goose Eye Brook. Follow the running water upstream past small waterfalls and a deep gorge carved out of the smooth rock. Rejoining the road, the path continues along the brook, sometimes crossing it, other times climbing the slope above it.

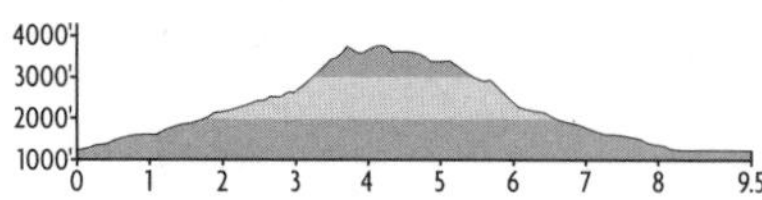

Passing large rocks, small ledges, and more cascades, the moderate climb reaches a campsite and the start of the loop in 2.5 miles. A sign recommends the use of the 1.5 mile northern branch for the ascent to minimize impact and erosion. Following the recommendation, stay right and continue along the shrinking brook, occasionally hopping over rocks from one side to the other. As the valley narrows, the trail climbs to the base of a large ledge where views of the deep cirque unfold. Following a short drop, the trail, aided by ladders and switchbacks, begins a slow, steady ascent up the mountain's steep, slide- and cliff-covered slope. You soon enter an old-growth spruce-fir forest, probably spared the saw because of the location's inaccessibility. Remember, this is eastern old-growth forest and very shallow soil; do not expect towering trees. Instead, notice the thick moss, diverse ages of vegetation, and lack of sawed-off stumps. At the top of the cirque, the footing eases over a long boardwalk, ending at the Mahoosuc Trail.

Turn left up the rocky side of Goose Eye Mountain's East Peak, a route that in recent years has been greatly improved by the installation of ladders and a boardwalk. A final push above tree line leads to the open summit with views in all directions, including the Presidential Range, northern New Hampshire, and Maine's western mountains. The loop resumes down the southwest face of the peak and quickly drops into a small saddle where the southern branch of the Wright Trail turns left. Goose Eye Mountain's West Peak, the bare summit included on the list of New England's Hundred Highest Mountains, is easily reached 0.4 mile ahead.

Upon returning from the West Peak, pick up the Wright Trail's 1.9 mile southern branch. The relatively flat path circles around the summit area and then joins a long ridge that descends east over a series of bald knobs. In and out of the woods, the trail climbs over each small peak, where views of the cirque below are particularly impressive. Beyond the final opening the trail descends abruptly right, swings left, levels off, and then quickly drops down to Goose Eye Brook. While traversing through the forest as it changes from evergreen to deciduous, look for the fiery orange breast of the tiny

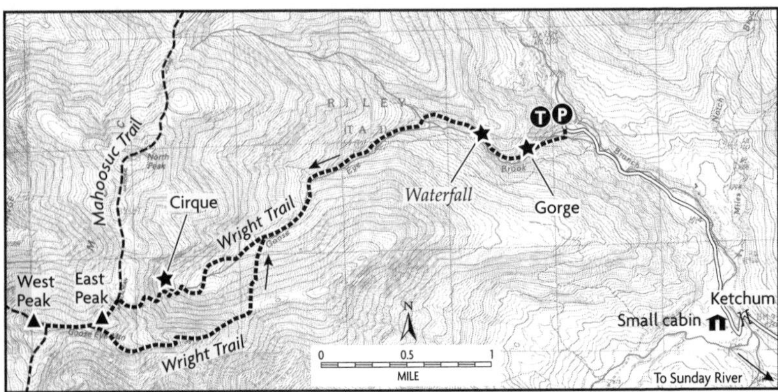

Goose Eye Cirque

Blackburnian warbler. This bird's high-pitched trill at the end of its call is often heard in transitional forests, and with a little patience you can spot their colorful feathers as they jump from limb to limb near the tops of trees.

Cross Goose Eye Brook at the base of a small cascade and turn right for the final 2.5 miles.

33 Grafton Notch

Round trip ■ 4.9 miles
Loop direction ■ Counterclockwise
Rating ■ Moderate–Difficult
Hiking time ■ 3 hours
Starting elevation ■ 1496 feet
High point ■ 2560 feet
Elevation gain ■ 1950 feet
Best season ■ May through October
Maps ■ USGS Old Speck Mountain
Contact/fee ■ Maine Bureau of Parks and Lands

Driving directions: Follow Route 2 east of Bethel. Turn left onto Route 26 in Newry. Continue 12.1 miles to a large parking area on the left, where the Appalachian Trail crosses Route 26.

Cascading streams tumbling down rocky mountain slopes serve as the backdrop for two short loops that together offer a nice half-day of hiking to the Eyebrow and Table Rock, scenic ledges in Maine's Grafton Notch. Each loop can be hiked individually as a shorter trip, and each can be extended by more than 5 miles to include one-way trips to the highest peaks in the region. For those looking for a multiple-day adventure, these same features can be visited along a brand-new 42-mile loop trail. Whatever your pleasure, Grafton Notch is a welcome addition to any hiking itinerary.

Both loops start on the parking area's north side. To reach the Eyebrow, follow the Old Speck Trail left (west) 0.1 mile. Turn right on the Eyebrow Trail, which meanders gradually past large rocks through a forest where helicopter-shaped seeds of maple trees rain down in summer. The route soon rises aggressively along the side of a large ledge. Carefully cross the ledge, which is often wet, and turn left, continuing up the steep climb. The trail moderates near the top of the rock face, where limited views are available. A final half-mile push leads to the Eyebrow and its eagle's-eye view of the narrow and steep walls of Grafton Notch.

From the high point the trail descends into the woods but emerges again onto open ledges before reaching the Old Speck Trail; to the right the summit of 4180-foot Old Speck Mountain can be reached in 2.7 miles. There a tower provides excellent views of the White Mountains and western Maine.

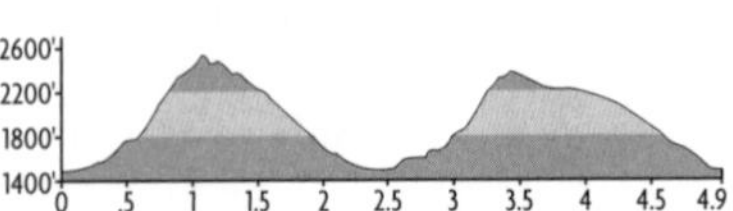

To complete the loop, continue left on the Old Speck Trail for the remaining 1.1 miles. Paralleling Cascade Brook the route descends rapidly, but the footing is fine and the

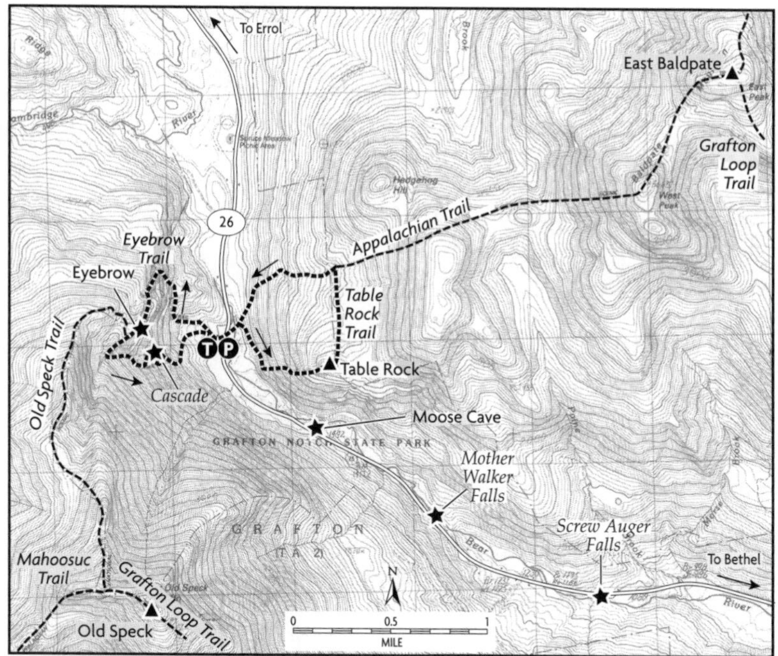

views of a number of waterfalls provide good resting spots along the way.

To reach Table Rock, follow the Appalachian Trail east. Cross Route 26 and in 0.1 mile turn right onto the Table Rock Trail. The 1-mile climb to the open ledge begins gradually, but near a small outcropping the trail ascends more quickly up rock steps. While climbing, take a few breaks and listen for the call of two small birds commonly heard singing in this area: black-throated green and black-throated blue warblers. With patience, both species can be observed flitting from branch to branch. The former, with its bright yellow face, prefers taller trees, while the latter, identified best by the small white patch on its grayish-blue wings, seeks lower locations.

The slope levels off as the trail passes through a small boulder field. Make your way through with care, and then up a narrow gully to the base of Table Rock. Veer right and climb over a number of large stones and past small caves that are popular spots for exploring. The path circles up to the short spur trail that leads to the top of Table Rock and its spectacular views of Old Speck Mountain and Grafton Notch. Watch your step—the cliff drops straight down. Fortunately, there are plenty of safe places to sit and enjoy the scenery away from the edge.

The return trip continues north and, with the exception of one short drop, is very gradual. In 0.5 mile turn left onto the Appalachian Trail, at a location 2.9 miles from the wide-open summit of East Baldpate, a wonderful destination

Grafton Notch from the Eyebrow Trail

with excellent views of the lakes and mountains of western Maine. The loop's 0.9-mile conclusion follows easy grades.

If you are interested in hiking Old Speck Mountain along with the Eyebrow loop, the trip is 7.8 miles, while the Table Rock loop with the Baldpates is an 8.3-mile trip. Both hikes should take about 6 hours. A new loop trail completed in 2005 connects the summits of East Baldpate and Old Speck Mountain. Along with the Appalachian Trail, the loop covers 42 miles, passes a number of shelters providing overnight accommodations, and visits the scenic summits of Sunday River Whitecap and Puzzle Mountain. For more information, contact the Maine Appalachian Trail Club. Additionally, two short trails to waterfalls and a loop to Moose Cave are available in Grafton Notch State Park, a few miles south. All three hikes make ideal afternoon destinations after scaling the Eyebrow and Table Rock.

34 Tumbledown Mountain

Round trip ▪ 6.5 miles
Loop direction ▪ Clockwise
Rating ▪ Moderate–Difficult
Hiking time ▪ 4 hours
Starting elevation ▪ 1100 feet
High point ▪ 3060 feet
Elevation gain ▪ 2400 feet
Best season ▪ June through October
Maps ▪ USGS Roxbury and Jackson Mountain
Contact/fee ▪ Maine Bureau of Parks and Lands

Driving directions: From the junction of Routes 156 and 142 in Weld, drive 2.4 miles north on Route 142. Turn left and at 0.5 mile turn right onto a dirt road that closes from November 1 to May 31. Pass Mountain View Cemetery in 2.1 miles and turn right. Follow the narrow public road 0.6 mile to a gate erected in 2005 to protect land from being damaged by public use. The area on the other side of the gate is privately owned; in 2005 the Maine Bureau of Parks and Lands, the town, and others were working with the landowner to improve signage, alleviate concerns regarding public use in the area, and address the lack of adequate parking. Until a long-term solution is reached, park along the side of the 0.6-mile road or along the main road.

Sweeping views, precipitous rocky slopes, and a large, high-elevation pond attract many visitors to western Maine's Tumbledown Mountain. Most visitors choose the Brook Trail, the shortest and least difficult path, but for a more interesting excursion the Parkers Ridge and Pond Link trails combined provide a slightly longer, less crowded alternative. While this is a good summer hike, the area's bountiful hardwood trees each autumn light up in oranges, yellows, and reds, making September and early October the most enjoyable time of year to scale this scenic peak.

Beginning at the gate, hike 0.2 mile straight on the road that goes through the center of the field area. Up a brief incline, reach the former location of a lean-to. The Little Jackson Mountain and Parkers Ridge trailheads begin here. Pick up the Parkers Ridge Trail, located the farthest to the left. While the trailhead lacks obvious signage, the route is well blazed and easy to follow. After crossing and paralleling a small stream, the trail swings left onto an old road. As the slope increases, climb up and over a pair of ledges, and then begin a steep climb under a dark evergreen canopy.

Your efforts will soon be rewarded as you emerge onto the rocky summit of Parkers Ridge. Especially stunning are views of Tumbledown Pond and the mountain's three peaks. To the south, Webb Lake lies surrounded by a ring of mountains composed of metamorphic rocks fused together from extreme pressure and heat beneath the earth's surface millions of years ago. To the contrary, the lake's bright blue waters sit atop a granite foundation that eroded more easily during the last ice age. Descend past the Pond Link and Brook trails to the shore of Tumbledown Pond, where there are ample places to rest and enjoy the scenery.

Continuing west up the open ledges, enter one last wooded section and scramble up a rock slab. At the top the trail swings left and proceeds to the barren summit of East Peak. The glaciers that shaped this rugged mountain smoothly polished the northern side while plucking rocks off the southern face. The result is today's "tumbledown" appearance, where one can safely stand at the edge of a high, steep ledge and gaze upon countless hills and peaks, including Mount Washington's imposing profile on the southwest horizon. If time and

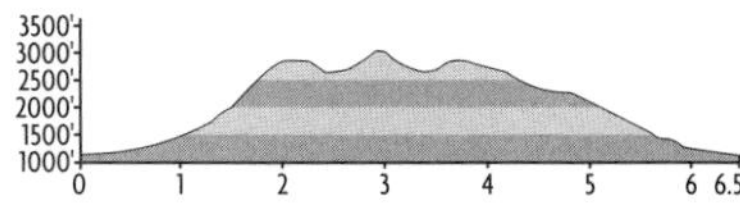

energy allow, hike 0.3 mile farther to West Peak, where additional interesting ledges, rock formations, and geologic features can be found. In the fall, Tumbledown is also a good location to see migrating geese. While Canada geese are more common, with luck, the V-shaped gaggle in the sky may be snow geese, their pure, white relatives.

Return to and turn left on the Pond Link Trail. Follow the path up through a picturesque birch forest, lined with ferns and wildflowers. Across a saddle and over a ledge with limited views the trail descends moderately over rocky ground. The footing becomes smoother near a small stream crossing. Stay straight at a trail junction. To the left the path leads to Little Jackson Mountain; however, with more than a 1000-foot climb to the wide-open summit, it is better to save this for a future non-loop day. Follow the Little Jackson Trail down the old road. Although washed out in places, the route is wide and easily passable. The steady descent winds through young but maturing hardwood forests, and before you know it you arrive at the gate and the end of the day's trek.

In 2005 a private landowner owned the beginning sections of the Parkers Ridge and Little Jackson trails. In fact, Tumbledown Mountain and many of the surrounding peaks have until very recently almost entirely been privately owned. However, inspired by the mountain's beauty, concerned citizens have partnered with the Land for Maine's Future Program, the federal

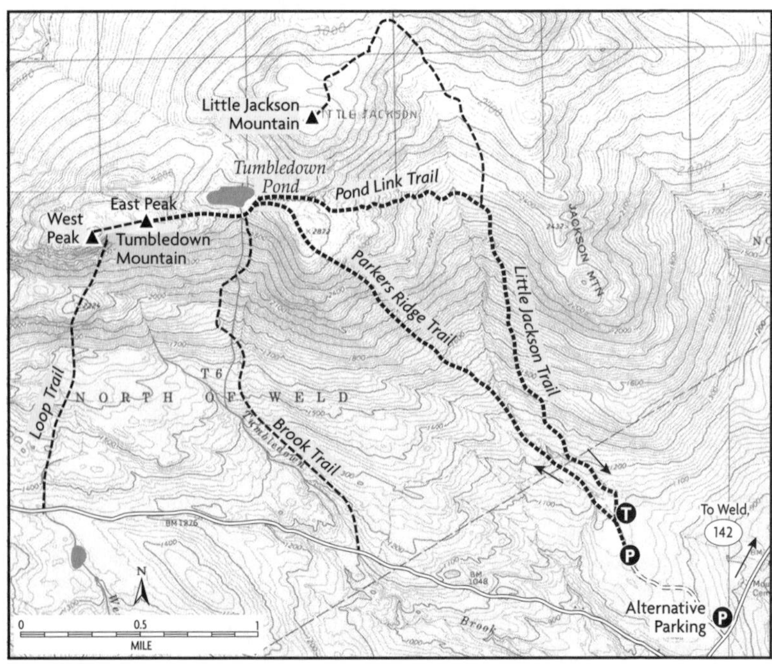

Tumbledown Pond

government, conservation organizations, and private landowners to protect, in the past decade, more than 25,000 acres in the region through easements and fee purchases. The Tumbledown Conservation Alliance and the Trust for Public Land continue to lead this effort.

35 Bigelows

Round trip ■ 13.2 miles
Loop direction ■ Counterclockwise
Rating ■ Strenuous
Hiking time ■ 8 to 10 hours (or 2 days)
Starting elevation ■ 1253 feet
High point ■ 4150 feet
Elevation gain ■ 3690 feet
Best season ■ May through October
Maps ■ USGS The Horns and Sugarloaf Mountain
Contact/fee ■ Maine Bureau of Parks and Lands

Driving directions: From Kingfield, take Route 27 north. Drive 3.3 miles past the Sugarloaf Ski Area entrance and turn right onto a dirt road. Follow the dirt road 1.6 miles to a parking area and information kiosk. The road continues another half-mile, but it is rough and parking is limited.

The most spectacular high-elevation hike in Maine outside of Baxter State Park, the loop over the Bigelow Range is a day-long adventure high above the sprawling expanse of Flagstaff Lake. Once slated to be the next big ski area in New England, Bigelow Mountain and 36,000 acres of surrounding landscapes were permanently protected when Maine voters went to the polls in 1976 and narrowly approved a measure to add the area to the state's public reserved lands. Thanks to their foresight, today the Bigelow Mountain Preserve is a hiker's paradise of steep slopes, bountiful wildlife, high-elevation alpine meadows, long, sweeping ridge lines, secluded mountain ponds, maturing actively managed forests, and scenic backcountry campsites.

From the parking area, follow the main road left for a half-mile to Stratton Brook Pond. Small stepping stones lead across the outlet where the old road continues past primitive campsites. Soon the Firewardens Trail veers sharply left and begins a gradual 1-mile ascent up a rocky slope and past a small wetland. At the intersection with the Horns Pond Trail, stay straight. The path remains along relaxing grades through nice hardwood forests. Enjoy; the climb is about to begin.

After turning left the trail heads steadily up the slope and arrives at the Moose Falls campsite. Maintained by the Maine Appalachian Trail Club (MATC), Moose Falls is the first of three backcountry camping locations found along the day's journey. Each of the sites is available on a first-come, first-served basis. The Bigelow ridge line lies 1 mile ahead beyond the hike's most demanding stretch. A series of rock steps leads up through the spruce-fir forest and ends in the saddle between West and Avery peaks, where a second MATC campsite is located.

The first stop along the ridge is the 4088-foot summit of Avery Peak, located 0.4 mile to the east, traveling north on the Appalachian Trail. Follow the short, rocky climb as it leads above the trees to breathtaking scenes of Flagstaff Lake and mountains stretching to the Québec border. The path carves its way through alpine vegetation to an old fire warden's building and 360-degree views. Return to the saddle and continue west (south on the AT) 0.3 mile to the wide-open summit of West Peak with its array of fragile alpine vegetation. The highest point along the ridge, West Peak's 4145-foot elevation provides the most expansive views of the Bigelow Range and the surrounding area.

Leading down over exposed rock, the trail reenters the forest and begins a steady descent; however, the slope quickly eases. A long section of modest elevation change follows through classic high-elevation spruce-fir forest. When cones are abundant, look

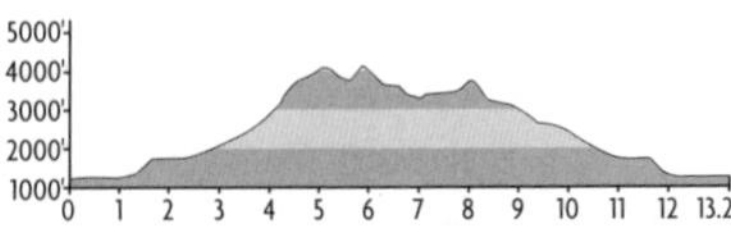

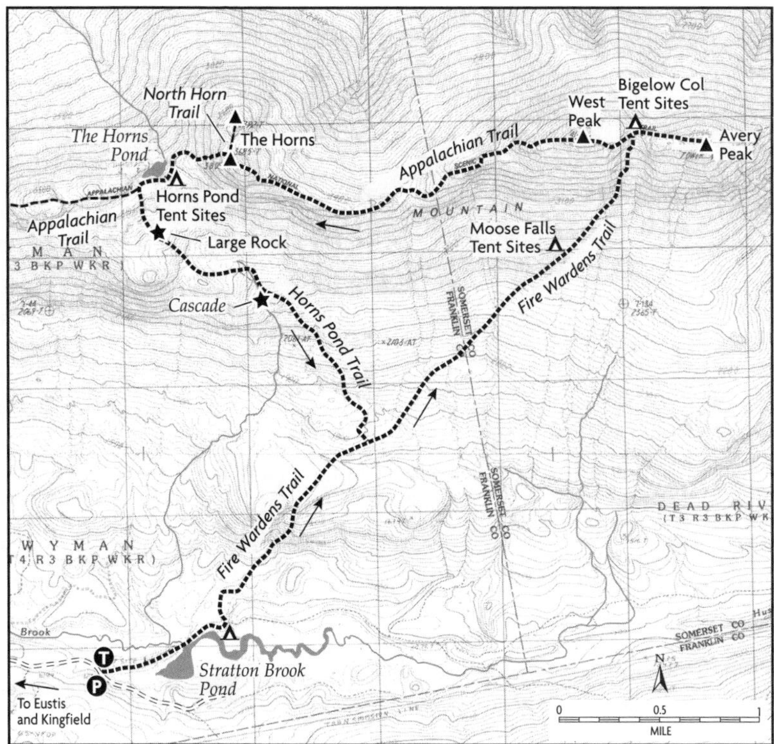

for flocks of white-winged crossbills, red, melodious birds. Uniquely adapted to peel away seed layers of cones, the tips of a crossbill's upper and lower bills do not touch, but instead form an X.

The easy grades end at the base of South Horn, where a short incline leads to a scenic rock perch a few hundred feet above the Horns Pond. Head steeply down the other side to the MATC campsite located above the pond's shore. Halfway down, a 0.2-mile spur leads right to North Horn, where views of Bigelow Ridge and Flagstaff Lake are excellent. From the campsite area, marked trails that avoid forest revegetation areas lead to the small, peaceful body of water guarded by rocky walls.

Continue 0.2 mile west and turn left onto the Horns Pond Trail. Follow this route through the thick forest where moss-covered ground is interrupted only by the many large boulders that dot the landscape. The trail circles around an especially large rock before descending to the edge of a bog. After crossing a small stream, a spur trail leads a few hundred feet to a bench with views of Sugarloaf Mountain and a small cascade. The Horns Pond Trail concludes along moderate grades before reaching the Firewarden's Trail. Turn right for the remaining 1.5 miles to the parking area.

Below Avery Peak

36 Little Moose Mountain

Round trip ■ 4.8 miles
Loop direction ■ Clockwise
Rating ■ Moderate
Hiking time ■ 3 hours
Starting elevation ■ 1650 feet
High point ■ 1825 feet
Elevation gain ■ 600 feet
Best season ■ May through November
Map ■ USGS Big Squaw Pond
Contact/fee ■ Maine Bureau of Parks and Lands

Driving directions: From Greenville, drive north on Routes 6/15. Cross under the railroad bridge in Greenville Junction and drive 3.6 miles to a dirt road on the left. Look for a sign indicating Little Moose Public Reserved Land. Follow the road 1.6 miles before turning left on a narrower road. The trailhead is 1.1 miles on the left with parking along the roadside.

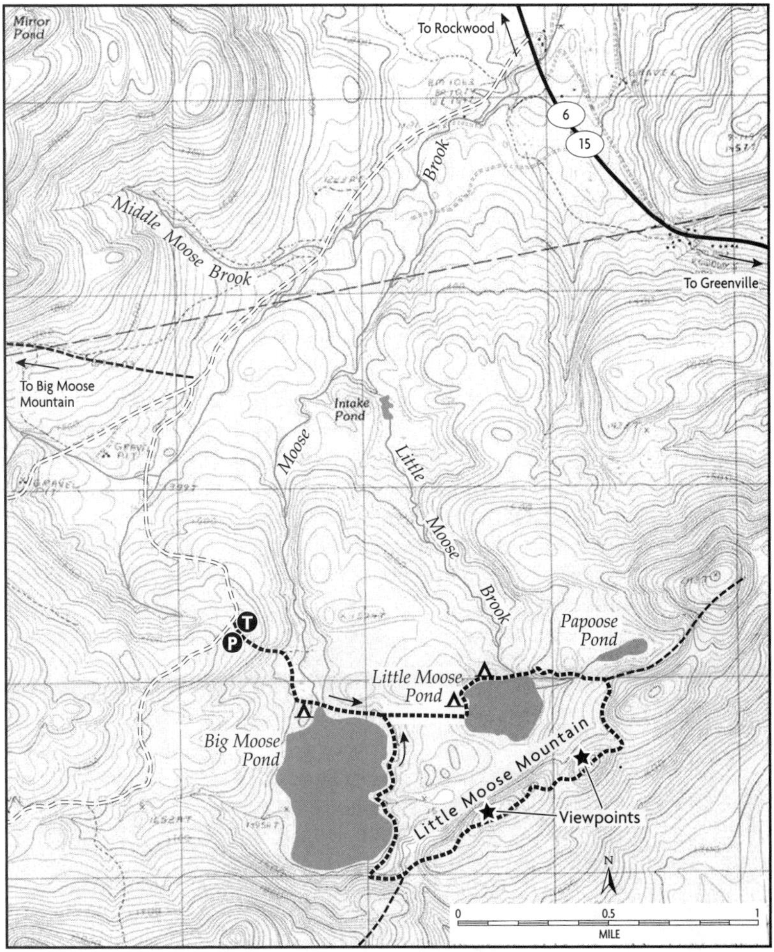

Northern Maine is a vast expanse of lakes, low ridges, and forests. The landscape is a patchwork of public reserves, forest industry land, and private conservation areas. With its abundance of wildlife and its relative remoteness, Maine's north woods lures and tempts each of us to explore its vastness. Yet for many the region can be difficult to visit and may appear daunting, especially for those new to the area. Adventuring for a half-day in the Little Moose Public Reserve, however, will provide even the most unfamiliar a firsthand introduction and a wonderful snapshot of the flora, fauna, and beauty the region has to offer.

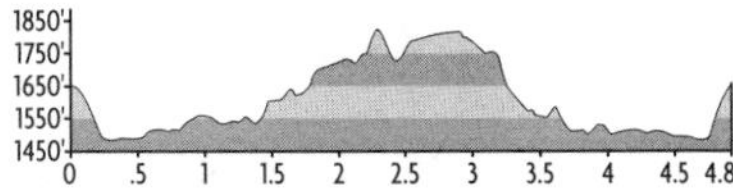

Begin the journey under the tall limbs of sugar maple trees, which are sure to shower you with shade during the heat of summer and bury you in bright orange leaves by late September. A long slate staircase leads into a valley where the trail passes a small wetland. At a junction a path leads straight to a campsite; stay left, quickly arriving on the rocky shore of Big Moose Pond. Formerly known as Big Squaw Pond, this site and others in the area were renamed Moose in 2000, when the Maine legislature eliminated all place names that used the pejorative term for Native American women. Above the water's distant shore stands a rock ledge, a scenic spot that lies ahead. First, cross over a cement dam at the pond's outlet and enter the woods where a short stroll ends at a trail junction and the start of the day's loop.

Follow the left branch toward Little Moose Pond. As you approach the shore the route veers left and circles around a small cove, passing primitive campsites. While uneven, the going is not difficult. Once across a small stream, hug the shore's edge for the last time and then climb out of the basin to the base of a large ledge. Remaining below the rock face, arrive at another intersection. The route left leads past Papoose Pond and over a small ridge to a hotel north of Greenville. Turn right.

From here the terrain changes dramatically. The ascent up Little Moose Mountain is gradual at first, but the slope becomes steeper as the route winds up the rocky landscape. Up and over a small knoll, head downhill and at a sharp left turn follow a spur straight to an open ledge perched high above

Big Moose Pond (photo by Maria Fuentes)

Little Moose Pond. The ledge offers views toward Mount Kineo, Moosehead Lake, as well as Big Moose Mountain.

Remaining on the ridge, the trail climbs over a number of small rocky summits, each with limited views, until reaching a second spur trail on the right. Hike up the path a few hundred feet to the finest view of the day, the wide-open ledge first seen from Big Moose Pond. From this vantage point countless other mountains are visible, including White Cap, Barren, Coburn, and Little and Big Spencer mountains. This is a great location to view the ridges that form a natural amphitheater. It is also a perfect setting for enjoying the haunting call of the common loon, a sound frequently heard echoing from the ponds below. Scan the water to find them, but be patient; loons are more adept at swimming than flying and thus spend considerable time underwater.

Leaving the open ledge, hike past a trail junction where a path leads left to the Notch Ponds. Stay right and wind down the short, steady descent that quickly ends on a level surface and arrives at the southern end of Big Moose Pond. Remaining near the shoreline, continue to the loop's conclusion. Head left to return to your car.

37 Mount Kineo

Round trip ■ 6 miles
Loop direction ■ Clockwise
Rating ■ Moderate–Difficult
Hiking time ■ 4 hours
Starting elevation ■ 1027 feet
High point ■ 1790 feet
Elevation gain ■ 760 feet
Best season ■ May through October
Maps ■ USGS Mount Kineo and Brassua Lake East
Contact/fee ■ Maine Bureau of Parks and Lands

Driving directions: Drive north on Routes 6/15 from Greenville to Rockwood. Turn right 1.5 miles past Moosehead Lake's second Kennebec River outlet. Follow the road 0.3 mile to the Rockwood Boat Launch. The trailhead is located on a peninsula on the other side of the lake. For a fee, a private boat runs 9 AM to 5 PM from Memorial Day weekend to Columbus Day, crossing hourly during the summer (every two hours on less busy days). Crossing the water by canoe is possible but can be dangerous if windy. The lake freezes solidly in the winter, allowing foot access. The shortest distance across the water is 0.7 mile.

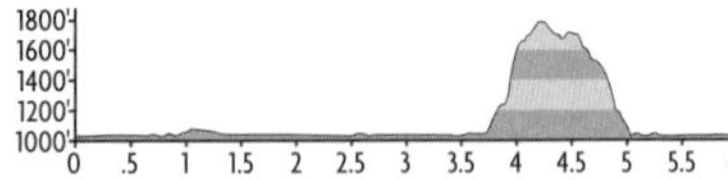

Rising above Moosehead Lake's deepest waters, Mount Kineo's 700-foot cliffs stand guard over the largest body of fresh water in Maine. Native Americans who ventured to this location in search of stone for tools described the mountain as a large moose slain by the gods. By the nineteenth century, Kineo lured countless tourists venturing north by train

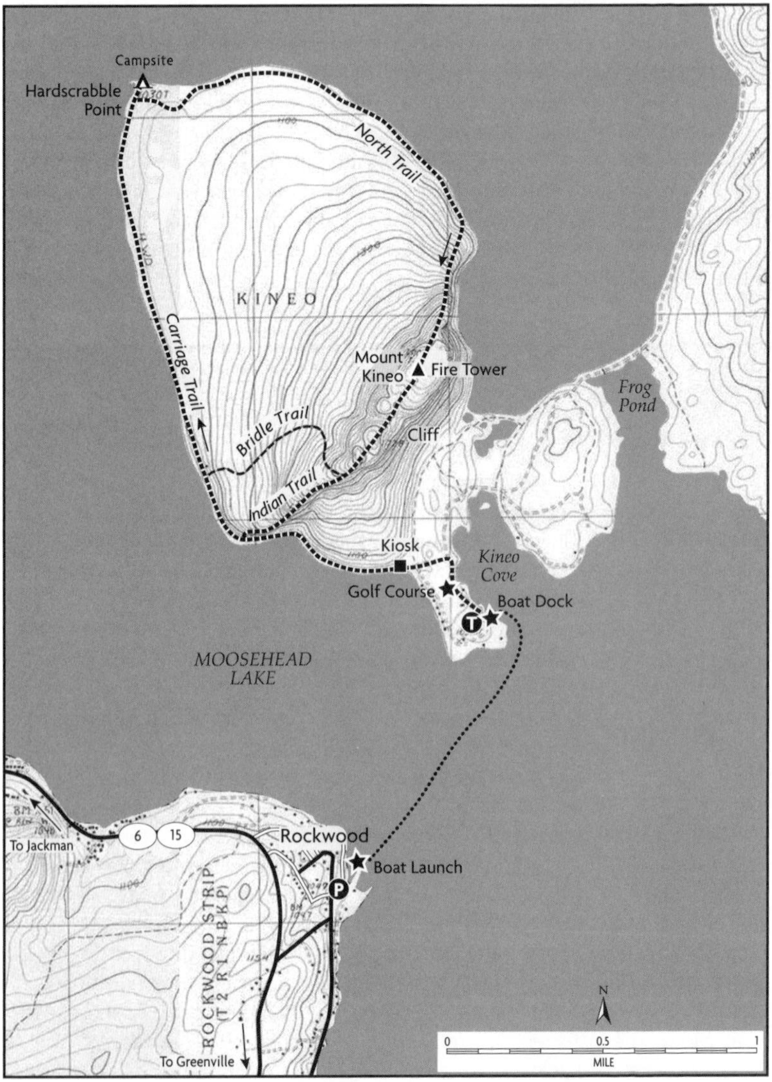

Mount Kineo's 700-foot cliff

and steamship to stay at the immense Victorian hotel that once stood beneath the towering cliffs. Today, summer homes still dot the shorefront, but in 1990 more than 800 acres on the peninsula were permanently protected as public reserved land, with assistance from the Maine Chapter of The Nature Conservancy and funding from the Land for Maine's Future Program. Thanks to these efforts, hikers can continue to scale Mount Kineo's steep slopes and enjoy one of the finest views in northern Maine.

From the boat follow the service road that parallels Kineo Cove, the small bay to the right. Watch out for stray balls from the nine-hole golf course as you make your way past a pro shop where the road swings left. The beginning section of the hike crosses private property; pay close attention to all signs. Near the far shore of the lake a small sign marks the start of the Carriage Trail, which, with only minor elevation changes, closely winds along the lake's rocky shore. Continue past the base of a talus slope, underneath the mountain's lower cliffs and beyond the start of the Indian Trail (marked by blue paint on the rock). Ahead you will find an old fire warden's cabin and a sign marking the start of the Bridle Trail, the easiest and safest route up. While most people choose to ascend the Indian Trail and hike down the Bridle Trail, a longer, quieter, and more enjoyable alternative is to continue straight on the Carriage Trail as it meanders along the flat shoreline for 2.1 miles to a primitive camping area at Hardscrabble Point.

From Hardscrabble Point join the North Trail for a trip around the peninsula's northern shore. The terrain remains relatively level for 1.5 miles. As you approach the base of Kineo Mountain, the North Trail swings right and begins a steady climb up the ridge. Pass under a stand of tall, stately maple and yellow birch trees, a sight not often experienced in the region, and then continue up switchbacks through the smaller spruce-fir canopy. In between steps, listen for the jovial "ank, ank, ank" call of the red-breasted nuthatch. These small, gray-backed birds creep up and down the trunks of evergreen trees, often in the company of chickadees. They invariably seem to "laugh" loudest after a hiker has stumbled across a rock or has slipped on a wet root.

Slowly the terrain moderates and after a few small climbs the trail ends beneath the summit tower. Scale the five sets of stairs that lead above the wooded summit to behold the immenseness of Moosehead Lake and the rolling hills and mountains that surround it in all directions.

The return trip to the dock is roughly 2 miles and takes anywhere from 60 to 90 minutes, something to keep in mind unless you are great swimmer! Gradually wind down the Bridle Trail. On the other side of a small knoll, the Indian Trail bears left. While the Bridle Trail is easier, the Indian Trail is far more scenic. Throughout the 0.4-mile drop to the shore of Moosehead Lake, the Indian Trail skirts atop the side of the sheer cliffs with one glorious view after another.

Once back to the Carriage Trail, turn left and retrace your steps back to the dock.

38 Gulf Hagas

Round trip ■ 9 miles
Loop direction ■ Clockwise
Rating ■ Moderate–Difficult
Hiking time ■ 6 hours
Starting elevation ■ 675 feet
High point ■ 1160 feet
Elevation gain ■ 670 feet
Best season ■ May through October
Map ■ USGS Barren Mountain East
Contact/fee ■ KI–Jo-Mary Multiple-Use Forest (day-use fee); Maine Appalachian Trail Conference

Driving directions: From Brownville Junction, follow Route 11 north for 4.8 miles. Turn left onto the road that leads to Katahdin Ironworks. The route quickly turns into a logging road and in 6.3 miles reaches a

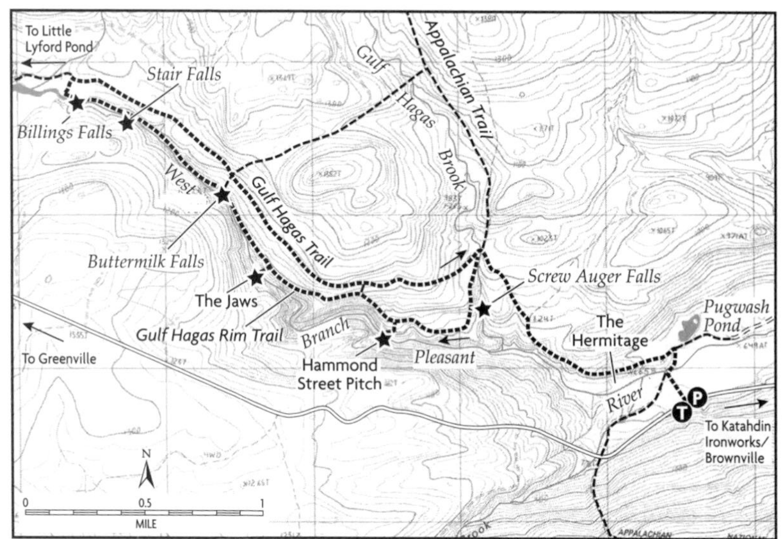

gatehouse. Stop, register, and pay the day-use fee. Continue across the bridge. At 3.4 miles stay left at a fork in the road (the road right leads to another less traveled road which ends at an alternative trailhead that avoids the river crossing on the described hike). In 3.1 miles pull into the large parking lot on the right. From Greenville, follow Pleasant Street past the municipal airport 3.6 miles to Big Wilson Stream. Continue up the logging road roughly 9 miles to Hedgehog Checkpoint. Stop, register, and pay the day-use fee. Ahead at a T intersection (to the left is Little Lyford Pond) turn right and drive 4.5 miles to the parking area on the left.

Described as the "Grand Canyon of Maine," Gulf Hagas is a deep gorge where rushing water continues to erode and smooth the slate walls that surround it. This scenic loop meanders through a tall pine forest, to the edges of steep precipices and amid the refreshing spray of crashing waterfalls. Gulf Hagas is unlike any other place in New England and, save for the dynamite that was used to aid the log drives that once took place here, it is a location that continues to change very little in the course of a human lifetime.

This most adventurous route to Gulf Hagas begins by fording the very river responsible for its creation. After a short walk, join the Appalachian Trail on the edge of the Pleasant River's West Branch. Passage through the running water is wide and rocky; however, the water level is typically below the knees. Chilly in the spring, the river is refreshing by midsummer. When crossing, use sandals and walking sticks to improve balance.

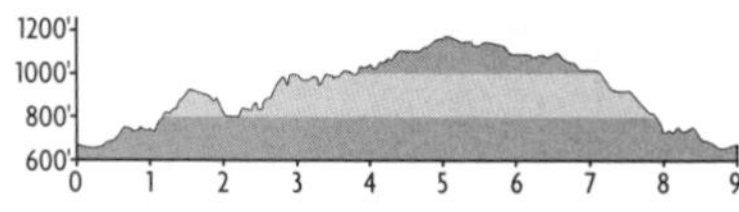

As with all water crossings, use extreme caution—especially in spring and after heavy rains. While crossing, scan the rushing water for the bobbing tails of spotted sandpipers. With large black spots on their chest, these medium-sized shorebirds enjoy hopping from rock to rock along the shores of rivers, ponds, and lakes.

With boots back on, continue along the trail 0.1 mile to a junction near Pugwash Pond. The route entering from the right is longer and avoids the river crossing, but it begins at a different parking area (see driving directions). Turn left and enter The Hermitage—site of a former homestead, now dominated by large white pines. Past the last of the big trees, begin a relaxing 1-mile climb away from the river. As the Appalachian Trail swings right, stay straight and jump across the rocks of Gulf Hagas Brook. A boulder and plaque on the other side commemorate the protection of this unique area by the National Park Service.

Turn left and join the Gulf Hagas Rim Trail as it meanders 3.2 miles along the Gulf Hagas Brook, at first, and then along the rim of the gulf itself. While the trail has very little overall elevation change, it does have a series of inclines and descents that result in a more difficult hike than many expect. The route is well marked and easy to follow, but in places you will need to watch your footing, especially when perched a few hundred feet above the

View into Gulf Hagas (photo by Andy Kekacs)

rushing river. Use extra care on the slate bedrock that abounds; it can be quite slippery when wet. Take advantage of the many side paths that lead to the following features in order of appearance: Screw Auger Falls, Hammond Street Pitch, the Jaws, Buttermilk Falls, Stair Falls, and Billings Falls. The views of the Jaws and Stair Falls are most impressive. While not a trail for vertigo sufferers, the path is ideal for those intrigued by the slow, steady, and awesome power of water—Gulf Hagas is paradise for Chinese philosophers. Along the way there are also two routes that lead right and quickly connect to the Gulf Hagas Trail; each provides a shorter loop option.

At the head of the gulf the trail swings away from the river before reaching a three-way intersection. To the left an old road leads to Little Lyford Pond camps, purchased by the Appalachian Mountain Club (AMC) in 2003. At the time of this book's production the AMC was in the process of developing a plan for the camp along with 37,000 acres of surrounding land they acquired in 2003 from the International Paper Company with funding from the Land for Maine's Future and Forest Legacy Programs.

The hike back begins right on the Gulf Hagas Trail, a path that gradually makes its ways through a peaceful northern hardwood forest. Once back to the Appalachian Trail, retrace your steps to the trailhead.

39 Turtle Ridge

Round trip ■ 8.5 miles
Loop direction ■ Counterclockwise
Hiking time ■ 6 hours
Starting elevation ■ 1090 feet
High point ■ 1630 feet
Elevation gain ■ 1200 feet
Best season ■ May through November
Maps ■ USGS Nahmakanta Stream and Wadleigh Mountain
Contact/fee ■ KI–Jo-Mary Multiple-Use Forest (day-use fee); Maine Bureau of Parks and Lands

Driving directions: From Brownville Junction, follow Route 11 north for 15.7 miles. Turn left onto Jo-Mary Road. In 0.2 mile arrive at a gate for the North Maine Woods. Register, pay the fee, and continue north on the dirt road. Travel for 15 miles through a second gate (no fee), and then enter the Nahmakanta Public Reserved Land. Drive another 1.2 miles across a small bridge to a parking area on the left. From Greenville, drive northeast toward Kokadjo. Continue approximately 2 miles past Kokadjo

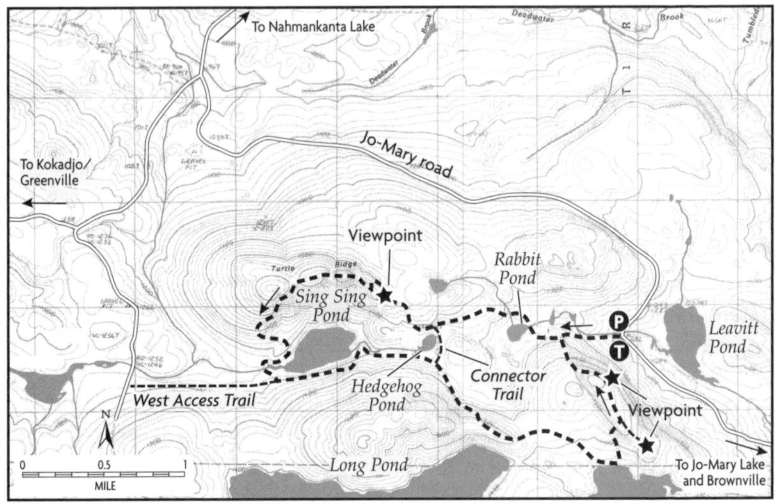

and turn right onto Second Roach Pond Road. Follow the signs that lead toward Nahmakanta Lake Camps. Continue 5 miles to a four-way intersection; turn left. Travel an additional 7.5 miles and turn left onto Penobscot Pond Road. Continue for five miles, past the boundary of the Nahmakanta Public Reserved Land, and then at a three-way intersection turn right onto the Jo-Mary Road. Travel 4 miles to the parking lot on the right just before a bridge.

In 1999 the Maine Bureau of Parks and Lands opened up this new trail in the 43,000-acre Nahmakanta Public Reserve. An 8.5-mile loop, the trip around Turtle Ridge is a pleasant journey over moderate, rolling hillsides. The well-constructed path winds through changing landscapes, past a collection of different-sized wetlands, and over rocky ridges with tremendous views of Baxter State Park. Despite its length the loop is a good choice for hikers of many levels, and for those interested in a shorter excursion a connector trail is available midway that allows for a 4.9-mile circuit. Either way, the loop is a great opportunity to experience northern Maine's remoteness and wildlife abundance.

From the parking area head south down the Jo-Mary road over the small bridge to where the path leads right into the thick forest. Climb gradually to an open ledge and the start of the loop. Turn right and hike over the exposed rock down to peaceful Rabbit Pond. Cross the outlet and head left back into the forest. The trail meanders across rolling terrain around small wetlands and past rocky knolls until reaching a trail junction. To the left a connector path leads to Hedgehog Pond and the

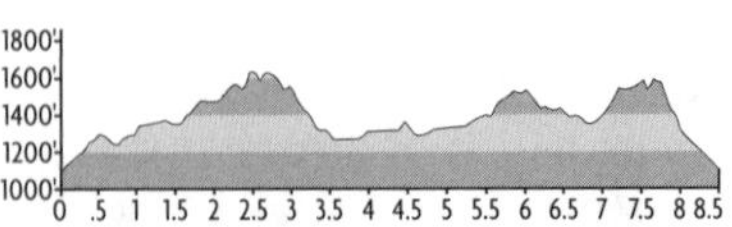

south side of the loop, providing a shorter option. Otherwise, stay right and head toward Turtle Ridge.

The route passes beneath the bottom of a large rock ledge. Swing right and follow the winding path up to a short spur trail that leads a couple hundred feet to the top of the ledge where tremendous views of Mount Katahdin await. The trail continues across the ridge, passing a series of small open vistas with views of Sing Sing Pond and White Cap Mountain. The evergreen forest on the ridge is a favorite destination for pine siskins, small brown, speckled birds that closely resemble goldfinches. Look for hints of yellow in their wings when in flight.

After the final ledge, descend down moderate grades through a nice hardwood forest. Leveling off, the path arrives at Sing Sing Pond. A number of sitting rocks are available near the water's edge, each providing pleasant views of Turtle Ridge's rocky slopes.

Turtle Ridge from Sing Sing Pond

The loud slap of a beaver tail may encourage you to move along, picking up the path along the water's edge. A bridge crosses the pond's outlet near a large cedar tree. From here the loop quickly reaches an old road, where a western access trail enters from the right. Turn left and follow the old road for about a mile before veering left and returning to a more interesting pathway. Pass a marshy wetland and the connector trail. Then begin a slow ascent through a flat, rocky landscape.

A short climb leads to a spruce-covered ridge, where a long, relaxing stroll ends at the shore of Henderson Pond. The largest body of water on the loop, Henderson Pond is a nice place to pause before beginning the loop's final ascent. The trail passes about 50 feet from the shore, but paths lead to the water's edge.

Beyond Henderson Pond the trail rises quickly, but thanks to a circuitous layout it is easier than one would expect. Halfway up, a side path leads 0.1 mile to a "viewpoint" that is largely overgrown. At the top of the ridge, however, the viewpoint north toward Baxter State Park is wide open and a great spot to finish the day. The final section descends moderately. Turn right at the trail junction to return to your car.

Nahmakanta is the state's largest public reserved property. The initial 26,000 acres of the reserve were first protected in 1990 with help from the Maine Chapter of The Nature Conservancy (TNC) and with funding from the Land for Maine's Future Program. In 2004 TNC acquired 41,000 acres of adjacent land, the Debsconeag Lakes Preserve that connects Nahmakanta with Baxter State Park. The three units comprise nearly 300,000 acres of contiguous conservation land.

40 Trout Brook Mountain

Round trip ■ 3.4 miles
Loop direction ■ Clockwise
Rating ■ Moderate
Hiking time ■ 2 hours
Starting elevation ■ 700 feet
High point ■ 1767 feet
Elevation gain ■ 1050 feet
Best season ■ May through October
Map ■ USGS Trout Brook Mountain
Contact/fee ■ Baxter State Park

Driving directions: Take Exit 264 from Interstate 95, drive north on Route 11 for 9.6 miles through Patten, and then turn left onto Route 159. Travel 9.9 miles into Shin Pond. Route 159 ends here, but the paved road continues straight 16.3 miles to the Matagamon Pond entrance to Baxter State Park. Register at the gate, then follow the Perimeter Road for 2.7 miles to a small parking area on the left.

Located in the quiet northeastern corner of Baxter State Park, the loop over Trout Brook Mountain is an excellent half-day trek that can be done in combination with a number of other short hikes in the area. Traversing classic northern Maine forests along gradual slopes, the journey leads to an open 1767-foot summit and a number of scenic ledges where nearby mountains and the endless expanse of Maine's vast north woods stand on display. Trout Brook Mountain is a good choice for people of all ages and for those who hike infrequently.

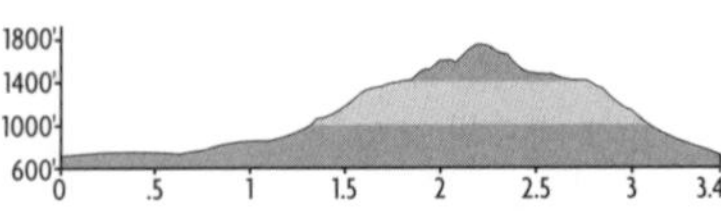

From the parking area, head left on the Five Ponds Trail. Rerouted in the 1990s, the beginning section of the trail crosses very flat terrain.

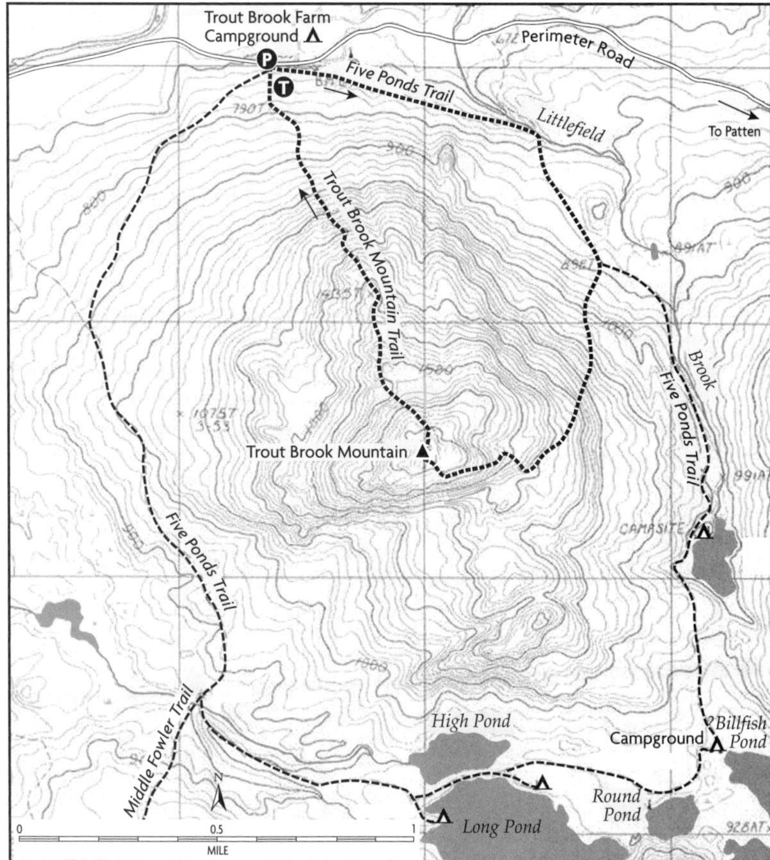

After a little more than a half-mile, approach Littlefield Brook. Here the path turns sharply right, joining the original trail to the five ponds. Leading south through the dense hardwood forests, the route remains easy and soon reaches the start of the Trout Brook Mountain Trail. Turn right and begin the ascent up the mountain.

While not difficult, the trail does climb more than 800 feet in 1.3 miles. The low elevation and thick vegetation provide excellent habitat for a number of songbirds. Listen for the boisterous whistlelike call of the solitary vireo, a small, common bird of northern New England. The vireo can be illusive, but when spotted its bluish-gray head, white eye-ring, and hint of yellow under its wings distinguish it from other similar-sounding birds.

As the trail nears the summit area the slope becomes a bit steep and eventually the forest thins. Climb up the rock and ledges that lead to the high point and enjoy the panoramic views. Especially impressive are the scenes south toward the five ponds area and the towering slopes of Traveler Mountain.

The loop continues north along a 1.3-mile descent. Passing through open areas the route offers excellent views of the bright blue waters of Grand Lake Matagamon. Farther north, the low, rolling hills and mountains of southern Aroostook County and the Allagash River Wilderness Waterway can be seen. With the exception of forest-managed lands, you will see few signs of human activity. The bottom half of the trail gradually moderates and passes through a grove of cedar trees before reaching the journey's end.

Looking across the parking area and the park's Perimeter Road, notice the large field. Now a campground, this is the former site of Trout Brook Farm, a location that once provided food and services to loggers harvesting forests in the surrounding area. Today most of Baxter State Park is off limits to timber harvesting. However, roughly 29,000 acres north and west of this trailhead continues to be managed as an experimental forest, fulfilling the wishes of the late Governor Baxter.

If you are looking for a cloudy-day hike, skip Trout Brook Mountain and instead remain on the Five Ponds Trail throughout. Leading 6 miles around the peak, the lowland path visits Littlefield, Billfish, and Long ponds, before swinging north and returning to the same parking area. Other than the esker between High and Long ponds, there is little elevation change throughout, and with a lot of water this loop provides an excellent opportunity to spot wildlife.

Young hikers near summit

41 South Branch Mountain

Round trip ■ 6.8 miles
Loop direction ■ Counterclockwise
Rating ■ Moderate–Difficult
Hiking time ■ 4.5 hours
Starting elevation ■ 1005 feet
High point ■ 2599 feet
Elevation gain ■ 2175 feet
Best season ■ May through October
Map ■ USGS Wassataquoik Lake
Contact/fee ■ Baxter State Park

Driving directions: See Hike 40 for directions to the Matagamon Pond entrance to Baxter State Park. Register at the gate, then follow the Perimeter Road for 7.1 miles and turn left. Continue straight for 2.3 miles where the road ends at a campground and parking area.

Like most non-Katahdin hikes in Baxter State Park, the 6.8-mile loop up and over the more diminutive South Branch Mountain is a scenic adventure where you are more apt to stumble upon a cow moose browsing with her calf than fellow hikers sharing the area's beauty. In addition to abundant wildlife, this loop passes two scenic ponds and climbs over an open summit still feeling the effects of a fire that swept through the area more than a century ago. With views of nearby Traveler Mountain and the more distant Mount Katahdin, the hike over South Branch Mountain is a scenic trip to a quiet corner in Maine's most famous state park.

Sign in near the ranger's station and then turn right. Walk through the picnic area to the pond's outlet. If the pond's level is low you should be able to hop across the rocks and remain dry; however, be prepared to ford the slow-moving stream. Safely across, follow the level trail to the banks of a small, wooded brook. Turn left and climb moderately alongside its bubbling water.

At 0.7 mile the trail leaves the brook and climbs steadily, at times steeply, to the northern summit of South Branch Mountain, also called Black Cat Mountain. Along the way the path emerges onto numerous open ledges with views north and east. Especially impressive are scenes of the South Branch ponds below. Up and over the viewless north summit, proceed across the fern-covered ridge and through a small saddle. A final push ends atop the 2585-foot south summit of the mountain. A few small trees, some low shrubs, and a carpet of wildflowers have established roots in the rocky soil,

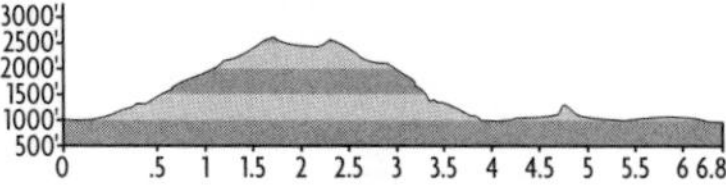

yet they do little to block the splendid views of the mountains, notches, and lakes that surround the area. South Branch Mountain is a great place to view much of Baxter Park's 200,000-plus acres and absorb the abundant silence.

The 1.9-mile descent to the Upper South Branch Pond begins through open meadows. The trail drops down on loose rock, but overall the footing is fine. About a half-mile from the summit the trail turns sharply left and passes the last unrestricted viewpoint. Weaving through the forest the trail gradually skirts across the talus-covered slope. A few steep and rocky sections demand some attention, but the path soon levels. After passing a spur trail that ends at a lean-to, cut across the thin area of land that divides the large pond on the left from a series of marshy beaver ponds on the right. Keep

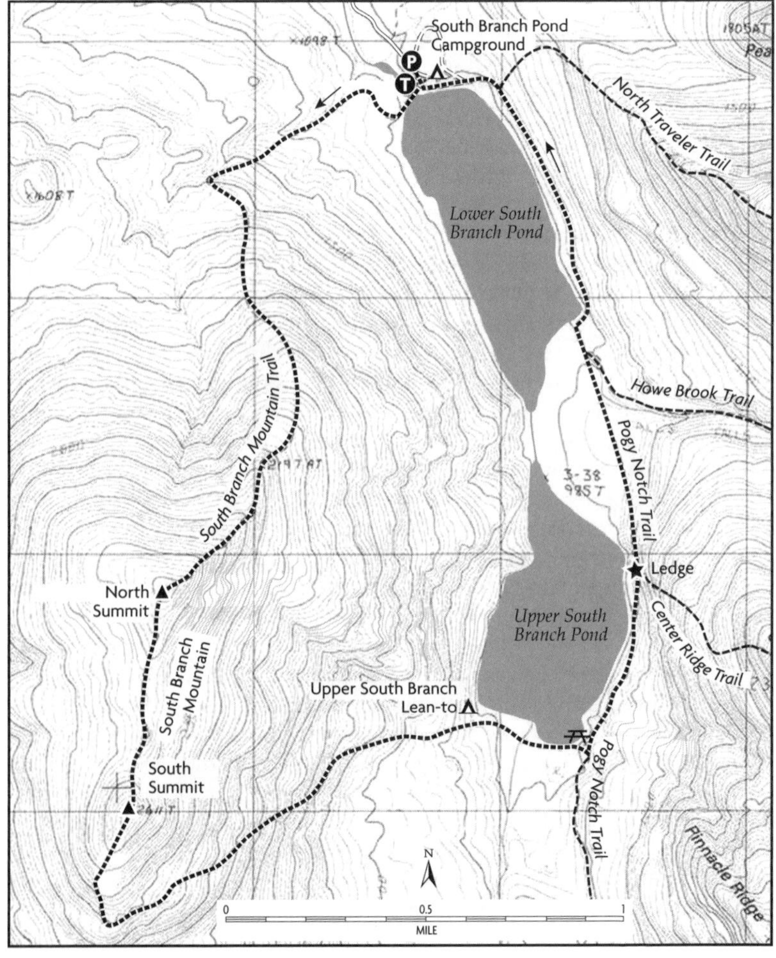

South summit of South Branch Mountain

your eyes open for moose, the largest animal in the area. If you are fortunate you might also catch a glimpse of a much smaller creature, the ruby-throated hummingbird. This tiny bird, attracted by red objects, buzzes endlessly from flower to flower, feeding its insatiable appetite for nectar.

Once through the wet area the trail climbs briefly to an intersection with the Pogy Notch Trail. The final 2.1 miles lead left along the Upper South Branch Pond's east shore. After crossing a small stream, ascend steeply but briefly up to a small ledge. At a junction where the Center Ridge Trail leads right, a few feet to the left a perch high above the pond provides a nice view of the sparkling blue water. Looming above the pond is recently conquered South Branch Mountain.

Continuing north on the Pogy Notch Trail, descend the short, rocky slope onto a flat pathway. With little elevation change remaining, enjoy the last 1.4 miles across a small stream and along the shore of the Lower South Branch

Pond. After passing the North Traveler Trail, the route reaches the campground. Turn left on the dirt road and follow it to the parking area, perhaps after enjoying a refreshing swim at the rocky beach.

South Branch Pond Campground is an excellent place to spend the night and take advantage of the canoe rentals. Consider exploring the pond by canoe on another day, or if you are looking for a full-day adventure, choose the recently completed loop over scenic Traveler Mountain. In 2004 the park completed a new path that connects the North Traveler Trail with the Center Ridge Trail. Now a loop beginning from the campground leads 10.6 miles across a barren landscape still recovering from a 1903 fire that blew through Pogy Notch, destroying much of the forest in the South Branch area. At 3541 feet, Traveler Mountain is the highest volcanic mountain in New England.

42 Brothers and Coe

Round trip	10.9 miles
Loop direction	Counterclockwise
Rating	Strenuous
Hiking time	8 to 9 hours
Starting elevation	1210 feet
High point	4140 feet
Elevation gain	3870 feet
Best season	May through October
Maps	USGS Doubletop Mountain and Mount Katahdin
Contact/fee	Baxter State Park

Driving directions: From Exit 244 on Interstate 95, follow Route 11 toward Millinocket. Drive 11.3 miles and turn right at a T intersection, following the sign to Baxter State Park. In 0.2 mile, turn left. Continue for 16.7 miles until reaching the Togue Pond Gatehouse. After registering, follow the Perimeter Road left 13.2 miles to a small parking area on the right.

While Mount Katahdin draws much of the attention from Baxter State Park visitors, it is not alone in providing hikers with stunning high-alpine adventures. This loop over the second highest ridge of mountains in the park travels through quiet mountain forests and up slide-scarred slopes to reach barren summits with 360-degree views of the lakes and mountains of Maine's north woods. While not as difficult as Mount Katahdin, this challenging hike is a perfect option for those

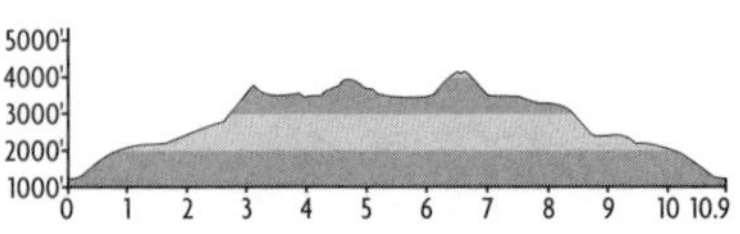

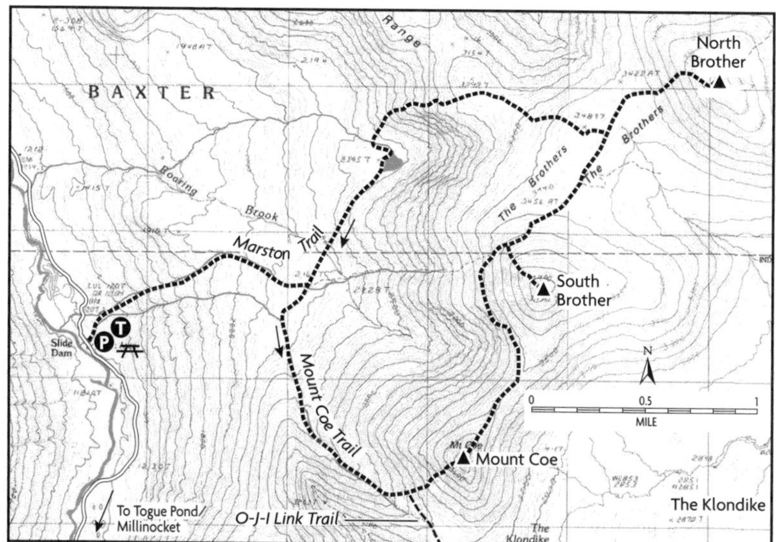

seeking solitude; its beauty is largely overlooked because of its neighbor.

From the parking area follow the Marston Trail over flat terrain through a beautiful grove of mature maple trees. At 0.2 mile the route swings right and begins a steady climb near a tumbling mountain stream. The climb continues while moderating and crossing a few small brooks.

At 1.3 miles turn right onto the Mount Coe Trail. Leading 1.9 miles to the summit of Mount Coe, the trail begins in a thick, moist evergreen forest but quickly emerges at the base of an enormously long slide. Using the slide as its pathway, the trail gradually climbs over a surface of loose rocks. The valley begins to narrow between Mount Coe and the steep walls of Mount O-J-I (named for the shapes of the slide scars once left on the other side of the mountain). Stay close to the small brook. After crossing it a few times the trail begins to pull away and climb more steeply. Through an open meadow of large rocks, continue to ascend the slope. The trail bends left onto a mostly solid rock surface that can be very slippery when wet.

Past the O-J-I Link Trail on the right, the route continues up the steep slide and soon becomes tree-free. Now on a wide-open swath of barren rock, carefully follow the blue blazes up toward the left side of the slide. The trail remains very steep and exposed, but the views are nothing short of breathtaking. At the top of the slide, reenter the woods and continue climbing 0.2 mile to the open summit of Mount Coe. Perched high above the impenetrable boggy area known as the Klondike, Mount Coe provides impressive views of Mount Katahdin.

Descend the very narrow ridge line over small knobs before turning left into the balsam-scented surroundings. Through the thick and quiet forest,

Mount Coe Summit (photo by Maria Fuentes)

follow the trail as it winds down, around, and eventually up the slope of South Brother Mountain. If you are lucky you may even stumble upon a spruce grouse; tamer than the more common ruffed variety (and not so easily startled), the male is identified by a bright red marking above its eye. A 0.3-mile spur leads right, culminating at the top of the 3930-foot peak where 360-degree views await.

The Mount Coe Trail continues straight, descending gradually for 0.7 mile, ending at an intersection with the Marston Trail. Before returning to the parking area, stay straight and head toward the summit of North Brother. The 0.8-mile journey crosses a number of wet, eroded areas, but quickly begins to climb more aggressively along drier, rockier terrain. Just below the summit the trail rises above tree line and enters the alpine zone where fragile plants and small colorful flowers are on display throughout the summer. A wooden sign marks the 4143-foot rocky summit and provides an optimum location to view much of Baxter State Park, Nesowadnehunk Lake to the west, and north toward Chamberlain and Chesuncook lakes.

Return back to the upper junction of the Mount Coe and Marston trails and turn right. Starting along a relaxing grade, the trail quickly begins a steady descent to a small pond tucked away in a large cirque carved out of the side of the mountain. Follow the switchbacks down the ridge, enjoying an occasional view of the placid water. As the trail begins to level off, it turns left, crosses the outlet, and soon reaches the shore.

From here the trail leads 0.8 mile back through a forest once decimated by blowdowns that is slowly regenerating. At the junction of Mount Coe and Marston trails, stay right for the final 1.3 miles.

43 Mount Katahdin

Round trip ■ 9.8 miles
Loop direction ■ Clockwise
Rating ■ Strenuous
Hiking time ■ 9 to 12 hours
Starting elevation ■ 1480 feet
High point ■ 5267 feet
Elevation gain ■ 4050 feet
Best season ■ May through October
Maps ■ USGS Mount Katahdin and Katahdin Lake
Contact/fee ■ Baxter State Park

Driving directions: From Exit 244 on Interstate 95, follow Route 11 toward Millinocket. Drive 11.3 miles and turn right at a T intersection following the sign to Baxter State Park. In 0.2 mile, turn left. Continue for 16.7 miles until reaching the Togue Pond Gatehouse. After registering, follow the park road right and drive 8.1 miles to the day-use parking area on the left.

Steeped in Native American lore and legend, Mount Katahdin has inspired people for countless centuries. Rising like a large island above the flat valleys and lesser peaks surrounding it, the mountain's headwalls and deep ravines are like no other. The rugged beauty of Mount Katahdin has lured visitors, experienced and novice hikers alike, for over 200 years. While many visitors underestimate the physical and natural challenges the mountain presents, those who are prepared and successfully complete the journey will have memories that last a lifetime.

The first challenge of hiking Mount Katahdin is successfully securing a parking space at one of three trailheads (see the Introduction for more general information on visiting Baxter State Park). On nice days, especially weekends, but even midweek during the summer, Katahdin's day-use parking areas may be full by 5:00–5:30 in the morning (the entrance gate at Togue Pond opens at 5:00 AM during the summer).

Of the three trailheads, the one at Roaring Brook is the most popular and the one that offers the most loop-hike possibilities. (By using either of the other two trailheads an 11-mile loop can be completed by following the Abol Slide Trail, the Hunt Trail, and 2 miles of the park Perimeter Road.) Begin your ascent from Roaring Brook by registering at the ranger station, where weather updates and other useful information are available. The park closes trails when weather forecasts predict severe conditions above tree line.

The fun begins on the Chimney Pond Trail. Follow this flat and rocky path 0.1 mile to the start of the Helon Taylor Trail. Leading 3.1 miles to the 4902-foot summit of Pamola Peak, the Helon Taylor Trail wastes little time in ascending Keep Ridge. Initially the climb is moderate through mixed hardwood forests. After a small plateau the trail descends briefly and crosses a small brook.

From here the trail begins to climb more aggressively. Meandering through the increasingly thin forest canopy, the trail emerges above tree line for the final 1.2-mile stretch. The terrain is steep but straightforward, and the views are spectacular. Upon reaching the top of Pamola Peak the first views of Chimney Pond basin and the summit of Mount Katahdin appear. The only thing between you and the top now is the infamous Knife Edge. Before continuing forward be sure that weather conditions are cooperative. Once on the middle of the Knife Edge, there is little room for error and no quick way to safety.

Leading 1.1 miles to the summit, pick up the Knife Edge Trail as it descends abruptly into a small gap in the ridge. A short and steep scramble on the other side leads to the top of Chimney Peak. Follow the Knife

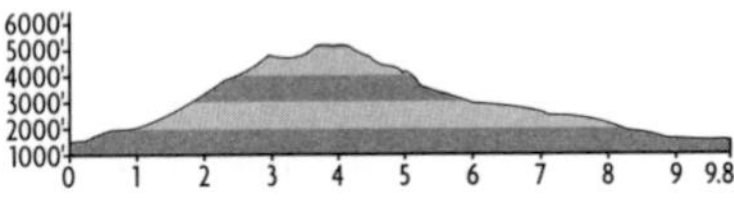

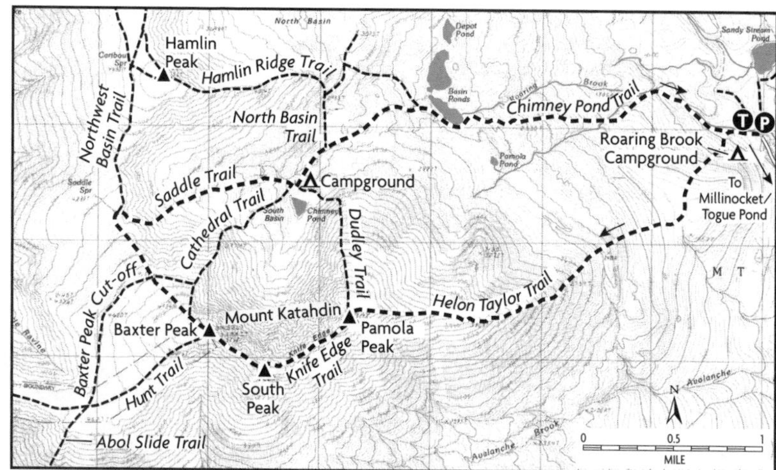

Edge Trail along the spine of the ridge. Rocky and exposed to the elements, there are a number of spots where extra caution is warranted, especially for those with shorter legs or in bad weather.

After narrowly skirting a fairly steep ledge the trail makes a final short descent before aggressively climbing up to the mountain's south summit. Only 0.3 mile of rocks and boulder-hopping stands between you and the highest point in Maine. The view from atop Mount Katahdin's Baxter Peak on a clear day seems endless. It is so tempting to gaze upon the beauty in all directions, but unfortunately, time constraints eventually require one to begin an often-underestimated descent.

Head down the Saddle Trail, which leads northwest toward nearby Hamlin Peak. Remaining above tree line for more than 1 mile, the trail drops quickly across the open terrain referred to as the Table Land. This is a good location to stay alert for water pipits, brown sparrow-sized birds often seen wagging their white-lined tail feathers. Common breeders in alpine areas throughout the western United States and northern Canada, Katahdin is one of the few places in New England where pipits are known to nest.

Upon reaching the saddle the trail turns sharply right and heads steeply down the talus Saddle Slide. As the half-mile slide ends, the trail moderates. Back under an evergreen forest, follow the rock-covered path to Chimney Pond where the dramatic walls of Baxter Peak and the Knife Edge stand 2000 feet above. The remaining 3.3 miles follow the Chimney Pond Trail, mostly moderate but rocky. A number of viewpoints exist along the way, including one from the shore of Basin Pond where the mountain serves as a stunning backdrop. In the evening, while resting your knees and cooling the soles of your feet, there will be plenty of memories to share over dinner.

For those wishing to avoid the Knife Edge, other, less-exposed trails are available for loop possibilities; for example, one 10.5-mile option would be to use the Chimney Pond Trail, ascend Baxter Peak via the Cathedral Trail, and descend down the Saddle Trail. A less-crowded 9.2-mile alternative would be to skip Baxter Peak all together and use the Chimney Pond, Saddle, and Hamlin Ridge trails. Hamlin Peak at 4751 feet is much less frequently visited, but nearly as spectacular as Baxter Peak. Some strong hikers also choose to hike Baxter and Hamlin peaks on the same day, a tremendous adventure if you have the stamina to complete it.

Katahdin's Knife Edge (photo by Maria Fuentes)

MAINE COAST

44 Wells Estuary

Round trip	5 miles
Loop direction	Counterclockwise
Rating	Easy
Hiking time	3 hours
Starting elevation	40 feet
High point	58 feet
Elevation gain	60 feet
Best season	Year round
Map	USGS Wells
Contact/fee	Laudholm Trust

Driving directions: Take Maine Turnpike's Exit 19 and follow Route 9 east into Wells. At the Route 1 junction, turn left at the light. Travel 1.5 miles and turn right onto Laudholm Road. Follow Laudholm Road for 0.5 mile and turn left. The Reserve's entrance is 0.1 mile on the right.

With 7 miles of trails, numerous potential loops, and 1600 acres of diverse habitats, the Wells Estuarine Reserve is an oasis of open space on Maine's southern coastline. Designated in 1984, it is one of twenty-six NOAA-designated estuarine research reserves in the country and the only one in Maine. It was established to conduct research, to convey findings to decision-makers, to provide natural resource education, to protect the land for wildlife and people, and to conserve the coastal resources of southern Maine. The Wells Estuarine Reserve is a public/private partnership, which relies in part on funding from the Laudholm Trust, a nonprofit organization. Federal, state, and local governments jointly own the property. This suggested loop leads through a representative cross-section of the reserve. Especially impressive in the spring during the height of bird migration, the reserve's natural beauty is on display twelve months a year.

Follow the walkway toward the barn and nineteenth-century farmhouse near the hilltop where a flagpole stands. Turn right and head down the paved driveway. On the right a sign in the field marks the start of the Muskie Trail. Follow this path through an open field often frequented by eastern bluebirds. With fiery orange breasts in brilliant contrast to bright

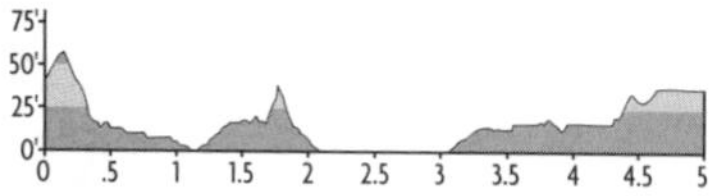

blue backs, bluebirds often pounce from overhanging branches onto unsuspecting insects below.

After crossing a road the path meanders around the field's edge. The shade of large white pines and red oaks offers a change in scenery near the start of the Pilger Trail. At the junction a short spur leads right through tall reeds to a viewing platform where geese, ducks, and herons frequently congregate.

The Pilger Trail, a short enjoyable stroll that soon emerges onto an open field, climbs a grassy slope before reentering the forest and ending at the Barrier Beach Road. On the other side of the road the loop continues along the Laird–Norton Trail. For now, however, turn right and follow the road over a causeway, past a gate to beautiful sandy Laudholm Beach. Besides

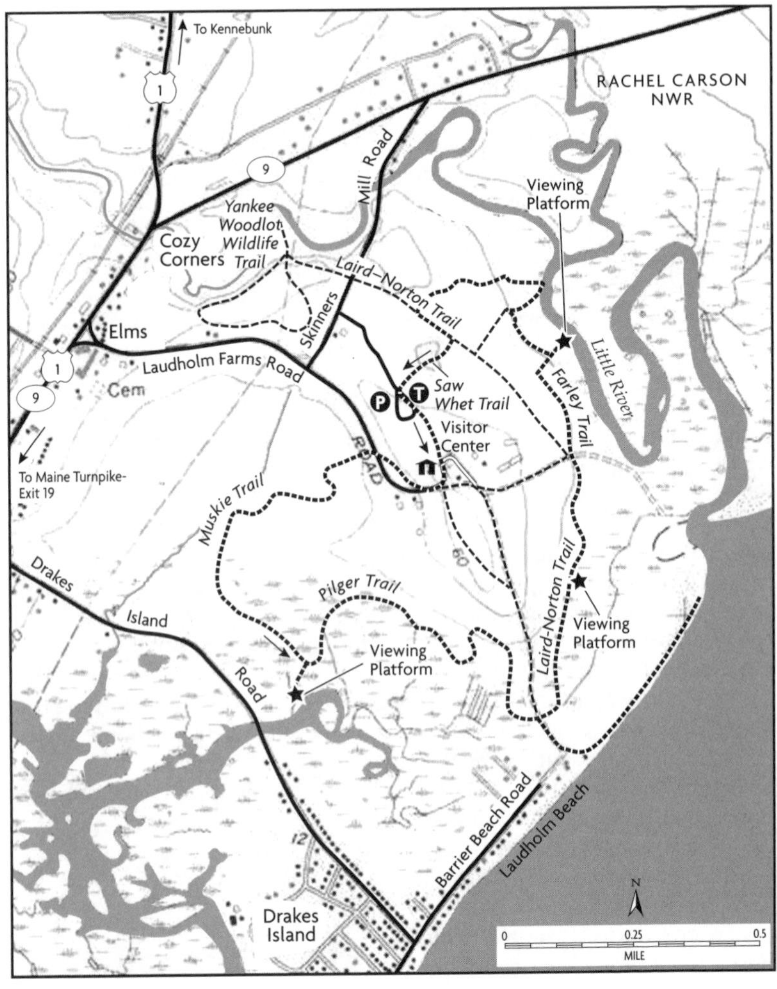

Laudholm Beach

being an ideal location for a relaxing oceanside excursion, the beach is a great place to see the endangered and federally protected piping plover. Please watch your step and obey all signs to avoid disturbing these tiny sand-colored shorebirds that nest and feed between the dunes and the water's edge. To the east the sand stretches undisturbed for over a quarter-mile before being interrupted by the Little River delta.

Return to the Laird–Norton Trail, following its winding boardwalk to a number of viewing platforms with views of the Little River estuary and its resident wildlife. Look for snowy egrets, tall, pure white birds with long black legs that hunt for small fish and crustaceans in the brackish waters. The river is also a popular destination for common goldeneyes, a black-and-white duck with a large white patch on its check.

As the boardwalk ends, head straight toward the field, but quickly veer right onto the Farley Trail, also called the Little River Loop. Staying close to the estuary the path quickly reaches another viewing platform. Continue straight to an intersection under a tall canopy of pines. Turn right and head over the needle-covered path toward the water's edge.

The trail swings inland and winds through the forest before reaching an open field. To the right a path leads through meadows and across a paved road to a quiet forested loop above the banks of a shady stream. This is a short, optional extension to an area teeming with warblers and other songbirds. The main loop continues left, but immediately veers right onto the Saw Whet Trail. Follow the wide path under large oak trees and over a tiny ridge to the entrance road. The parking area is located a few hundred feet left.

Head home or enjoy a picnic lunch under one of the many large shade trees that surround the homestead. A small museum within the farmhouse provides good information about the human and natural history of the area. For a short hike nearby along the opposite side of the Little River, head back to Route 9 and follow it less than a mile east to the Rachel Carson National Wildlife Refuge and the 1-mile loop there.

45 Wolfe's Neck Woods

Round trip ■ 2.8 miles
Loop direction ■ Clockwise
Rating ■ Easy
Hiking time ■ 1.5 hours
Starting elevation ■ 15 feet
High point ■ 95 feet
Elevation gain ■ 160 feet
Best season ■ Year round
Map ■ USGS Freeport
Contact/fee ■ Maine Bureau of Parks and Lands

Driving directions: Starting from Route 1 in downtown Freeport, turn onto Lower Mast Road (across from the L.L. Bean store). Follow Lower Mast Road 2.3 miles until you reach Wolfe Neck Road on your right. Take Wolfe Neck Road 2.2 miles to the entrance of the state park. Turn left and follow the road past the fee station to the parking area. During the off-season, park on the field side of Wolfe Neck Road and walk 0.2 mile up the driveway to the summer parking area.

Located on a long peninsula that juts into scenic Casco Bay, Wolfe's Neck Woods State Park is 233 acres of shady forests and rocky shoreline. In 1969 Freeport residents Mr. and Mrs. Lawrence M. Smith generously donated this land to the state for the establishment of the park. Today, Wolfe's Neck Woods is dissected by numerous trails that offer visitors of all ages a variety of short hiking opportunities. In addition to self-guided hikes, visitors are drawn to Wolfe's Neck's naturalist-led walks, presented throughout the summer.

Begin the loop to the left of the restrooms, on the edge of the picnic area. Follow the White Pines Trail, which leads left near a sign describing the characteristics of Maine's state tree. This well-groomed path soon arrives at a junction. Continue straight joining the Foliage Trail, a nearly half-mile long circuit that leads to the edge of a field, then weaves around a pleasant

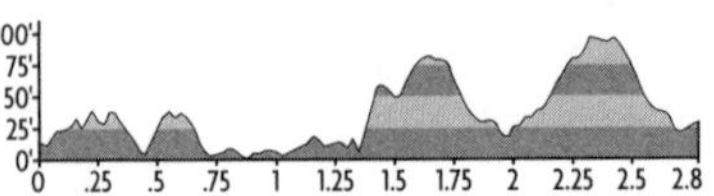

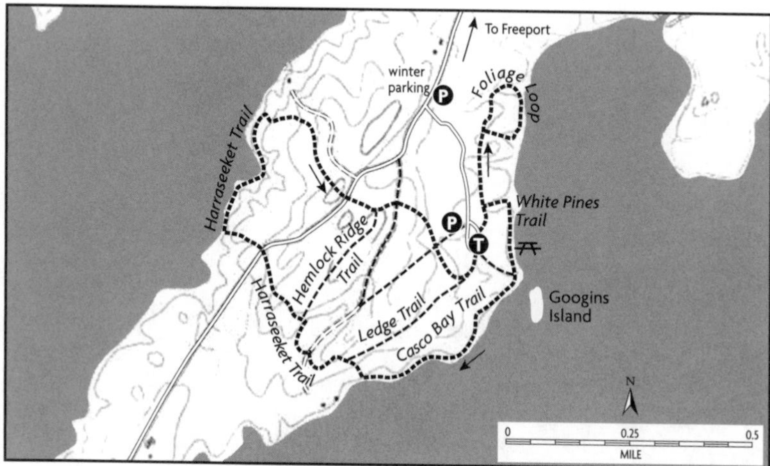

grove of hardwood trees. Upon returning to the White Pines Trail, turn left and head toward the bay. Once near the water's edge the trail bends to the right and hugs the shoreline with viewpoints, benches, and information signs scattered along the way.

The salt marsh to your left is a good place to spot shorebirds and gulls, particularly during low tide. In the deeper water, look for the long necks of double-crested cormorants. Adept swimmers and fishers, in the water cormorants appear loonlike in shape and in habit, but are more slender, more upright, and a bit larger. On land, double-crested cormorants stand upright, and up close they clearly exhibit small orange patches under their bills.

A popular spot on the shorefront is Googins Island, famous for its nesting ospreys. Beyond Googins Island the Casco Bay Trail leads across slightly more uneven but not difficult terrain. Down the series of rock steps a short side trail leads left to a great view of Casco Bay and its many islands. The journey continues past a number of tall oak trees for roughly a half-mile before ending at the Harraseeket Trail. To the left a spur trail leads down to a small beach, but watch your step on the rocks.

Follow the Harraseeket Trail right, beginning the trek across the Wolfe Neck peninsula. After climbing a low ridge, where the Ledge Trail leads 0.3 mile right to the parking area, the route levels off briefly and then drops down to a woods road. Cross the road (the parking area 0.4 mile right), pass through a small wetland, and follow the well-marked path around ledges in the shade of a thick evergreen forest. Past the Hemlock Ridge Trail, descend to, then cross Wolfe Neck Road. Continue along the needle-covered trail as it quickly reaches the banks of the Harraseeket River.

Once at the river the trail swings right and then meanders above the water along the rolling landscape past numerous viewpoints. Near a large rock the path returns inland and climbs to and crosses back over Wolfe Neck Road,

Rocky shore of Casco Bay

soon intersecting the Hemlock Ridge Trail once again. Continue straight over the hill and across an overgrown road. Descend through the young forest, following the trail as it eventually swings left back to the parking area.

46 Bradbury Mountain

Round trip ■ 3.2 miles
Loop direction ■ Counterclockwise
Rating ■ Easy
Hiking time ■ 1.5 hours
Starting elevation ■ 253 feet
High point ■ 485 feet
Elevation gain ■ 280 feet
Best season ■ Year round
Map ■ USGS North Pownal
Contact/fee ■ Maine Bureau of Parks and Lands

Driving directions: Take Exit 22 off Interstate 295 in Freeport. From the south, turn right off the exit; from the north, turn left. You immediately arrive at a T intersection. Turn left and travel 4.5 miles to Pownal Center. Turn right on Route 9. The entrance to the park is 0.5 mile on the left, with plenty of signs along the way.

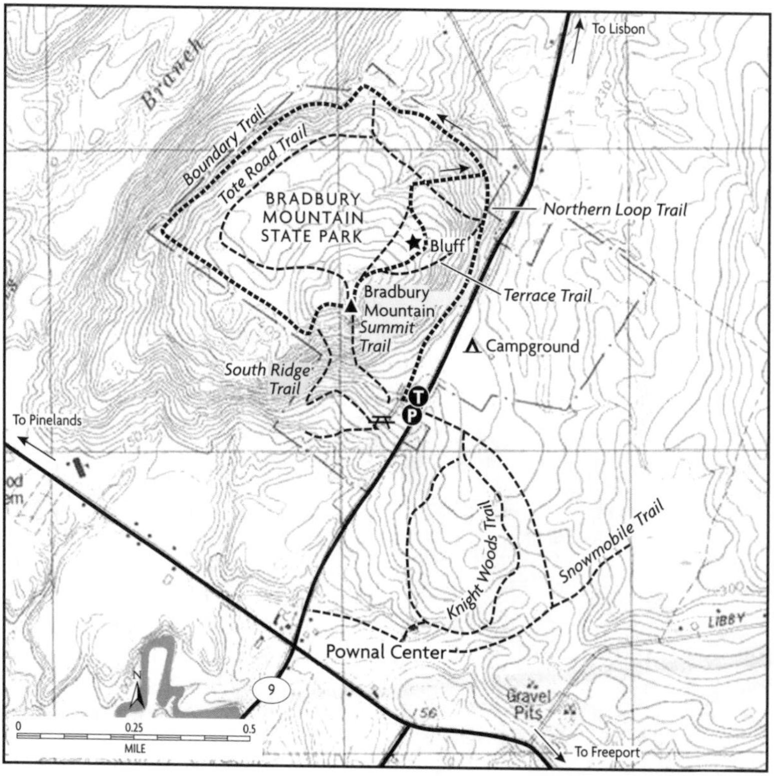

Bradbury Mountain State Park is nearly 600 acres of open space within a half-hour's drive of Portland. Surrounded by a growing and increasingly fast-paced community, Bradbury provides a window into the region's agrarian past. The mountain, once a stopping place for Native Americans traveling to the ocean, more recently was home to livestock, a vineyard, an inn, small mines, and a ski lift. Today the park is a popular destination for hiking and snowshoeing, as well as mountain biking and horseback riding. With a campground, picnic tables, a small playground, and easy-to-moderate terrain, Bradbury Mountain State Park is a perfect place to bring the whole family for a relaxing outing in the woods any time of year.

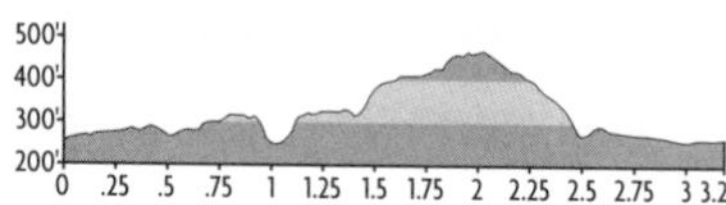

The park offers many different loop options from as little as 1 mile to as long as 3.5 miles. All the trails are well blazed and easy to follow, and most end atop the 485-foot summit of Bradbury Mountain. The quickest, steepest ascent is the Summit Trail. However, for a more interesting journey, follow a path that reaches the open ledge more circuitously, such as this option that begins on the Northern Loop Trail.

Leave the northeast corner of the parking area for a half-mile hike along the wide footpath. Cross level terrain while passing many historical features, including a cattle pound, stone walls, and a mine where feldspar was gathered to make china. After passing a junction with the Terrace and Ski trails, continue straight to the start of the Boundary Trail. Traveling through a wide diversity of habitats, this trail lives up to its name by hugging the park boundary line for 1.5 miles. Tall red oaks and small wetlands line the trail's beginning, habitat frequented by black-and-white warblers, a small zebralike bird that is most often seen creeping up tree trunks searching for food.

After passing over several small mounds, descend and cross over a tiny streambed; a short climb up a steep hemlock-covered slope follows. At the boundary's westernmost corner, the trail turns sharply left and after crossing a rock wall ends at the South Ridge Trail. Turn left and head 0.3 mile to the summit of Bradbury Mountain. From the open ledge views stretch south toward the ocean and the Portland skyline.

Stonewall leads through hemlock forest.

Departing the summit, follow the Northern Loop Trail briefly and in 0.1 mile turn right onto the Terrace Trail. Another 0.1 mile farther, turn left onto the Bluff Trail, which descends gradually to a short spur trail that leads to a bluff with pleasant views of the surrounding countryside. From the bluff continue a few hundred feet down the trail, meeting once again with the Northern Loop Trail. Remain on this route as it makes its way down the mountain. As the path levels and passes the start of the Boundary Trail, stay right for the final 0.5-mile hike back to the parking area.

If you are not ready to return to civilization, consider a short adventure on the other side of Route 9, where a 1.5-mile loop begins across from the park headquarters. Here the Knight Woods Trail provides an opportunity to enjoy more of Bradbury Mountain State Park's beautiful forests and abundant wildlife. The Land for Maine's Future program, in partnership with the Pownal Land Trust, is also in the process of acquiring land in a 7-mile corridor that will connect Bradbury State Park with the nearby Pinelands Public Reserve property. The Pinelands, located in New Gloucester, is the site of two gradual 1.5-mile loop hikes located near the banks of the Royal River. When the Bradbury-Pinelands project is completed, the result will be nearly 3000 acres of contiguous conservation land.

47 Dodge Point

Round trip ■ 4.2 miles
Loop direction ■ Counterclockwise
Rating ■ Easy–Moderate
Hiking time ■ 2 hours
Starting elevation ■ 155 feet
High point ■ 270 feet
Elevation gain ■ 450 feet
Best season ■ Year round
Map ■ USGS Bristol
Contact/fee ■ Maine Bureau of Park and Lands

Driving directions: From downtown Wiscasset, travel east on Route 1 for 6.2 miles. Turn right and in 0.2 mile turn right again (to the left is downtown Newcastle in 0.8 mile). Follow River Road 2.5 miles to a sign and parking area on the left. From Boothbay, follow Route 27 north for 2.7 miles and turn right onto River Road. Drive 6.9 miles to the parking area on the right.

With more than 500 acres and over 8000 feet of frontage on the tidal waters of the Damariscotta River, the Dodge Point Public Reserve is a four-season family destination where New England's ever-changing scenery is on constant display. In addition to natural beauty, Dodge Point showcases human history, including an old mill site and brickyard, cellar holes and rock walls, and stands of large trees grown under the watchful eyes of a small woodlot owner whose trustees sold the land to the state in 1989. The preserve is a perfect location for a short, leisurely hike. Better yet, extend the day, pack a lunch, and take advantage of the many picnic locations along the shore. With waterfowl diving, seals foraging, and cool breezes blowing,

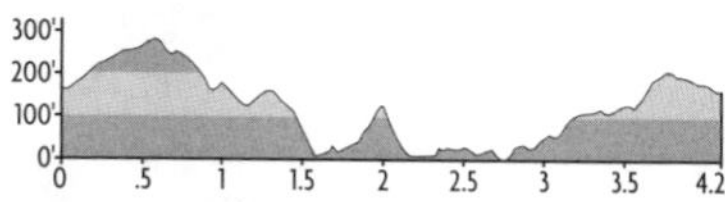

the peaceful surroundings will send you home refreshed whichever option you choose.

Begin on Old Farm Road beyond the gate. This wide path loops 2.2 miles around the property and provides an excellent, no-nonsense route, especially nice for cross-country skiing. Head up a small incline in 0.1 mile and turn right onto the narrower Timber Trail. Winding over boardwalks and through small wetlands, the trail slowly climbs around the side of a low hill.

After reaching the height of land and passing through a firebreak, the path slowly descends. Climb over a small stone wall and then turn right back onto Old Farm Road. Gradually make your way down the side of a steep hill.

As the route levels, join the interpretive trail on the right. Follow this path 0.2 mile to a small dock on the river. During colder months this is a great location to spot loons as well as long-tailed and bufflehead ducks. Long-tailed ducks are black and white with long, pointy tails. Buffleheads

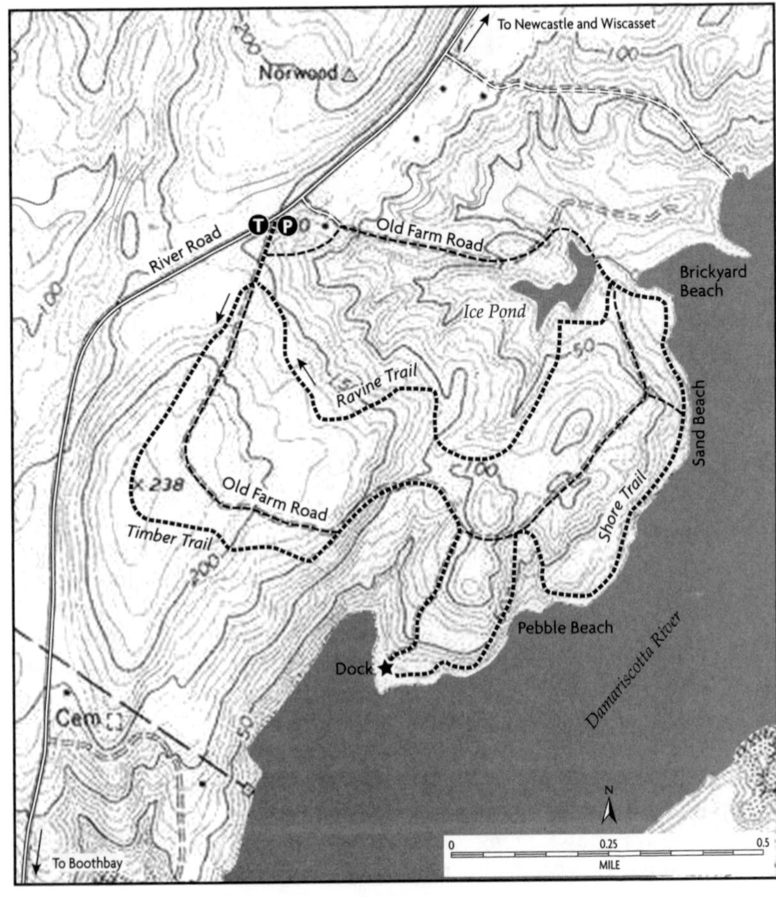

Picnicking on the Damariscotta River (photo by Craig Romano)

are much smaller, gregarious black ducks with large white patches on the backs of their heads. Both spend considerable time feeding beneath the water's surface.

For the next 1.3 miles follow the Shore Trail's scenic journey north winding along the river. You will pass many side paths that lead to small beaches. Level for the most part, the trail climbs briefly near a small streambed before descending along the other side. Take your time and explore the many quiet spots, and relax in the shade of the tall pines and oaks that grow along the shore. The final waterfront location is Brickyard Beach, a mudflat popular for shellfish harvesting. Aptly named, the beach is also strewn with the remains of bricks produced here, as early as the 1600s. At one time there were nearly thirty brickyards in the region employing two hundred locals.

The trail eventually swings inland and returns once again to Old Farm Road. Follow the road right a few hundred yards to the start of the Ravine Trail. Before taking this path, check out the Ice Pond and small dam a few dozen feet ahead. This is a good location to spot turtles sunning on fallen trees.

The Ravine Trail circles around the pond and slowly ascends on the edge of a small ravine. After leveling off, the route swings right and cuts through a dark evergreen forest, only to emerge onto an old road lined with large sugar maple trees. Turn left off the road. Hike over a few small inclines and arrive one last time on Old Farm Road. Turn right to complete the circuit. Before leaving, stop at the small kiosk for information about the Damariscotta River Association, a local land trust that helps the state manage the property.

In addition to being a stand-alone preserve, Dodge Point is also part of the River-Link Corridor Project, a multiple-conservation-organization initiative to establish a 10-mile stretch of protected freshwater and tidal streams, forests, shorelands, and trails connecting the Sheepscot and Damariscotta rivers. The Land for Maine's Future Program is helping to advance this ambitious project by supporting acquisition of several parcels and easements along the trail and wildlife corridor. When complete, the corridor will stretch from Whitefield to Boothbay Harbor, incorporating conserved properties in Newcastle, Edgecomb, and Boothbay.

48 Mount Megunticook and Maiden Cliff

Round trip ■ 6.8 miles
Loop direction ■ Clockwise
Rating ■ Moderate–Difficult
Hiking time ■ 4 hours
Starting elevation ■ 210 feet
High point ■ 1380 feet
Elevation gain ■ 1670 feet
Best season ■ Year round
Maps ■ USGS Camden and Lincolnville
Contact/fee ■ Maine Department of Conservation, Bureau of Public Lands

Driving directions: From Route 1 in downtown Camden, follow Route 52 north toward Lincolnville Center. In 2.8 miles, just before approaching Megunticook Lake, turn right onto a driveway that leads up a short hill to the start of the Maiden Cliff Trail.

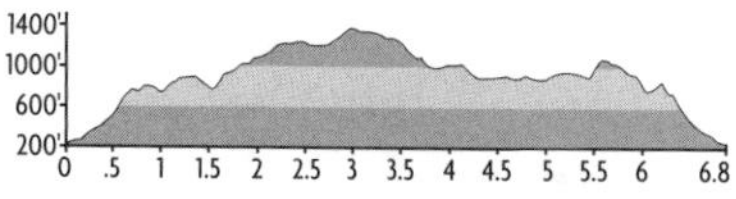

Views of distant islands and boat-filled harbors from one ledge, and scenes of rolling hills, farmland, and a deep blue lake from another, highlight this loop's many attractions. The journey, which leads past two popular Camden Hills State Park destinations, completes a figure-eight circuit while also passing through some of the state park's quieter locations. Two loops in one, the hike can be completed as described or as two shorter, separate adventures. Whichever option you choose, you will not go home disappointed any time of the year.

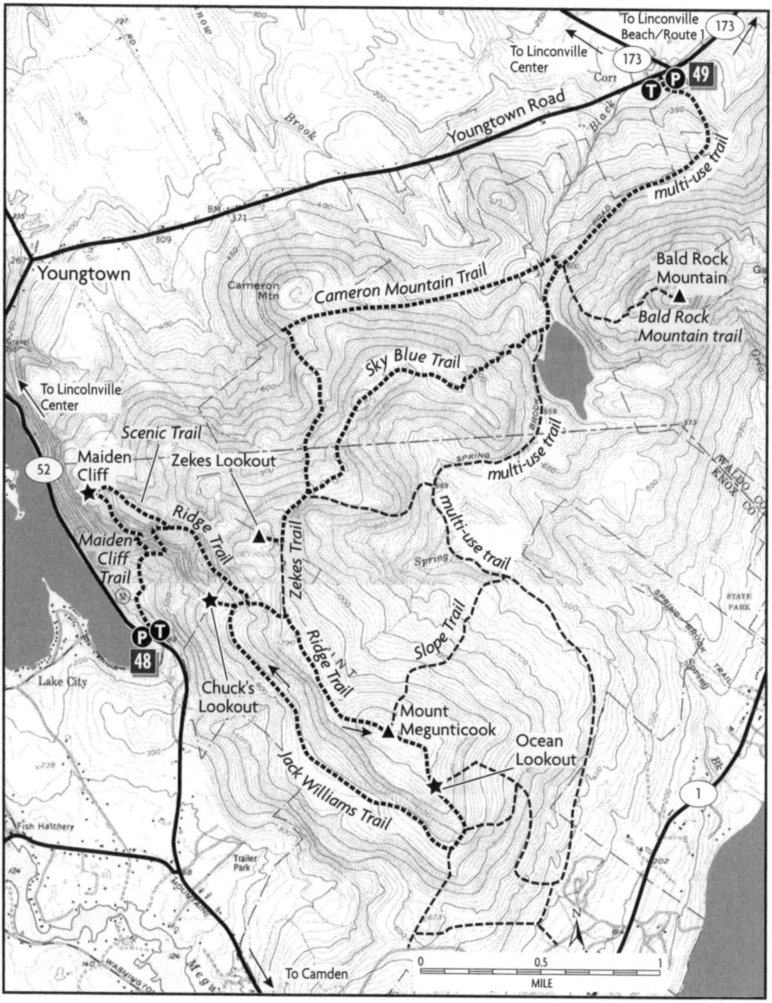

Begin along the wide footpath as it carves through a narrow, rock-covered ravine. Under the shadows of tall pines and hemlocks, ascend to a large boulder and trail junction 0.5 mile from the parking area. Stay left and climb up short switchbacks that culminate on a flat oak-covered ridge. At a three-way intersection, turn left onto a short spur trail that ends atop Maiden Cliff. From this high vantage point the views of Megunticook Lake are stunning. While not very scary, the top of the cliff can be dangerous for those who wander down the steep slope. It is wise to heed the warning from the metal cross that has been erected in the memory of a young girl who plunged to her death in 1864.

Return to the woods and pick up the Scenic Trail, which leads left up a short rocky slope. Above, the trail traverses a series of wide-open ledges with views that were captured in the 1993 movie *The Man Without a Face*.

At the bottom of the final ledge lies a junction with the Ridge Trail. To the right the path leads less than 1 mile down to the parking area, offering a modest 2.1-mile loop. To complete the longer hike, continue straight on the Ridge Trail. Descend briefly before beginning a gradual ascent of the northwest shoulder of Mount Megunticook. Abruptly, the hardwood trees give way to evergreens; under the darkening canopy, pass the Jack Williams Trail on the right. Use caution in this area during cold weather; with limited snow cover, the ground may be icy. Stay left as the Ridge Trail climbs to a small wooded ledge with distant views of the ocean. Over level terrain the trail continues through a pleasant stretch of ferns and rock formations.

A final climb ends atop the wooded summit of Mount Megunticook, the park's highest point. Rather than stopping here, press on a half-mile down the ridge to the spectacular Ocean Lookout. Perched above a cliff face, the Ocean Lookout, while popular, provides plenty of locations to spread out, enjoy the scenery, and, even on the hottest of summer days, be refreshed in cool ocean breezes. The lookout is also an excellent vantage point to marvel at the countless islands and inlets of Penobscot Bay and to gaze upon the distant mountains of Acadia National Park "downeast."

The loop continues southeast and quickly descends the mountain. In between watching your step and enjoying the views, listen for the boisterous call of the American goldfinch. This small, bright yellow bird (mostly brown in the winter) may be heard while flying rollercoaster-fashion between the stunted oak trees.

Beyond an intersection with the Adam's Lookout Trail the slope flattens. Turn right on the Jack Williams Trail, which provides a wonderful and seldom-used loop opportunity along the base of the cliff. Work your way across the low plateau beneath the limbs of large deciduous trees. As you approach the ridge, a short path leads left to Chucks Lookout, a viewpoint similar in appearance but not nearly as popular as Maiden Cliff.

The route ascends briefly, then ends at the Ridge Trail. Turn left toward

Opposite: Penobscot Bay from Ocean Lookout

Maiden Cliff and, at the intersection with the Scenic Trail, turn left again. Over open ledges follow the trail down to a small streambed. After veering right the path ends at the Maiden Cliff Trail 0.5 mile from the trailhead.

49 Zekes Lookout

Round trip ■ 7.2 miles
Loop direction ■ Counterclockwise
Rating ■ Moderate
Hiking time ■ 4 hours
Starting elevation ■ 265 feet
High point ■ 1190 feet
Elevation gain ■ 1100 feet
Best season ■ Year round
Map ■ USGS Lincolnville
Contact/fee ■ Maine Department of Conservation, Bureau of Public Lands

Driving directions: From Route 1 in Lincolnville Beach, follow Route 173 (across from the Isleboro Ferry Terminal) 2.2 miles west. Turn left onto Youngtown Road. From the junction of Routes 52 and 173 south of Lincolnville Center, follow Route 173 east 2.9 miles before turning right onto Youngtown Road. Once on Youngtown Road, the parking area is immediately on the left.

Camden Hills State Park is a popular destination for hikers throughout the year, particularly on summer weekends. While most folks are drawn to a handful of popular vistas, the park is also big enough to support quiet destinations as well, such as Zekes Lookout. While the views are not as breathtaking as at other area locations, the journey to Zekes Lookout offers visitors more subtle rewards. In fact, while enjoying the peaceful forest surroundings along the way, you are more apt to be interrupted by a melodious chorus of warbling songbirds than the rowdy shouts of fellow hikers.

Begin along a wide multiple-use trail enjoyed mostly by hikers, cross-country skiers, and snowshoe enthusiasts. Climbing moderately and surrounded by the large trunks of oaks, maples, and pines, listen for the hammering sound of New England's largest woodpecker. Pileated woodpeckers, red-crowned black-and-white birds, have left their signature deep, rectangular holes in cavities of decaying trees throughout this area.

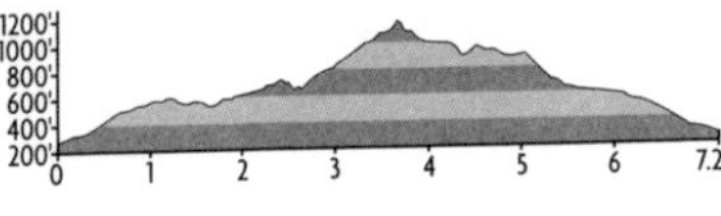

After traveling about a mile the route levels before approaching the

Camden Hills State Park

Bald Rock Mountain Trail, a popular half-day, non-loop family hike that provides excellent views of Penobscot Bay. Just beyond, turn right onto the Cameron Mountain Trail. Down the hill (and snowmobile trail) a few hundred feet, swing left to begin a relaxing stroll along the wide path. Surrounded by the growing vegetation, it is hard to picture this area without forests, but the numerous stone walls are clear evidence of an agrarian past. Slowly the trail makes its way toward Cameron Mountain, a bald, privately owned blueberry-covered hill adjacent to the state park. Stay on the trail while passing the mountain, and drop down the other side of the hill.

At an intersection of woods roads, the trail bears left and crosses a small stream. Follow the path as it winds steadily through the spruce-fir forest, arriving at the start of the Sky Blue Trail in 0.8 mile. This route will provide the day's descent, but for now continue straight a hundred yards and turn right onto the Zekes Trail. After a half-mile under the gnarled branches of oak trees, reach a side trail on the right marked by a sign and small cairn. A brief scramble leads to Zekes Lookout and distant views of Penobscot Bay. Not as impressive as they probably were in the past, the views are nice and offer a pleasant backdrop for a quiet lunch.

Return to the Sky Blue Trail, which despite its name is enjoyable for its shady forests. Pass over a few low ridges and near small wetlands, where the vegetation occasionally shifts abruptly from deciduous to coniferous, depending on the direction of the slope. Mainly gradual, the trail drops more quickly toward the end before reaching an old road. Turn left and then left again, rejoining the multi-use trail 1.6 miles from the parking lot.

A number of alternative loops, some as long as 10 miles, can be completed from this trailhead. In addition to the Cameron Mountain and Sky Blue trails described, one could use the Zekes Trail and the Slope Trail. All four routes originate from the multi-use trail. The Slope Trail climbs to the summit of Mount Megunticook, the highest peak in the area, and can be connected to the other three options via the Ridge Trail. Also note that this section of Camden Hills State Park, although open for year-round use, is available for hunting in season. Be sure to wear orange when appropriate, and keep in mind that Maine prohibits Sunday hunting.

50 Ducktrap River

Round trip	4.4 miles
Loop direction	Clockwise
Rating	Easy–Moderate
Hiking time	2 hours
Starting elevation	215 feet
High point	250 feet
Elevation gain	120 feet
Best season	Year round
Map	USGS Lincolnville
Contact/fee	Maine Department of Conservation, Bureau of Public Lands

Driving directions: From Lincolnville Beach follow Route 1 north for 1 mile, and then turn left onto Ducktrap Road. In 0.7 mile turn right onto Tanglewood Road. Continue down the dirt road 1 mile to a parking area on the left.

Hugging the shores of a winding salmon river, the loop through the Ducktrap section of the Camden Hills State Park is a relaxing stroll through a nicely forested landscape. The loop circles a property dissected with a number of trails that offer numerous short- and medium-length options. The Ducktrap River area is a popular destination year-round, luring many

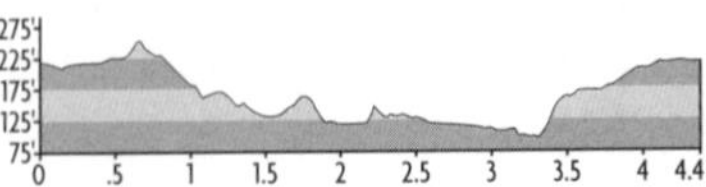

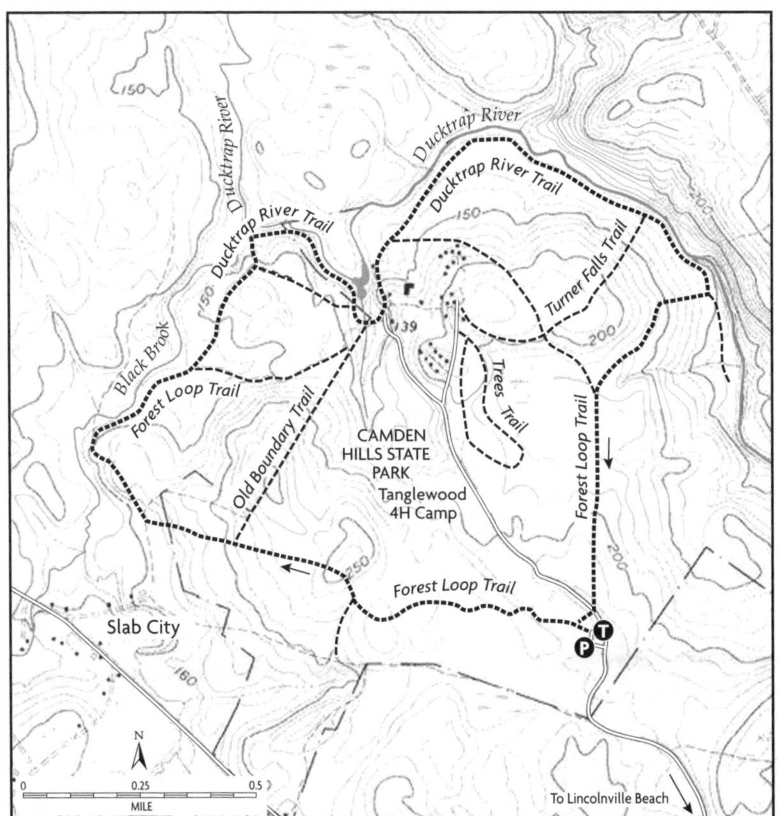

cross-country skiers in the winter, bird-watchers in the spring and summer, and leaf-peepers in early autumn.

The route heads quickly into the forest near a small kiosk and in a few hundred feet reaches the start of the Forest Loop Trail. Stay left and follow the path through the mixed forest dominated by large white pine trees. In and around small wetland areas, meander across gently rolling terrain and soon climb gradually up a dry oak-covered ridge. Stay straight and hike down the hillside into the darkening forest. After passing an opening in the forest canopy where the Old Boundary Trail leads right, continue straight, descending to an old woods road. The trail turns right and follows the road, eventually paralleling Black Brook. Remain along the path through some marshy wetland areas.

At a junction turn left onto the Ducktrap River Trail and climb up a small hill before descending to the shore of Black Brook at its confluence with the Ducktrap River. The trail continues along the side of the river where ample places are available to enjoy the peaceful flowing water. Proceed quietly and you may happen upon the beautifully colored wood duck. A small, shy waterfowl, the wood duck when startled quickly takes off while emitting a high-pitched whistle. Stay close to the river as the route passes a few intersections, crosses a small stream, and arrives at the Tanglewood 4-H Camp. Run by the University of Maine Cooperative Extension, Tanglewood provides a number of educational programs for kids and adults focused on forest management and ecology.

Remain along the riverbank, picking up the Ducktrap River Trail on the north side of the camp. Stay close to the water and enjoy the flat terrain and quiet scenery of this peaceful trail. The silence occasionally may be broken by the echoing call of the belted kingfisher. A bluish-gray bird with a crest and large beak, the kingfisher occasionally hovers before crashing into the water seeking nourishment. The river slowly flows between tall banks and under the long limbs of numerous shade trees. As the water begins to bend and change direction, the surrounding forest briefly opens.

Back under a dark evergreen forest, the trail drops aside a long section of rapids. Pick up the second trail that leads right and follow it up a small incline out of the secluded valley. The path continues gradually through

Ducktrap River

young forests. Turn left back onto the Forest Loop Trail. Upon reaching a wide dirt road, hike straight across and in a few hundred feet arrive at the loop's conclusion. Turn left to return to the parking area.

The Ducktrap River is one of eight rivers in Maine with runs of native Atlantic salmon. Thanks to the efforts of the Coastal Mountains Land Trust, the Ducktrap Coalition, and the Land for Maine's Future Program, more than 82 percent of the land bordering the river is now owned by a conservation organization, protected by an easement, or is part of Camden Hills State Park.

51 Champlain Mountain

Round trip ■ 5.5 miles
Loop direction ■ Clockwise
Rating ■ Moderate–Difficult
Hiking time ■ 4 hours
Starting elevation ■ 55 feet
High point ■ 1058 feet
Elevation gain ■ 1400 feet
Best season ■ Late June through early October
Map ■ USGS Seal Harbor
Contact/fee ■ Acadia National Park

Driving directions: The loop begins at the Village Green on Route 3 in the center of Bar Harbor. While there is limited public parking, the Green is within walking distance of many places of lodging and can be reached using the Island Explorer shuttle service from a number of locations, including the national park visitor center in Hulls Cove.

Automobiles have traditionally been the preferred mode of transportation in Acadia National Park, a park often plagued by air pollution and haze. In response, public and private interests, including the Friends of Acadia, L.L. Bean, and the National Park Service, have joined to establish the Island Explorer propane-powered shuttle service. Providing free bus transportation throughout the park, the Island Explorer uses established routes and runs throughout the day from late June to early October. While stopping at the most popular destinations, shuttles also will pull over at any safe location along their routes. In addition to reducing pollution (and park entrance fees for those traveling alone or in pairs, at $5 per person compared to $20 per vehicle), the Island Explorer conveniently provides an unlimited number of loop

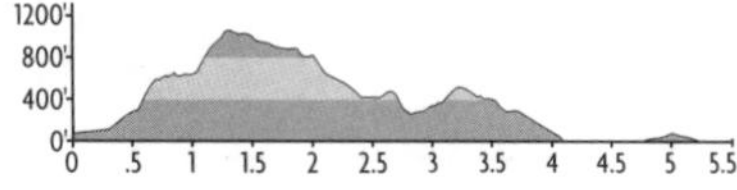

options, such as this classic hike that visits popular attractions in the park. As you pass the overflowing parking areas along the journey, you will be happy that your only concern is how many photos to snap of the waves crashing into the rocks below. (Island Explorer information was gathered in 2004. Contact the National Park Service for updates and schedules.)

At the Village Green in the heart of Bar Harbor, hop aboard an Island Explorer shuttle for Sieur de Monts Spring and the Wild Gardens of Acadia.

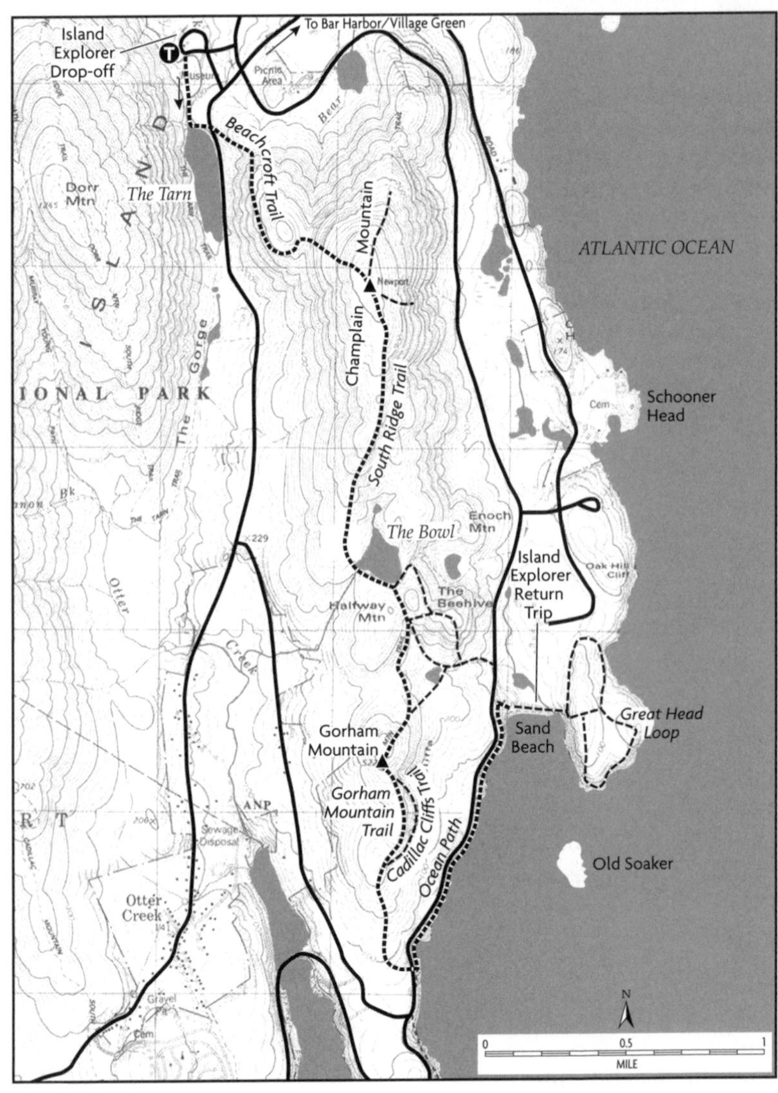

Beachcroft Trail

Ten minutes later arrive at the gardens, where a short trail weaves through an illustrative collection of native plant species found on Mount Desert Island. To the left of a small nature center, follow the 0.4-mile path that leads to the Tarn. At the north shore of the small pond, turn left, cross Route 3, and join the Beachcroft Trail as it gradually switchbacks up the steep slope. The footing here consists of a series of flat stones laid out perfectly, one example of the fine stonework and trail maintenance in evidence throughout the park, thanks to many decades of trail stewardship. Looking back as you ascend, you'll see below the clear blue waters of the Tarn reflecting the rugged east face of Dorr Mountain.

Circling around Huguenot Head, a small peak on the ridge, the 1.1-mile trail descends to a saddle before climbing steeply up rock ledges to the summit of Champlain Mountain. The mountain, named for the French explorer who discovered and named Mount Desert Island in 1576, stands at 1058 feet above Frenchman Bay.

A relaxing 1.6-mile stroll down Champlain's attractive South Ridge Trail ensues. Duck in and out of the stunted pine trees that have established roots within the inhospitable rocky surface, and follow the trail as it steadily descends past countless ocean vistas before reaching a small stream crossing. Beyond sits the Bowl, a large, secluded pond that is home to beaver and other resident wildlife. With the assistance of a boardwalk, make your way along the shore and turn right at the pond's south shore. Passing through a birch forest of white bark and bright green leaves, continue through the young forest that has sprouted following the infamous fire of 1947, which burned over 17,000 acres of forest on Mount Desert Island. Stay straight past a trail junction and then turn right for the 0.2-mile climb to the summit of Gorham Mountain. Although perched at only 525 feet above sea level, the mountain's proximity to the ocean provides excellent views and cool, refreshing breezes.

Heading west down the Gorham Mountain Trail, quickly reach the Cadillac Cliffs Trail on the left. This interesting route weaves around a series of rock faces once submerged beneath the sea. Take the slightly more difficult Cliffs Trail or continue straight; the two paths intersect below.

Upon reaching the Gorham Mountain Trail's conclusion, pick up the Ocean Path on the opposite side of the Park Loop Road. The Ocean Path, flat and well-manicured, passes many of the most visited sites in the park. There are plenty of opportunities for taking photos as well as viewing wildlife such as the common eider, a large black-and-white sea duck (females and young are dark brown) that spends hours diving for food along the shore. Otter Cliffs, a scenic spot above the ocean, lies 0.5 mile to the right.

For the 1-mile completion of the loop, turn left and head past Thunder Hole, a popular spot where the ocean crashes loudly between the rocks, especially as the tide rises. Continue to beautiful Sand Beach where Island Explorer shuttles arrive every half-hour for the return trip to the Village Green. If you have the time and energy, Sand Beach and the 1.5-mile loop to Great Head that begins on the beach's eastern end are both enjoyable destinations.

52 Dorr and Cadillac Mountains

Round trip ■ 6.5 miles
Loop direction ■ Counterclockwise
Rating ■ Difficult
Hiking time ■ 4 hours
Starting elevation ■ 55 feet
High point ■ 1532 feet
Elevation gain ■ 1700 feet
Best season ■ April through November
Map ■ USGS Seal Harbor
Contact/fee ■ Acadia National Park

Driving directions: Follow Route 3 through the center of Bar Harbor. Past the Village Green, the road turns sharply right. From here drive 2.1 miles to the Sieur de Monts entrance. Turn right and follow the road to a parking area. From late June to early October the Island Explorer shuttle provides free bus transportation from the Village Green to Sieur de Monts Spring and the Wild Gardens of Acadia (see Hike 51).

This loop leads to the highest point on America's east coast and the most comprehensive view of Acadia National Park. Before scaling Cadillac Mountain, the journey includes a scenic climb up and over the bald summit of Dorr Mountain and a short scramble through a narrow notch that picturesquely frames the distant ocean. The return trek winds down a flat, open ridge, passes a long a series of cascades and flumes, and concludes near the edge of a wetland teeming with wildlife. The hike, 6.5 miles in length, has significant elevation change and a couple of rugged sections to ensure that you earn all of the many rewards along the way.

Begin at the nature center at the Wild Gardens of Acadia and head straight toward the Abbe Museum (this is the original Abbe Museum, still open seasonally, while the Abbe Museum's new, expanded museum in downtown Bar Harbor is open year-round). Turn left across a bridge and follow the path to the north end of the Tarn. Pick up the Kurt Diederich Trail on the right and ascend the series of rock steps that wind up the steep slope. At 0.4 mile turn left onto the East Face Trail, and continue more gradually up the ridge. The mixed pine forest has many openings providing splendid views, and the footing is excellent.

After passing the upper end of the Dorr Ladder Trail, follow the route as it swings right and heads up the slope more steadily. At the crest of the ridge, turn left toward the large summit cairn a few hundred feet away, 1.7

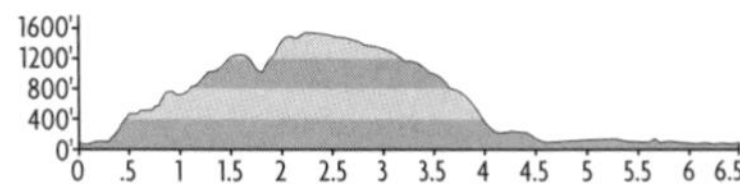

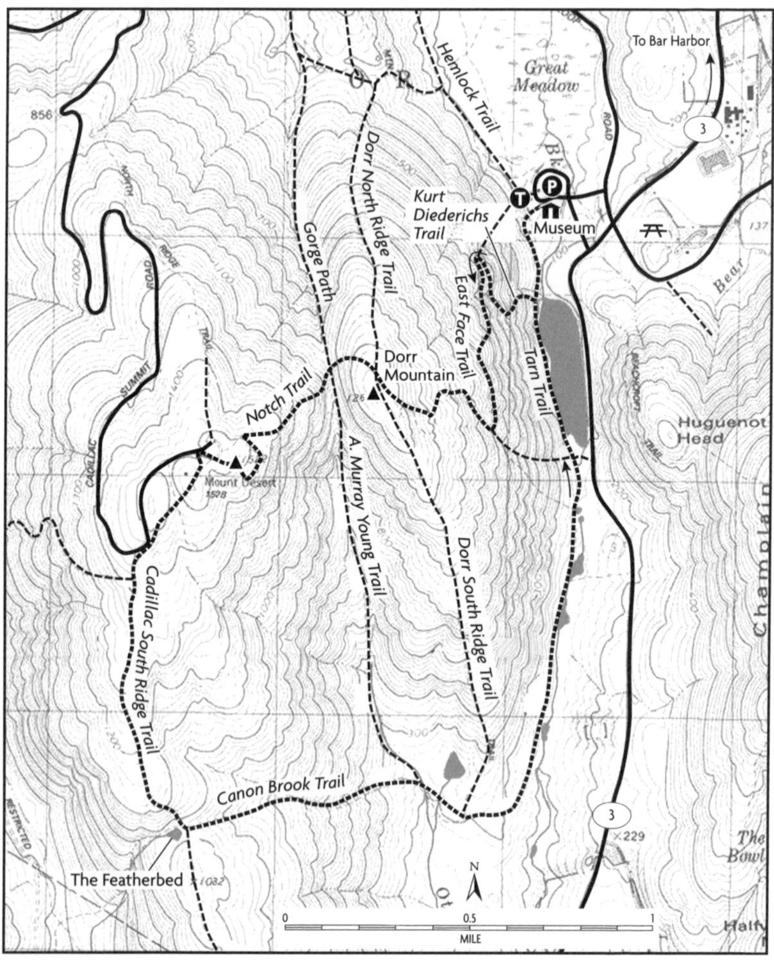

miles from the parking area. Named for George B. Dorr, Acadia's first superintendent, this 1270-foot mountain is an ideal location to view the eastern side of Mount Desert Island and the islands and inlets of Frenchman Bay.

The 1-mile hike to Cadillac begins down Dorr Mountain's north ridge. In 0.1 mile, head left, soon dropping into a narrow notch. While wise to avoid when icy or wet, the hike down is very scenic with interesting rock formations and ledges. The ascent up Cadillac's east shoulder begins just past a four-way intersection deep in the notch. Requiring some scrambling at first, the trail eases near the summit. From the barren peak, expansive views of islands, mountains, and bays await. Only a few trees and hordes of tourist (most having driven up), block the abundant scenery. While on the summit, take advantage of the nicely paved path that loops past informative signs.

When ready to leave the crowds behind, head for the Cadillac South Ridge Trail, which begins near a large sign where cars enter the summit area. At first along a dirt road, the path climbs over a few small inclines and approaches the auto road. Veer left, leaving developed Cadillac Mountain behind, and enter the treeless south ridge. The sidewalk-like journey eventually ends when the trail drops to the Featherbed, a small, secluded pond 1.2 miles from the summit.

From the Featherbed, pick up the Canon Brook Trail. Following a small stream much of the way, this path is gradual at both ends, but in between drops swiftly while passing a series of cascades, waterfalls, and small flumes. Occasionally crisscrossing open ledges, the route is not always obvious but remains near the stream.

Upon reaching the confluence of two brooks under the shade of cedar trees, cross to the intersection with the A. Murray Young Trail on the other side. Stay right and continue past Dorr Mountain's South Ridge Trail.

The final 1.7 miles begin on a relaxing stretch of hiking along a series of ponds and streams. The wetlands provide ideal habitat for beaver, otter, and

Dorr Mountain summit cairn

many birds, including the great blue heron. The largest wading bird in the Northeast, the heron stealthily moves in shallow waters before propelling its long powerful beak at fish, amphibians, and other small prey. The series of wetlands ends at the Tarn. Follow the rocky path along the west shore. Pass the start of the Kurt Diederich Trail and return to the Wild Gardens.

A number of shorter loop options are possible from the same starting point. Dorr Mountain's South and North Ridge trails are both very pleasant. Combined with the Tarn Trail they form a nice 5.5-mile loop. Either also provides a nice descent after climbing Dorr Mountain's east face. For quieter hikes, consider the A. Murray Young Trail and the Gorge Path. Both lead through the notch between Dorr and Cadillac mountains.

53 Jordan Pond

Round trip ■ 5.4 miles
Loop direction ■ Clockwise
Rating ■ Moderate–Difficult
Hiking time ■ 4 hours
Starting elevation ■ 320 feet
High point ■ 1190 feet
Elevation gain ■ 1670 feet
Best season ■ April through November
Maps ■ USGS Southwest Harbor and Seal Harbor
Contact/fee ■ Acadia National Park

Driving directions: From Acadia National Park's Hulls Cove Visitor Center, follow the park road south for 3 miles. Turn right and continue 4.4 miles to the hikers' parking lot for the Jordan Pond area. As an alternative, from June to October, the Island Explorer shuttle bus offers free transportation from Bar Harbor's Village Green (see Hike 51).

Like most of the water bodies on Mount Desert Island, Jordan Pond is long and narrow. Running north-to-south, the pond is a classic reminder of the glacial history that shaped the landscape. In addition to its bright blue waters and mountain scenery, Jordan Pond is an ideal location to begin any number of loop hikes, from flat 1-mile nature trails to all-day adventures over the highest elevations in the park. The following half-day journey showcases the best of Jordan Pond and opens the door to limitless future travels.

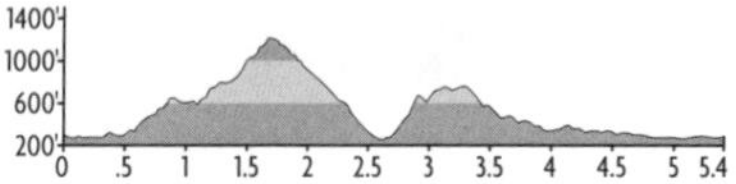

From the parking area take the wide path down to Jordan Pond.

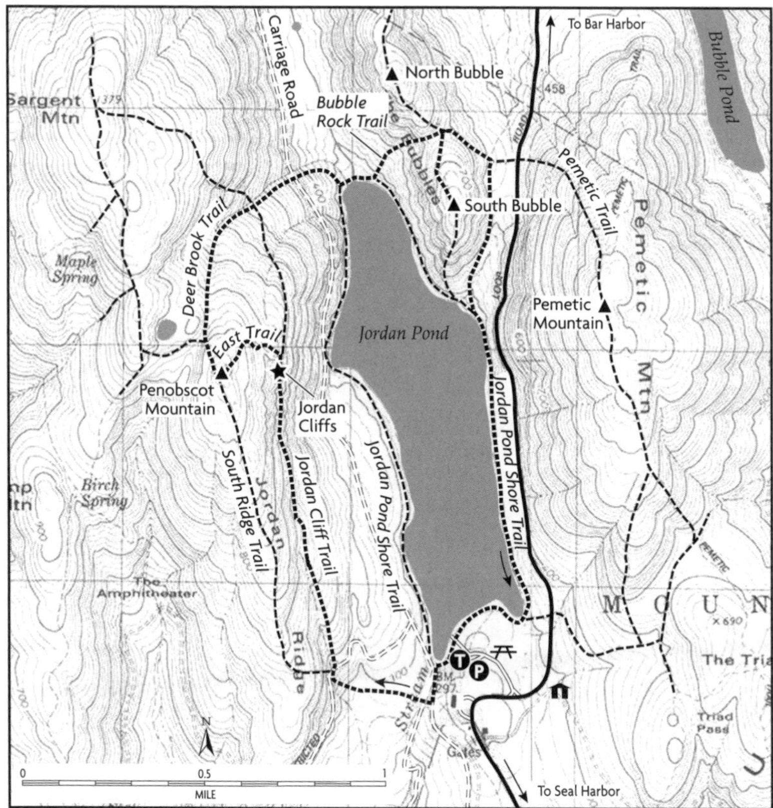

Looking north, the steep sides of Penobscot and Pemetic mountains frame the view as bookends with the Bubbles' famous rounded profiles straight ahead. Turn left and follow the shoreline until reaching a carriage road. Follow the carriage road left for 0.1 mile before turning right (west) onto the Penobscot Mountain South Ridge Trail.

Once across a small bridge, the trail winds through thick forests, climbing gradually to an intersection. The most direct route to Penobscot Mountain's summit is straight on the South Ridge Trail; however, for steep drop-offs and ladders, turn right onto the Jordan Cliff Trail. Keep in mind that the South Ridge Trail may be the only option if the Jordan Cliff Trail is closed to protect nesting peregrine falcons. These rapid-flying black-masked birds of prey continue to become more prevalent inhabitants of Acadia National Park and other cliff-face locations in northern New England. Built to be aerodynamic, peregrines tuck in their wings and dive toward their prey.

The Jordan Cliff Trail quickly heads across a carriage road and up the narrowing ridge. Ascending across ledges and through forest, the route emerges

Jordan Pond and the Bubbles

atop a large talus slope. Looming ahead is the cliff, while the views of the sparkling blue water below are tremendous. Carefully make your way in and out of the trees, around ledges, and up the side of the mountain. At the base of the cliff the journey becomes quite exposed and very steep. Using iron rungs inserted in the bedrock, scramble up a thin gap in the ledge. The trail soon levels off and reaches a junction with the Penobscot East Trail. Turn left for a half-mile trek across a mostly open ridge. The journey ends atop the 1190-foot summit of Penobscot Mountain, where panoramic views abound.

Continue the loop by heading north on the Sargent Mountain Pond Trail. A brief descent leads to the start of the Deer Brook Trail on the right. (Sargent Mountain Pond is 0.1 mile west on the other side of a small knoll, while Sargent Mountain can be reached 0.6 mile farther along the Sargent Mountain South Ridge Trail; see Hike 54.) Follow the Deer Brook Trail down alongside a small streambed. While not difficult the route is quite rocky. Continue straight through a four-way intersection where the Jordan Cliff Trail enters from the right and a trail that leads 0.8 mile to Sargent Mountain leaves left. Cross the carriage road below and proceed to the north shore of Jordan Pond. Here, the Jordan Pond Shore Trail leads 1.6 miles back to the parking area along either side of the pond; however, along the west shore the footing is more rugged.

For the finest view of Jordan Pond, head left 0.1 mile east before joining the 0.4-mile Bubble Rock Trail on its steep, rocky journey toward the two rounded peaks. From the saddle follow the well-groomed footway right to South Bubble's summit and its glorious views of Jordan Pond.

Return to the saddle, then follow the Bubble Rock Trail right (east) 0.3 mile toward the Park Loop Road. If you have not had enough open, high-elevation hiking for the day, you can continue across the road up a steep 0.5-mile climb to the top of Pemetic Mountain. From there, trails lead south 1.5 miles back to the lower end of Jordan Pond. For a more relaxing alternative, pick up the Jordan Pond Carry Trail that enters the forest to the right, just before reaching the Park Loop Road. This trail leads 0.4 mile south to Jordan Pond where a very flat and relaxing 1-mile journey on the Jordan Pond Shore Trail leads left along the east shore of the pond back to the parking area. If you have time, visit the Jordan Pond House, which serves delicious lunches, teas, and dinners in season.

54 Sargent Mountain

Round trip	5.2 miles
Loop direction	Clockwise
Rating	Moderate–Difficult
Hiking time	4 hours
Starting elevation	245 feet
High point	1320 feet
Elevation gain	1900 feet
Best season	April through November
Map	USGS Southwest Harbor
Contact/fee	Acadia National Park

Driving directions: From the junction of Routes 102 and 198 north of Somesville, follow Route 198 southeast toward Northeast Harbor. The parking area is located 4.1 miles ahead on the right side of the road, just before Upper Hadlock Pond.

The relative quietness of Mount Desert Island's second highest summit is a wonderful alternative to the crowds typically encountered atop Cadillac Mountain. With no buildings, radio towers, or automobile traffic, the most significant Sargent Mountain question to ask is which hiking trails

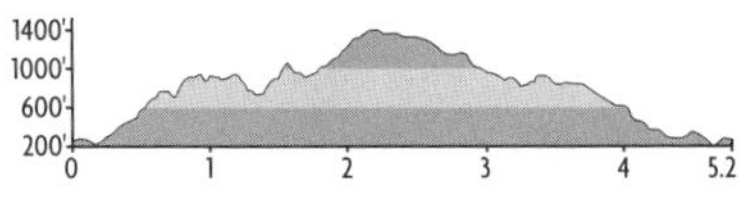

to choose for the day's adventure. This suggested route from the west is a very scenic option that combines numerous barren summits, a long enjoyable ridge walk, a bubbling mountain stream, a quaint waterfall, and an assortment of interesting geological features.

Carefully cross the busy highway and enter the forest at the cedar post. Stay right on the Hadlock Brook Trail and at 0.3 mile turn left toward Bald Peak. Immediately you'll reach the first of four carriage road crossings on the day's journey; be alert for bicyclists at each one. The trail climbs gradually, but after crossing a second carriage road the terrain becomes much steeper. Up a solid rock slope you are soon rewarded with views of the ocean and the village of Northeast Harbor.

Wandering in and out of the forest, steadily make your way to Bald

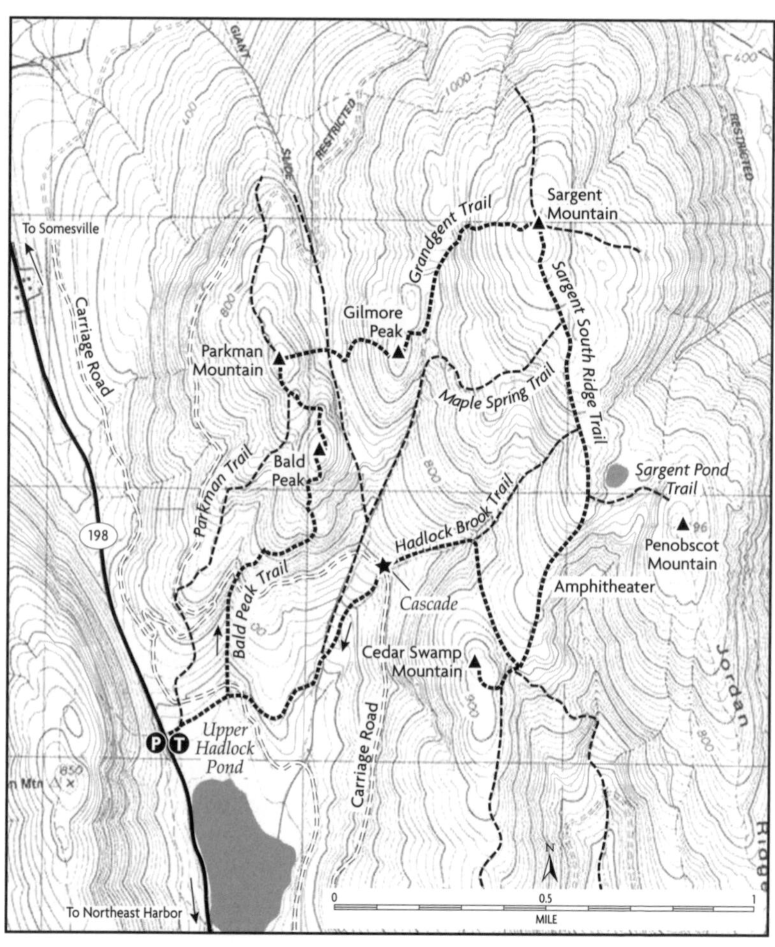

Peak's open summit. Standing in the shadow of higher ridges, this destination, 0.9 mile from the start, provides the first of many exceptional vistas. From here, descend to the north, soon passing through a small depression. At a junction turn right, climbing a few hundred feet to Parkman Mountain's rocky top and its views of Somes Sound.

Bridge over Hadlock Brook

From the summit follow the route that leads northeast toward Sargent Mountain. The trail descends 0.2 mile into a shady, boulder-covered notch to an intersection where trails lead north and south. Continue straight, joining the 1-mile Grandgent Trail, which wastes little time ascending the 1036-foot treeless summit of Gilmore Peak. Another brief descent leads to a small brook crossing and a long forested wetland. A final climb up the steep slope leads through the thinning forest to a large cairn on Sargent Mountain's barren high point, a perfect spot to gaze upon the islands, inlets, mountains, and bays that are unique to and define Maine's special coastline.

Begin the descent down the Sargent Mountain South Ridge Trail. At first the elevation changes very little across an open expanse that often captures the shadows of the long, soaring wingspans of bald eagles. These majestic symbols of the nation have made an incredible comeback in recent decades and are now commonly spotted in the park and in much of coastal Maine. In 0.8 mile pass a trail that drops 0.1 mile left to Sargent Mountain Pond. Swing right and descend above the rim of the Amphitheater, a wide bowl carved out of the slope. In a small notch at a four-way intersection, continue straight, climbing 0.1 mile to an unmarked trail that leads right a few hundred feet, ending atop Cedar Swamp Mountain. This is an excellent vantage point to observe the many peaks, valleys, and ridges traversed on the loop.

Return to the four-way intersection and turn left, entering a thick spruce forest. Descend to and join the Hadlock Brook Trail in 0.4 mile. Follow the flowing water down the mountain for roughly half of the final 1.1 miles. Near the first carriage road crossing, a small waterfall drops a few dozen feet under a beautifully constructed stone bridge, one of many built in the park with the help of John D. Rockefeller, Jr. and his family. Rejoin the trail across the carriage road and enjoy the relaxing final stretch to Route 198.

There are countless other loop hikes available from this parking area. The upper section of the Hadlock Brook Trail and the Maple Spring Trail provide more direct journeys to Sargent Mountain's summit. Also a number of short loops can be completed, including a very pleasant 2-mile trip using the Bald Peak and Parkman Mountain trails.

55 Beech Mountain and Cliff

Round trip ■ 3.6 miles
Loop direction ■ Counterclockwise
Rating ■ Moderate
Hiking time ■ 2 hours
Starting elevation ■ 460 feet
High point ■ 839 feet
Elevation gain ■ 780 feet
Best season ■ April through November
Map ■ USGS Southwest Harbor
Contact/fee ■ Acadia National Park

Driving directions: Beginning north of Somesville at the junction of Routes 102, and 198, drive south on Route 102 for 0.9 mile before turning right. Drive 0.3 mile farther, then turn left. Follow the road for 3.1 miles to a dead end and small parking area on the right.

A popular destination on the quieter half of Mount Desert Island, this loop over Beech Mountain is two hikes in one. The 2.4-mile trip over Beech Mountain and the 1.4 mile-circuit around Beech and Canada cliffs separately offer expansive views, interesting natural features, and a degree of difficulty that is appropriate for hikers of all ages. Joining them together simply doubles the pleasure. Enjoying the scenery of Mount Desert Island in midsummer or marveling at the diversity of bright autumn colors, hikers will find Beech Mountain and its surrounding cliffs to be a perfect destination from spring to late fall.

Begin the hike at the northwest corner of the parking area near one of the island's signature cedar posts. The wide trail quickly splits in half. While both options lead to the summit, follow the more scenic one that continues to the right. Quickly wrapping around the thickly forested slope,

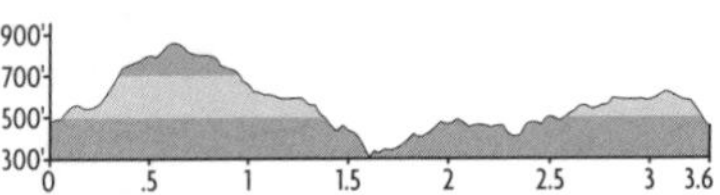

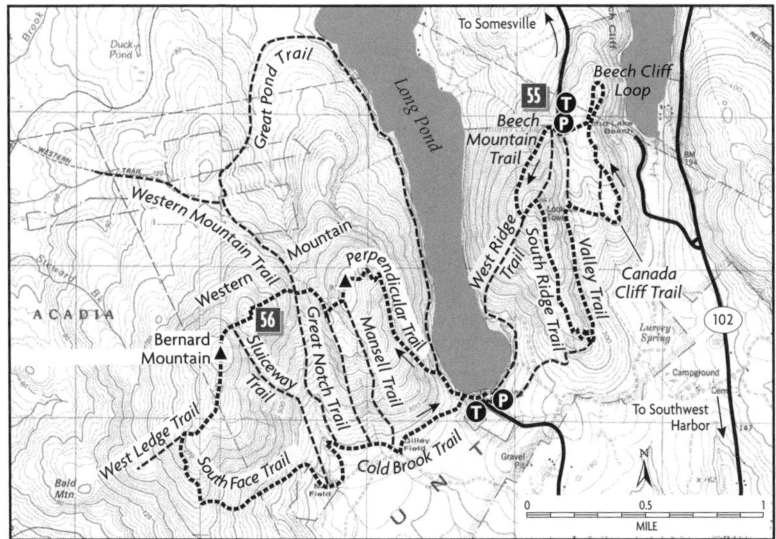

the path gradually climbs up the mountain. Demanding modest effort, the trail begins to ascend through thinning forest where views of Long Pond's expansive shoreline spread out below. To the west, across the bay that bears its name, stands the rounded summit of Blue Hill.

Slowly make your way up through open and semi-open ledges; while not difficult, the footing may be slippery if wet. After leveling off, the route passes by the West Ridge Trail on the right. Cut through the last swath of forest, up the rock steps, and arrive at the summit tower. Only a few stories tall, the tower stands amidst a panoramic view of Acadia National Park, countless bays and islands, and small rocky ridges toward the mainland. With ample places to spread out below, the summit is also an ideal location to enjoy a picnic lunch.

Rejoin the hike by starting down the South Ridge Trail. For the most part, the descent along the ridge is picturesque and very relaxing. However, some caution is required in a few instances where the path drops over small rocks and ledges. Weaving in and out of the forest, make your way along the rocky ridgeline.

At a final viewpoint the trail swings left and reenters the forest for good. Once under the dark evergreen canopy, follow the route as it gradually switchbacks down the steep mountain slope. Aided by an abundant number of rock steps, the trail soon reaches the aptly named Valley Trail below. Turn left here and head 0.9 mile to the start of the Canada Cliff Trail.

Skirting beneath the steep and rocky slope, the Valley Trail pleasantly meanders through a shady, mixed evergreen-hardwood forest. In the shadows of the long tree limbs, the fragile fronds of numerous species of ferns abound,

Beech Mountain Cliff

some taking root on the ground and others atop the countless boulders strewn across the valley floor. In addition to the area's flora, keep your eyes open for local fauna. The forest provides excellent habitat for many species of songbirds. If you are lucky, you may spot an American redstart darting from branch to branch. This tiny warbler, mostly black, displays red (females and young show yellow) in patches on its wings and frequently fanned-out tail.

The path ascends a bit before reaching a junction with the Canada Cliff Trail. The left trail leads 0.2 mile back to the parking area. Turn right toward Canada Cliff. After ascending a small ridge the path descends into a forested wetland where boardwalks end at another trail junction. Stay right and head up the small ledge into the patchy forest atop Canada Cliff. Between the trees are glimpses of Southwest Harbor and the Cranberry Islands in the distance.

The route slowly climbs up the slope. At an intersection, veer right and ascend through an open area with views of Beech Mountain's summit tower. Over a small crest in the ridge the trail reaches the first of many dramatic views of Echo Lake. Once past the Beech Ladder Trail, continue to the Beech Cliff Loop. Staying right, follow the exposed trail as it skirts high above Beech Cliff. Safe as long as you remain on the trail, the loop provides spectacular views of the area.

After circling around a small knoll, the loop winds back. Turn right for the final 0.2 mile to the parking area.

56 Western Mountain

Round trip ■ 4.9 miles
Loop direction ■ Counterclockwise
Rating ■ Moderate–Difficult
Hiking time ■ 3 hours
Starting elevation ■ 70 Feet
High point ■ 1071 feet
Elevation gain ■ 1500 feet
Best season ■ April through November
Map ■ USGS Southwest Harbor
Contact/fee ■ Acadia National Park

Driving directions: From the junction of Routes 198 and 102 north of Somesville, drive 5.8 miles south on Route 102, then turn right onto Seal Cove Road. In 0.5 mile turn right onto Long Pond Road. Follow Long Pond Road 1.3 miles to a pumping station and small parking area on the south shore of the pond.

Mansell Mountain, Knight Knubble, and Bernard Mountain are the westernmost peaks on Mount Desert Island. Not as barren and rocky as other Acadia mountains, this cluster (combined, they form Western Mountain) is more noteworthy for the thick spruce-fir forests that cover its slopes. This area is also one of the quieter sections of the park, and with numerous trails crisscrossing the landscape it is a location ripe for loop hikers. From the pumping station one can choose 3-mile adventures, trips exceeding 7 miles, as well as this

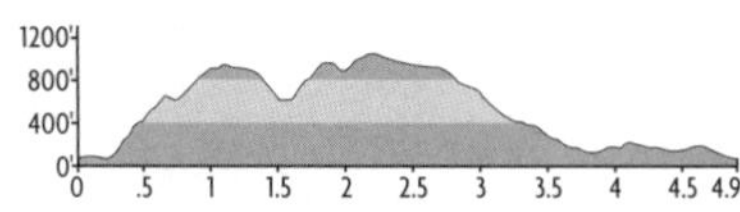

4.9-mile traverse of the range. Whatever the choice, be prepared for well-constructed trails, dense mountain forests, and quaint scenic vistas.

Pick up the trail behind the pumping station and quickly cross the Acadia National Park boundary. The path leads toward the western side of Long Pond after passing a junction with the Cold Brook Trail. Continue straight for 0.2 mile to the start of the Perpendicular Trail. The Great Pond Trail continues ahead, along the shore, before swinging left to join the Western Mountain Trail north of the Great Notch. Turn left onto the Perpendicular Trail, which aggressively leads up the steep slope of Mansell Mountain.

Switchbacks and expertly constructed rock steps aid the ascent, first through a talus slope and then up a narrow notch. The route soon swings right and descends under a long rock ledge. At the end of the huge slab, veer left alongside a small mountain stream. Crisscrossing the running water one stone bridge after another, the relentless 0.8-mile climb eventually ends atop a wide-open ledge with tremendous views of Long Pond, Southwest Harbor, and the Cranberry Islands.

Continuing up the ridge, follow the trail through the moss-covered forest over the wooded summit of Mansell Mountain and past the trail that bears its name. Across semi-open ledges the route swings right and then descends into a tall grove of spruce trees. Emerging from the forest, climb a narrow ridge of exposed rock called the Razorback. Here there are good views toward Bernard Mountain and Blue Hill Bay.

Continue in a northwesterly direction back into the forest and descend

View from Perpendicular Trail

deep into the Great Notch, a narrow depression on the ridge. The path climbs quickly up the other side and soon reaches a spur trail on the left that leads to a viewpoint of the ocean. After crossing over wooded Knight Knubble, drop into Little Notch where the Sluiceway Trail leads left into the dark forest. One last 0.2-mile climb leads past a western viewpoint and to the wooded top of Bernard Mountain.

The route continues pleasantly along the ridge over moderate terrain. At a cedar post, the West Ledge Trail leads straight. Turn left and remain on the South Face Trail. The wide footway winds down gradually at first, then the incline increases; however, the descent is straightforward and relaxing. Scan the tall tree trunks for the camouflaged plumage of the brown creeper, a small bird that is easily overlooked. Once spotted, the creeper is unmistakable because it is one of the few birds to creep up the sides of trees.

Before you know it the South Face Trail's 1.5-mile journey down ends at a small parking area. Start along the road but immediately turn left on the road leading to the reservoir. Up a short hill, turn right and follow the wooded trail that parallels the main road for 0.3 mile to Gilley Field. From here stay left on the Cold Brook Trail, which ends 0.4 mile ahead on the shore of Long Pond. Turn right to reach the pumping station.

If you are looking for a longer, 7.5-mile hike, follow the Great Pond and Western Mountain trails into Great Notch. From here turn right (west) to traverse Bernard Mountain and descend via the South Face Trail. Shorter loops can also be completed using the Mansell Mountain and Razorback trails, which are mostly ridge walks, as well as the Great Notch and Sluiceway trails, which follow valley ways. Each of the four trails is roughly 1 mile long.

57 Ship Harbor

Round trip ■ 1.4 miles
Loop direction ■ Clockwise
Rating ■ Easy
Hiking time ■ 1 hour
Starting elevation ■ 45 feet
High point ■ 55 feet
Elevation gain ■ 35 feet
Best season ■ Year round
Map ■ USGS Bass Harbor
Contact/fee ■ Acadia National Park

Driving directions: Drive south on Route 102 from Southwest Harbor. Turn left onto Route 102A and follow it 4.6 miles to the trailhead and parking area on the left.

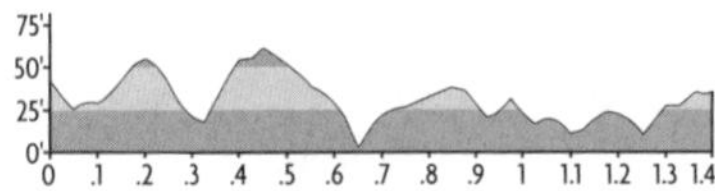

America's national parks are full of long, difficult routes to spectacular locations. Equally impressive are our park's many nature trails—trails that showcase the flora and fauna preserved by those who have gone before us for the betterment of the countless generations that follow. The Ship Harbor Trail in Acadia is one such place where Mount Desert Island's rugged coastline, thick evergreen forests, and sea life stand on display accessible to the vast majority of park visitors. Visit Ship Harbor throughout the year, witness the changing tides, marvel at the rising and setting sun, and take in the abundant beauty of Maine's unique coast.

The well-manicured, easy-to-follow trail weaves down over the grassy slope and quickly enters the forest. At the first intersection, stay left and follow the path as it meanders over the gently rolling terrain through spruce, fir, and cedar. The moist air sustains a thick ground cover of mosses. Down the hillside a second intersection is reached; stay left, once again climbing over a small ridge. In between the forested areas, the trail passes through small openings. Scan the sky for the many gulls gliding in the ocean breezes; herring and great black-backed gulls are especially common. Both gulls are large birds, the former distinguished by its gray back, black wingtips, and a red mark on its yellow beak. The black back of the latter is unmistakable. Continue down the trail to the southern tip of the loop. Here rock and exposed ledges provide excellent spots to kick back and enjoy the scenery, including waves crashing onto the shore, sailboats visiting nearby islands, and sea life in tidal pools. On a hot sunny day in July, there are few places in Maine cooler than the end of the Ship Harbor peninsula.

The return journey from the tip of the peninsula follows the eastern shore of Ship Harbor, soon reaching the harbor's mouth. From ledges a few dozen feet above, watch the water rush in the narrow opening as high tide approaches

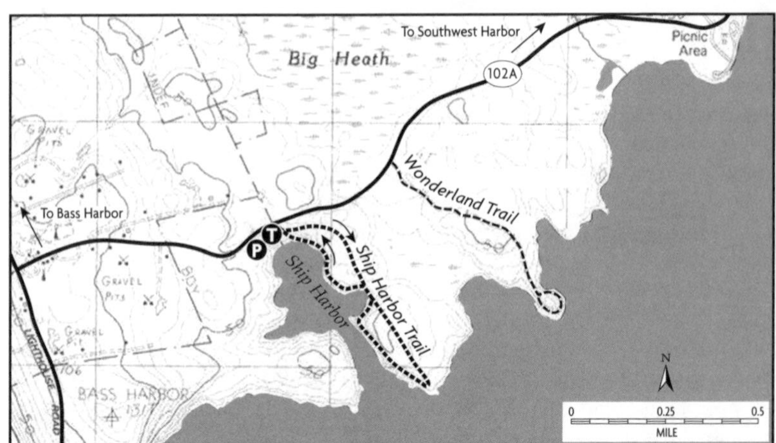

Ship Harbor Trail (photo by Maria Fuentes)

and cascade out during low tide. This is the trail's rockiest section, but it soon returns to a more groomed condition. Stay left at the intersection and continue skirting around a small cove that is often teeming with bird life. The final stretch leads to a small outcrop high above the harbor. Veer right down the slope and turn left one last time for the final section back to the parking area.

If you are looking for another short hike in the area, travel east along Route 102A a few tenths of a mile. Here the Wonderland Trail travels a similar distance down a nearby peninsula. Another good excursion to combine with Ship Harbor is a trip to the Cranberry Islands. From Southwest Harbor, boat trips are available throughout the day. Islesford (Little Cranberry Island) is especially nice and houses a small museum with interesting exhibits.

58 Black Mountain

Round trip ■ 5.1 miles
Loop direction ■ Counterclockwise
Rating ■ Moderate–Difficult
Hiking time ■ 3 hours
Starting elevation ■ 200 feet
High point ■ 1090 feet
Elevation gain ■ 900 feet
Best season ■ April through November
Maps ■ USGS Sullivan and Tunk Lake
Contact/fee ■ Maine Bureau of Parks and Lands

Driving directions: Follow Route 1 for 14 miles east of Ellsworth. Turn left onto Route 183 and continue 4.2 miles past a set of railroad tracks. Turn left onto a dirt road near a sign for the Donnell Pond Public Reserved

Land. At 0.4 mile, stay left and head toward Schoodic Mountain (the road right leads to an alternative parking area for Black Mountain). Continue 1.8 miles on the main road, past a number of roads veering left, until reaching a parking area at the bottom of a hill.

Located less than 30 minutes from downtown Ellsworth, the Donnell Pond Public Reserved Land encompasses more than 15,000 acres of lakes, mountains, and forests. Protected in stages with the help of Maine Coast Heritage Trust, the Maine Chapter of the Nature Conservancy, the Frenchman Bay Conservancy, and the Land for Maine's Future Program, the reserved land includes five mountains that exceed 900 feet in elevation, 40 miles of freshwater shoreline, and a 1940-acre ecological reserve managed for scientific research. With a similar geology and topography as Acadia National Park, the area provides outdoor adventurers with comparable opportunities but without the crowds. There are a number of loop hikes from which to choose, from 3-mile hikes to 10-mile journeys. This intermediate-level trip to Black Mountain also provides access to a longer backcountry excursion.

The Black Mountain Trail leads right near a stream at the lower end of the parking area. After a short climb the path levels while joining an old road. Passing wet terrain and through a thick wall of evergreens, the path emerges into a sunnier grove of northern hardwoods. At a cairn where roads once intersected, continue straight (northeast). A few hundred feet farther, veer left at a second cairn and head toward the base of Black Mountain. Aided by rock steps, make a steep ascent among boulders and around ledges.

The trail moderates near a junction where the Schoodic Beach Trail leads left. This route will complete the day's journey, but first venture ahead to the open east summit of Black Mountain by way of the west summit. The first half-mile stretch along the ridge is relaxing, with the aroma of spruce and fir in the air. Carve your way through the moss-covered ground to the mountain's west peak. Stay right, drop into a small saddle (here a path leads right to the alternative parking area), and begin the final ascent to the east summit. As the route passes onto the open ledge, look closely for the stone cairns that lead to the summit's 360-degree vista. Named for War of 1812 veteran and wealthy timberland owner Colonel John Black, the 1100-foot mountain provides exceptional views of Mount Desert Island and Frenchman Bay, as well as vistas of the reserved land's numerous lakes and ponds and surrounding ridges.

Return to the Schoodic Beach Trail and turn right. Before descending, the path meanders along the top of the ridge with occasional views of Donnell Pond and the rocky slopes of Schoodic Mountain. As the level terrain ends, a steep descent begins. Fortunately, switchbacks provide relief for the knees and the drop is brief. Level off near a small stream before joining an old road to the left. Follow the blue blazes carefully. One spot is particularly tricky, as the road stays straight while the trail bends right. Drop

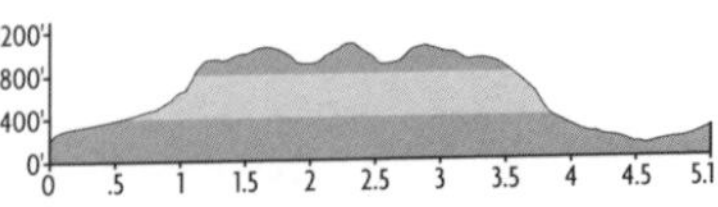

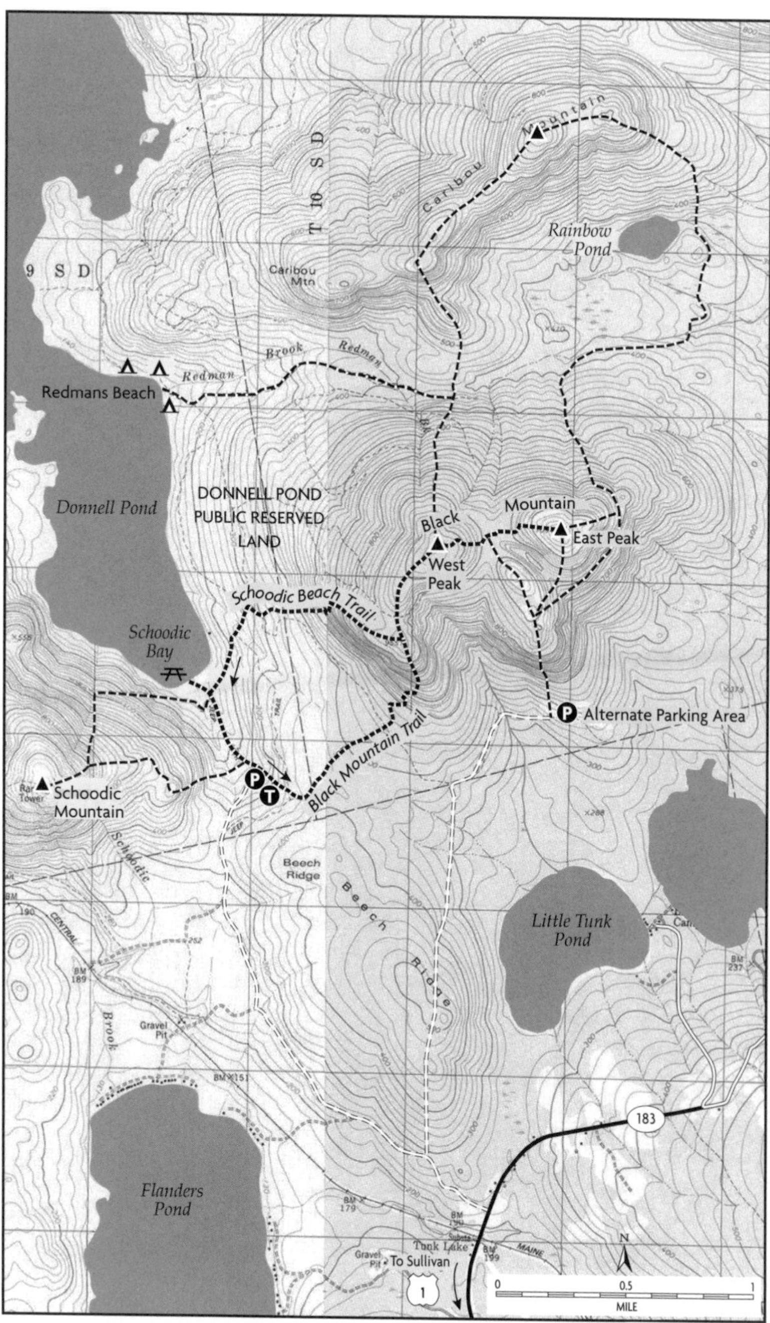
Caribou Mountain
T 10 S D
9 S D
Caribou Mtn
Rainbow Pond
Redmans Beach
Redman Brook
Donnell Pond
DONNELL POND PUBLIC RESERVED LAND
Black Mountain
West Peak
East Peak
Schoodic Beach Trail
Schoodic Bay
Black Mountain Trail
Alternate Parking Area
Schoodic Mountain
Beech Ridge
Little Tunk Pond
Gravel Pit
Flanders Pond
183
Tunk Lake
To Sullivan
1
0
0.5
1
MILE
N

Below Black Mountain's summit

down and across some small streams to a second, more developed road. To the right is Donnell Pond and Schoodic Beach, a beautiful, long swimming area and a refreshing place to cool down on a hot summer day. To the left an easy half-mile walk ends at the parking lot.

If you are looking to double your pleasure and find solitude, extend the Black Mountain hike by using the 5.5-mile trail that connects the east and west summits. This extension, which scales the scenic ridge of Caribou Mountain, will result in a 10.1-mile hike and add nearly 1000 feet of additional elevation gain. However, the increased effort required is greatly rewarded. The rarely used trail passes countless streams and wetlands, crosses fields of boulders, scales vista-covered ridges, and visits neighborhoods that are home to moose, beaver, and other wildlife. The many habitats along the way provide ideal breeding ground and nesting sites for many diverse species of birds. If you are fortunate you may hear the piercing cry and see the long, white wingspan of the osprey. Sometimes referred to as the fish hawk, this black-masked predator tucks in its pointy wings as it plunges into water searching for food.

59 Cutler Coast

Round trip ■ 10 miles
Loop direction ■ Clockwise
Rating ■ Difficult
Hiking time ■ 5 hours
Starting elevation ■ 200 feet
High point ■ 300 feet
Elevation gain ■ 1000 feet
Best season ■ Year round
Map ■ USGS Cutler
Contact/fee ■ Maine Bureau of Parks and Lands

Driving directions: The trailhead is located on Route 191 north of Cutler. From Route 1 in East Machias, follow Route 191 for 16.9 miles, past the center of Cutler to the parking area on the right. From Route 189, halfway between Whiting and Lubec, follow Route 191 south for 10 miles and turn left into the parking area.

While Maine is famous for its rugged coastline, from June to September many of the most scenic spots are overrun with visitors. To the contrary, the 12,000-acre Cutler Coast Public Reserve, located along Maine's less traveled Bold Coast, offers crowd-free viewing of nearly 5 miles of ocean scenery

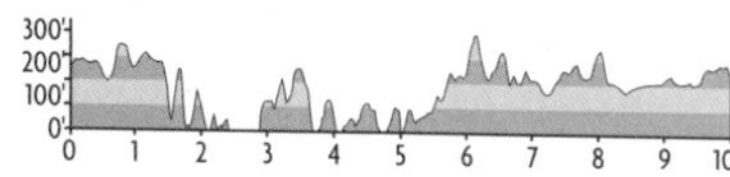

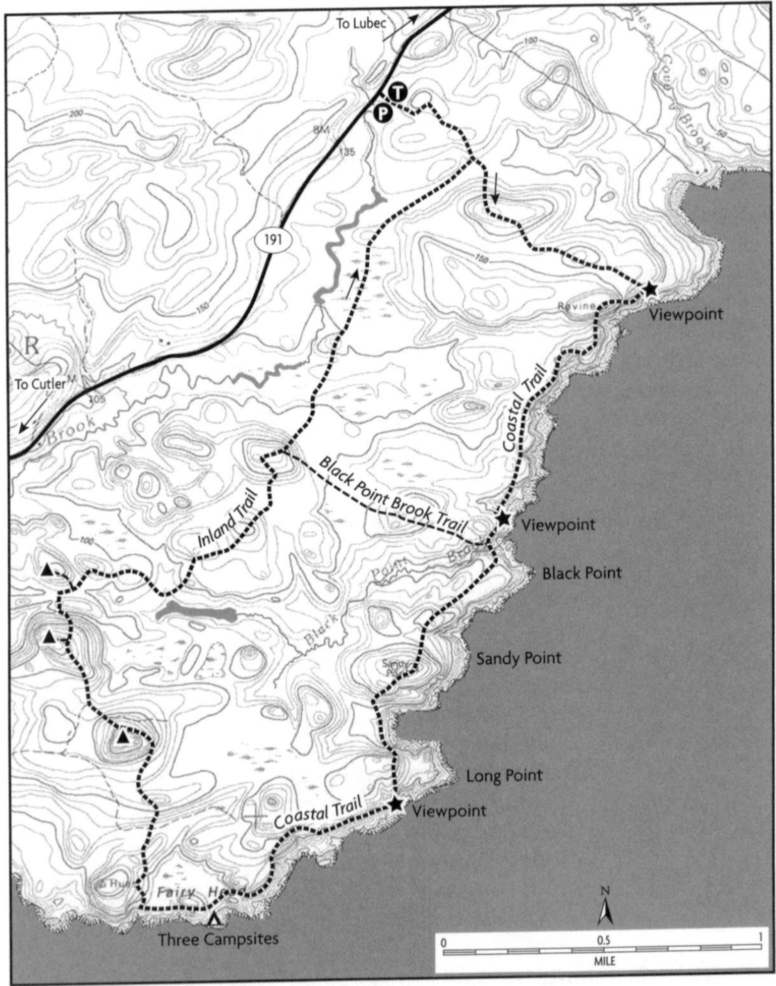

as spectacular as any other stretch in Maine and beyond. Protected by the state in the 1990s with the help of Maine Coast Heritage Trust and the Land for Maine's Future Program, the Cutler Coast is a land of rugged, rocky cliffs where cool temperatures sail in on refreshing sea breezes even during the hottest weeks of the summer. The reserve offers hikers two loop options, a 5.8-mile and a 10-mile journey, as well as three primitive campsites for overnight adventures. Whether half-day, full-day, or multiple-day, a sojourn to the Cutler Coast is a memorable opportunity to spot whales, moose, and countless species of birds.

Tunnel through the dense evergreen forest 0.4 mile to a junction with the Inland Trail. Continue straight on a relaxing 1-mile journey over small ridges and across boggy areas frequented by moose. Reaching the Coastal Trail, which leads right, check out the scenic vantage point on the short spur left. Down the rock steps and out onto an open ledge, use care; it is a long way to the water. The circling seabirds, crashing surf, and salt air surround a landscape of steep ocean cliffs. Across the water lies New Brunswick's rugged Grand Manan Island. Scan the surf for black guillemots, dark, ducklike birds with white wing patches and bright orange feet. These common ocean residents of eastern Maine often feed near shore.

From here the trail heads southwest, following the shore high above the water. Overall the elevation changes very little, but the route is far from flat. Passing steep walls and secluded rock beaches, the trail winds through forest and open meadows, passing one spectacular vista after another. At 1.5 miles the Black Point Brook Trail leads 0.8 mile to the Inland Trail, providing a 5.8-mile option.

While the southern coastline is not as dramatic, the longer loop is well worth the effort. Leaving the stone beach at Black Point Brook Cove (Black Point Brook being the last reliable fresh, albeit orange, water for the campsites that are 2 miles ahead), hike up a small wooden ladder and enter the forest. Across low, rolling terrain, the trail traverses open meadows and passes a small cove, before climbing through an attractive birch forest lined with ledge and ferns.

Maine's Bold Coast

Farther down the coast the trail emerges onto the wide-open expanse of Long Point. During August and September, in particular, Long Point is a great location for spotting whales swimming in the distant waves. The small island on the horizon is Machias Seal Island, the site of a large Atlantic puffin colony, as well as home to razorbill auks, arctic terns, and gray seals. Boats visit the island throughout the summer, leaving from Jonesport and Cutler—a great excursion to cap off any trip to Washington County.

The Coastal Trail continues past three campsites, each available on a first-come, first-served basis, and through an interesting notch in the woods. After crossing the outlet of a small bog, the route leaves the ocean and joins the Inland Trail (no sign). During late spring and summer, be prepared for insects on this less-windy and wetland-filled part of the loop. Apart from the bugs the trail is very pleasant. Along the way a number of hills with short paths lead to limited views.

After passing a large beaver pond, the route climbs to a semi-open knob and intersects the Black Point Brook Trail. Stay straight, down the hill, and through a wet marshy area where "witchity-witchity-witch" rings from the undergrowth. This is the call of the common yellowthroat, which when flushed from the marshy vegetation will exhibit a bright yellow body in contrast to its dark black mask.

Up and over a partially wooded ridge, reenter the shady evergreen forest and gradually make your way back. Turn left at the trail junction for the final 0.4 mile to the parking area.

60 Shackford Head

Round trip ■ 3 miles
Loop direction ■ Counterclockwise
Rating ■ Easy–Moderate
Hiking time ■ 2 hours
Starting elevation ■ 40 feet
High point ■ 173 feet
Elevation gain ■ 300 feet
Best season ■ Year round
Map ■ USGS Eastport
Contact/fee ■ Maine Bureau of Parks and Lands

Driving directions: From Route 1 in Perry, follow Route 190 south toward Eastport. At 6.4 miles the road turns sharply left near a gas station. Stay straight, turning off Route 190, but turn immediately to the right onto Deep Cove Road. Follow this road 0.7 mile; turn left onto the dirt roadway that leads to the parking area.

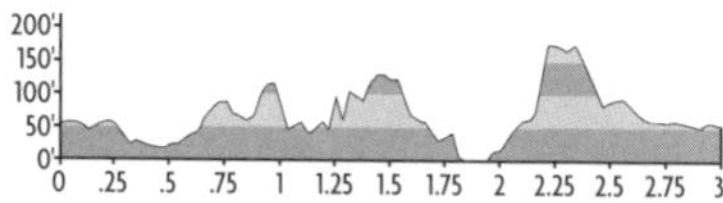

In 1783, John Shackford of Newburyport moved from western Massachusetts to what was then the easternmost section of the Bay State. He anchored his ship in Eastport and began a new life. In 1989, a little more than two centuries later, the state of Maine with the help of the brand-new Land for Maine's Future Program purchased the 90-acre peninsula once owned by Shackford. Today the land, owned by the Department of Conservation and jointly managed by the city of Eastport, offers easy hiking trails past classic Downeast Maine scenery.

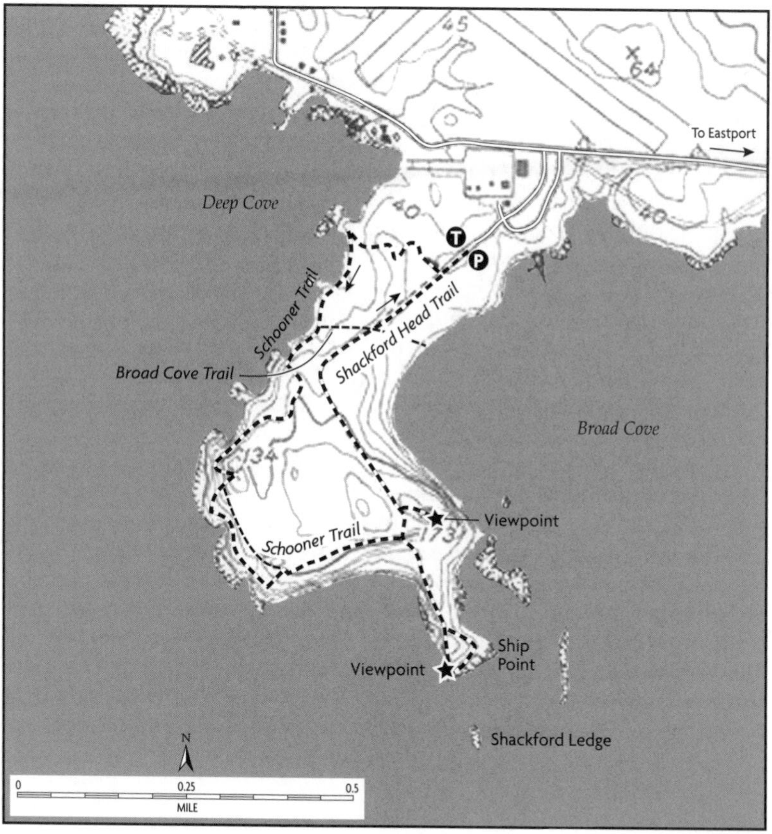

Shackford Head abounds with seals bobbing in the rapidly changing tides, bald eagles soaring in the salt breezes, and thick carpets of wildflowers flourishing in the moist air. In addition to natural beauty, the rocky location also offers a glimpse into the region's human history, recent and distant. With working waterfronts and towering church steeples on the horizon, Shackford Head is surrounded by the very communities that shaped the political philosophy of Franklin Delano Roosevelt, the most influential president of the twentieth century.

Follow the Shackford Head Trail from the parking area and quickly reach the start of the Schooner Trail. Turn right onto the much narrower path and wind through the thick spruce forest to the edge of Deep Cove. Here the trail hugs the rocky coastline, occasionally passing unmarked paths that lead to open bluffs or pebble beaches. Throughout the summer the trail is lined with a lush carpet of wildflowers, most notably the bunchberries with their white clover-shaped flowers, four deep-green leaves, and red fruits. Although the trail is easy, the terrain is not flat. However, the short climbs encourage you to stop and listen to the numerous songs that pierce through the blowing wind, such as the buzzing chorus of the diminutive northern parula warbler. With a little persistence and luck, you may catch a glimpse of their blue backs, yellow throats, and red necklaces here and in other mixed forest habitats along Maine's eastern coast.

After descending to a scenic meadow overlooking the water, the trail splits. The upper half continues through the forest, while the lower half remains near the water. Both paths meet once again as the trail climbs through an open ridge with views of Ship Point, the tip of Shackford Head.

Returning to the forest, the trail ends at a three-way intersection. Stay right and head down a short, steep slope. While not dangerous, the footing is loose and slipping a possibility. After the ground levels the trail splits, forming a short loop. Stay right and climb the small incline to Ship Point, a great place to scan the water for seals, cormorants, and a variety of sea ducks. Complete the loop around the point while passing a rocky beach where 412-million-year-old snail and mussel-like fossils have been found.

Back up the hill to the three-way intersection, to the right a sign points to Shackford Head. Follow this spur trail a few hundred feet to the open summit and its 180-degree views of the cliffs of Grand Manan Island, Roosevelt's family land on Campobello Island (now the Roosevelt-Campobello International Park), the picturesque Lubec hillside, and Eastport's deep-sea cargo pier.

From Shackford Head, return to the main trail. Turn right and follow the wide, well-groomed path as it meanders through the shady forest. Along the way a short 0.2-mile trail leads right to a small beach on Broad Cove. Across a boardwalk through a marshy area, the path ends at the parking area a few hundred yards beyond.

Before leaving, check out the historic markers that detail the salvaging of metal from Civil War ships that occurred here in the early twentieth century. The valued resource was recycled and used in the First World War. Also check out downtown Eastport, the first U.S. city each day to feel the warm rays of the sun, as long as they make their way through the dense fog.

Opposite: Schooner Trail

SCHOONER
TRAIL

Additional Hike Options

Hike Number and Name	Option	Miles	Difficulty	Hike Duration
1 Pisgah State Park	Kilburn Loop	6.3	Moderate	Half-day
2 Pack Monadnock	South Pack Monadnock	2.8	Moderate	Half-day
6 Mount Cardigan	Clark/Cathedral Forest Trails	5.6	Moderate	Half-day
7 Mount Whiteface	Tom Wiggin Trail	8.2	Difficult	Day
7 Mount Whiteface	Hedgehog Mountain	6.2	Moderate	Day
8 Jennings Peak	Sandwich Dome	8.9	Difficult	Day
9 Tripyramids	Scaur	3.4	Moderate	Half-day
10 Mount Moosilauke	Gorge Brook and Snapper Ski Trails	7.6	Difficult	Day
11 Franconia Notch	Cannon Balls	10.6	Difficult	Full-day
15 Hedgehog Mountain	Boulder Loop	3.1	Moderate	Half-day
16 Mount Chocorua and the Three Sisters	Sister only	8.1	Difficult	Day
18 Green Hills Preserve	Pudding Pond	1.6	Easy	Half-day
20 Arethusa Falls and Frankenstein Cliff	Ammonoosuc Lake	1.8	Easy	Half-day
22 Crawford Notch	Webster and Jackson	6.5	Moderate–Difficult	Day
22 Crawford Notch	Mount Pierce	6.6	Moderate–Difficult	Day
25 Mount Madison	Kelton and Inlook Trails	4.5	Moderate	Half-day
26 Carter Dome	Wild River	6.5	Moderate	Half-day
27 Imp Face	Middle Carter	9.9	Difficult	Day
28 Wild River	Highwater and Wild River Trails	5.5	Moderate	Half-day
29 Baldfaces	Meader Ridge	9	Difficult	Day
33 Grafton Notch	Grafton Loop Trail	42	Difficult	Multi-day
33 Grafton Notch	Old Speck	7.8	Difficult	Day
33 Grafton Notch	East Baldpate	8.3	Difficult	Day
37 Mount Kineo	Bridle and Indian Trails	4	Moderate	Half-day
38 Gulf Hagas	Cut-off Trail (near Buttermilk Falls)	6.5	Moderate	Half-day

Hike Number and Name	Option	Miles	Difficulty	Hike Duration
39 Turtle Ridge	Connector Trail	4.9	Moderate	Half-day
40 Trout Brook Mountain	Five Ponds Trail	6	Moderate	Day
41 South Branch Mountain	Traveler Mountain	10.6	Strenuous	Full-day
43 Mount Katahdin	Hamlin Peak	9.2	Strenuous	Full-day
44 Wells Estuary	Rachel Carson NWR	1	Easy	Half-day
46 Bradbury Mountain	Knight Woods Trail	1.5	Easy	Half-day
48 Mount Megunticook and Maiden Cliff	Maiden Cliff only	2.1	Easy–Moderate	Half-day
51 Champlain Mountain	Great Head	1.8	Easy–Moderate	Half-day
52 Dorr and Cadillac Mountains	Dorr, North and South Ridge Trails	5.5	Moderate–Difficult	Day
53 Jordan Pond	Jordan Pond Loop	3.2	Easy	Half-day
54 Sargent Mountain	Parkman and Bald Mountains	2	Easy–Moderate	Half-day
55 Beech Mountain and Cliff	Beech Mountain only	2.4	Moderate	Half-day
56 Western Mountain	Great Pond Trail	7.5	Moderate–Difficult	Day
58 Black Mountain	Caribou Mountain Extension	10.1	Difficult	Day
59 Cutler Coast	Black Point Brook Cut-off	5.8	Moderate	Half-day

APPENDIX

Landowners

Acadia National Park
P.O. Box 177
Bar Harbor, ME 04609
(207) 288-3338
www.nps.gov/acad/index.htm

Appalachian National Scenic Trail
NPS Park Office
Harpers Ferry Center
Harpers Ferry, WV 25425
(304) 535-6278
www.nps.gov/appa/

Appalachian Mountain Club
5 Joy Street
Boston, MA 02108
(617) 523-0636
www.outdoors.org

Baxter State Park
64 Balsam Drive
Millinocket, ME 04462
(207) 723-5140
www.baxterstateparkauthority.com/index.html

Dartmouth Outing Club
113 Robinson Hall
Hanover, NH 03755
(603) 646-2429
www.dartmouth.edu/~doc/

Maine Bureau of Parks and Lands
22 State House Station
Augusta, ME 04333
(207) 287-3821
www.maine.gov/doc/parks

NH Division of Parks and Recreation
172 Pembroke Road
P.O. Box 1856
Concord, NH 03302-1856
(603) 271-3556
www.nhstateparks.org/index.html
www.nhtrails.org/

New Hampshire Audubon
3 Silk Farm Road
Concord, NH 03301-8200
(603) 224-9909
www.nhaudubon.org

North Maine Woods
92 Main Street
Ashland, ME 04732
(207) 435-6213
www.northmainewoods.org

The Nature Conservancy
New Hampshire Chapter
22 Bridge Street, 4th Floor
Concord, NH 03301
(603) 224-5853
www.nature.org

Wells National Estuarine Reserve
342 Laudholm Farm Road
Wells, ME 04090
(207) 646-1555
www.wellsreserve.org

White Mountain National Forest
719 Main Street
Laconia, NH 03246
(603) 528-8721
www.fs.fed.us/r9/white/

Land Conservation Programs

Land and Community Heritage
Investment Program
10 Dixon Avenue
Concord, NH 03301
(603) 224-4113
www.lchip.org

USDA Forest Service
Forest Legacy, Northeastern Contact
P.O. Box 640
Durham, NH 03824
www.fs.fed.us/spf/coop/programs/loa/flp.shtml

Land for Maine's Future Program
38 State House Station
Augusta, ME 04330-0038
(207) 287-1487
www.maine.gov/spo/lmf

Land Conservation Organizations

Appalachian Mountain Club

Founded in 1876, the Appalachian Mountain Club (AMC) is America's oldest conservation and recreation organization. The AMC promotes the protection, enjoyment, and wise use of the mountains, rivers, and trails of the Appalachian Mountain region. They encourage people to enjoy and appreciate the natural world, because successful conservation depends on this experience. The AMC manages huts, cabins, lodges, tent sites, and other overnight locations that are mentioned throughout the book. Contact the main office for more information or to make reservations. The AMC also maintains more than 1400 miles of trails throughout the northeast.
Appalachian Mountain Club
5 Joy Street
Boston, MA 02108
(617) 523-0636
www.outdoors.org

Friends of Acadia

The Friends of Acadia (FOA) work to protect the outstanding natural beauty, ecological vitality, and cultural distinctiveness of Acadia National Park and the surrounding communities. Their activities include supporting trail-maintenance efforts and the Island Explorer shuttle service.
Friends of Acadia
43 Cottage Street
P.O. Box 45
Bar Harbor, ME 04609
(800) 625-0321
www.friendsofacadia.org

Friends of the Wapack

The Friends of the Wapack (FOW) maintain the Wapack Trail and other trails along its corridor. They also work closely with private landowners and are seeking to permanently protect the entire trail through easements and other voluntary agreements.

Friends of the Wapack
P.O. Box 115
West Peterborough, NH 03468
www.wapack.org

Maine Appalachian Trail Club

The Maine Appalachian Trail Club (MATC) is a volunteer, nonprofit trail-maintenance club that manages 267 miles of the Appalachian Trail in Maine, its facilities and corridor. The club maintains trails and lean-to sites along the Appalachian Trail corridor. The MATC also has a highly successful Caretaker/Ridgerunner Program, with a goal of providing trail stewards at high-use locations along the Appalachian Trail in Maine; here a focused program of hiker education should address negative impacts at areas of high use and make a major positive contribution to the trail experience.

Maine Appalachian Trail Club
P.O. Box 283
Augusta, ME 04332-0283
www.matc.org

Maine Audubon

Maine Audubon works to conserve Maine's wildlife and wildlife habitat by engaging people of all ages in education, conservation, and action. Maine Audubon manages a number of centers, camps, and sanctuaries encompassing more than 3000 acres around the state.

Maine Audubon
20 Gilsland Farm Road
Falmouth, ME 04105
(207) 781-2330
www.maineaudubon.org

Maine Coast Heritage Trust

Maine Coast Heritage Trust (MCHT) conserves and stewards Maine's coastal lands and islands for their renowned scenic beauty, outdoor recreational opportunities, ecological diversity and working landscapes. MCHT promotes the conservation of natural places statewide by working with land trusts, communities and other partners. Since 1970, MCHT has helped permanently protect more than 125,000 acres and more than 250 entire coastal islands. MCHT also runs the Maine Land Trust Network, a service that fosters the growth and professionalism of Maine's ninety local land trusts.

Maine Coast Heritage Trust
Bowdoin Mill
One Main Street, Suite 201
Topsham, ME 04086
(207) 729-7366
www.mcht.org

The Nature Conservancy

The Nature Conservancy (TNC) is an international land conservation organization with a mission to preserve the plants, animals, and natural communities that represent the diversity of life on Earth by protecting the lands and waters they need to survive. TNC's Maine Chapter has helped protect more than 870,000 acres of natural lands in the state, while the New Hampshire Chapter has worked to protect more than 121,000 acres of critical natural lands, including thirty preserves.

New Hampshire Chapter
22 Bridge Street, 4th Floor
Concord, NH 03301
(603) 224-5853
www.nature.org

Maine Chapter
14 Maine Street, Suite 401
Brunswick, ME 04011
(207) 729-5181
www.nature.org

New Hampshire Audubon

New Hampshire Audubon seeks to protect and enhance New Hampshire's natural environment for wildlife and for people. New Hampshire Audubon staffs seven visitor centers around the state and manages more than 8000 acres of land located in over forty wildlife sanctuaries.

New Hampshire Audubon
3 Silk Farm Road
Concord, NH 03301-8200
(603) 224-9909
www.nhaudubon.org

Randolph Mountain Club

The Randolph Mountain Club (RMC) maintains a network of nearly 100 miles of hiking trails, principally on the northern slopes of Mount Madison, Mount Adams, and Mount Jefferson in the Presidential Range of the White Mountain National Forest.

Randolph Mountain Club
P.O. Box 279
Gorham, NH 03581
www.randolphmountainclub.org/index.html

Society for the Protection of New Hampshire Forests

Founded in 1901, the Society for the Protection of New Hampshire Forests (SPNHF) is dedicated to protecting the state's most important landscapes while promoting the wise use of its renewable natural resources. The SPNHF has helped to protect over one million acres of open space in the state; effectively promotes good land stewardship through education and by example; and advocates for public policies that encourage the wise conservation of natural resources. They played a leadership role in the establishment of the White Mountain National Forest in 1911.

Society for the Protection of New Hampshire Forests
54 Portsmouth Street
Concord, NH 03301
(603) 224-9945
www.spnhf.org

Trust for Public Land

The Trust for Public Land (TPL) is a national, nonprofit land conservation organization that conserves land for people to enjoy as parks, community gardens, historic sites, rural lands, and other natural places, ensuring livable communities for generations to come. Since the TPL began working in New Hampshire in 1987, they have protected nearly 60,000 acres. The TPL began working in Maine in 1993 and has since protected nearly 50,000 acres.

Trust for Public Land
Northern New England Field Office
3 Shipman Place
Montpelier, VT 05602
(802) 223-1373
www.tpl.org

Wonalancet Out Door Club

Established in 1892, the Wonalancet Out Door Club (WODC) maintains 52 miles of trails in the southern White Mountain region in and around the Sandwich Mountain Wilderness.

Wonalancet Out Door Club
HCR 64, Box 248
Wonalancet, NH 03897
www.wodc.org

INDEX

U

W

Z

ABOUT THE AUTHOR

Jeff Romano has been hiking in New England for more than thirty years. He has scaled many of the region's highest peaks, hiking hundreds of miles of the region's trails and traveling to most of the region's wild places. In addition to his love of hiking, Jeff is an avid bird-watcher who especially enjoys the dozens of small, colorful warblers summering in New England each year. After growing up in southern New Hampshire, he earned a bachelor of arts in politics from Saint Anselm College and a juris doctorate from Vermont Law School. Jeff has worked on a handful of political campaigns and for a number of nonprofit organizations, and currently coordinates public policy activities for Maine Coast Heritage Trust, a statewide land trust that focuses on the conservation of Maine's unique coastline. When not in his office or in the State House in Augusta, Jeff is often found with his family on one of the many hiking trails in Maine and New Hampshire. He lives in Hallowell with his wife Maria and their son, Anthony.

Author and son (photo by Maria Fuetes)

THE MOUNTAINEERS, founded in 1906, is a nonprofit outdoor activity and conservation club, whose mission is "to explore, study, preserve, and enjoy the natural beauty of the outdoors. . . . " Based in Seattle, Washington, the club is now the third-largest such organization in the United States, with seven branches throughout Washington State.

The Mountaineers sponsors both classes and year-round outdoor activities in the Pacific Northwest, which include hiking, mountain climbing, ski-touring, snowshoeing, bicycling, camping, kayaking, nature study, sailing, and adventure travel. The club's conservation division supports environmental causes through educational activities, sponsoring legislation, and presenting informational programs.

All club activities are led by skilled, experienced instructors, who are dedicated to promoting safe and responsible enjoyment and preservation of the outdoors.

If you would like to participate in these organized outdoor activities or the club's programs, consider a membership in The Mountaineers. For information and an application, write or call The Mountaineers, Club Headquarters, 300 Third Avenue West, Seattle, WA 98119; 206-284-6310. You can also visit the club's website at www.mountaineers.org or contact The Mountaineers via email at clubmail@mountaineers.org.

The Mountaineers Books, an active, nonprofit publishing program of the club, produces guidebooks, instructional texts, historical works, natural history guides, and works on environmental conservation. All books produced by The Mountaineers Books fulfill the club's mission.

Send or call for our catalog of more than 500 outdoor titles:

The Mountaineers Books
1001 SW Klickitat Way, Suite 201
Seattle, WA 98134
800-553-4453
mbooks@mountaineersbooks.org
www.mountaineersbooks.org

The Mountaineers Books is proud to be a corporate sponsor of The Leave No Trace Center for Outdoor Ethics, whose mission is to promote and inspire responsible outdoor recreation through education, research, and partnerships. The Leave No Trace program is focused specifically on human-powered (nonmotorized) recreation.

Leave No Trace strives to educate visitors about the nature of their recreational impacts, as well as offer techniques to prevent and minimize such impacts. Leave No Trace is best understood as an educational and ethical program, not as a set of rules and regulations.

For more information, visit *www.LNT.org*, or call 800-332-4100.

OTHER TITLES YOU MIGHT ENJOY FROM THE MOUNTAINEERS BOOKS

Best Hikes with Dogs: New Hampshire and Vermont
Lisa Densmore
60 hikes selected to delight your dog (and you) in New Hampshire and Vermont—all close to urban areas.

An Outdoor Family Guide to Acadia National Park
Lisa Golan Evans
Comprehensive guide to family-friendly outings.

BEST HIKES WITH CHILDREN SERIES
Guides to day hikes for families, with tips for keeping kids interested and fostering in them a love of nature.

Best Hikes with Children: in Vermont, New Hampshire & Maine, 2nd Edition
Cynthia Copeland & Thomas Lewis

Best Hikes with Children in Connecticut, Massachusetts, and Rhode Island, 2nd Edition
Cynthia Copeland & Thomas Lewis

NORTHERN FOREST CANOE TRAIL MAPS
Thirteen **Maps** cover all sections of this 740-mile paddle trail through New York, Vermont, New Hampshire, Quebec, and Maine. Here are three:

Map 6 - Northeast Kingdom: Vermont/ Quebec, Lake Memphremagog to Connecticut River
Map 7 - Great North Woods: New Hampshire, Connecticut River to Umbagog Lake
Map 8 - Rangeley Lakes Region: Maine, Umbagog Lake to Rangeley Lake

---

Available at fine bookstores and outdoor stores, by phone at 800-553-4453 or on the web at *www.mountaineersbooks.org*

THE MOUNTAINEERS BOOKS